Banking and Insurance Management

Banking and Insurance Management

Adam Lerwick

RANDOM

RANDOM PUBLICATIONS

NEW DELHI (INDIA)

Banking and Insurance Management

ISBN 978-93-5111-443-7

Published in 2014 in India by

RANDOM PUBLICATIONS

4376-A/4B, Gali Murari Lal, Ansari Road
New Delhi-110 002
Phone : +91-11-43580356, +91-11-23289044
e-mail: randomexports@gmail.com, sales@randompublications.com,
info@randompublications.com

Reprinted 2025

Type Setting by: Friends Media, Delhi-110089
Printed at : Replika Press Pvt. Ltd.

Preface

Due to their influential status within the financial system and upon national economies, banks are highly regulated in most countries. Most nations have institutionalised a system known as fractional reserve banking, in which banks hold only a small reserve of the funds deposited and lend out the rest for profit. They are generally subject to minimum capital requirements based on an international set of capital standards, known as the Basel Accords. Banking in its modern sense evolved in the 14th century in the rich cities of Renaissance Italy but in many ways was a continuation of ideas and concepts of credit and lending that had its roots in the ancient world. In the history of banking, a number of banking dynasties have played a central role over many centuries. The oldest existing bank was founded in 1472. Banks act as payment agents by conducting checking or current accounts for customers, paying cheques drawn by customers on the bank, and collecting cheques deposited to customers' current accounts. Banks also enable customer payments via other payment methods such as Automated Clearing House (ACH), Wire transfers or telegraphic transfer, EFTPOS, and automated teller machine (ATM). Banks borrow money by accepting funds deposited on current accounts, by accepting term deposits, and by issuing debt securities such as bank notes and bonds. Banks lend money by making advances to customers on current accounts, by making installment loans, and by investing in marketable debt securities and other forms of money lending. Banks provide different payment services, and a bank account is considered indispensable by most businesses and individuals. Non-banks that provide payment services such as remittance companies are normally not considered as an adequate substitute for a bank account.

Insurance is the equitable transfer of the risk of a loss, from one entity to another in exchange for payment. It is a form of risk management primarily used to hedge against the risk of a contingent, uncertain loss. An insurer, or insurance carrier, is a company selling the insurance; the insured, or policyholder, is the person or entity buying the insurance policy. The amount of money to be charged for a certain amount of insurance coverage is called the premium. Risk management, the practice of appraising and controlling risk, has evolved as a discrete field of study and practice. The transaction involves the insured assuming a guaranteed and known relatively small loss in the form of payment to the insurer in exchange for the insurer's promise to compensate (indemnify) the insured in the case of a financial (personal) loss. The insured receives a contract, called the insurance policy, which details the conditions and circumstances under which the insured will be financially compensated. Insurance involves pooling funds from *many* insured entities (known as exposures) to pay for the losses that some may incur. The insured entities are therefore protected from risk for a fee, with the fee being dependent upon the frequency and severity of the event occurring. In order to be an insurable risk, the risk insured against must meet certain characteristics. Insurance as a financial intermediary is a commercial enterprise and a major part of the financial services industry, but individual entities can also self-insure through saving money for possible future losses.

This book has been intended as a manual for students of this subject.

I would like to thank my team for standing beside me throughout my career and writing this book. My special thanks go to "Random Publications" who have published the book.

—Adam Lerwick

Contents

1

History of Banking in India

Without a sound and effective banking system in India it cannot have a healthy economy. The banking system of India should not only be hassle free but it should be able to meet new challenges posed by the technology and any other external and internal factors.

For the past three decades India's banking system has several outstanding achievements to its credit. The most striking is its extensive reach. It is no longer confined to only metropolitans or cosmopolitans in India. In fact, Indian banking system has reached even to the remote corners of the country. This is one of the main reason of India's growth process.

The government's regular policy for Indian bank since 1969 has paid rich dividends with the nationalisation of 14 major private banks of India.

Not long ago, an account holder had to wait for hours at the bank counters for getting a draft or for withdrawing his own money. Today, he has a choice. Gone are days when the most efficient bank transferred money from one branch to other in two days. Now it is simple as instant messaging or dial a pizza. Money have become the order of the day.

The first bank in India, though conservative, was established in 1786. From 1786 till today, the journey of Indian Banking System can be segregated into three distinct phases. They are as mentioned below:

- Early phase from 1786 to 1969 of Indian Banks
- Nationalisation of Indian Banks and up to 1991 prior to Indian banking sector Reforms.

- New phase of Indian Banking System with the advent of Indian Financial & Banking Sector Reforms after 1991.

To make this write-up more explanatory, I prefix the scenario as Phase I, Phase II and Phase III.

Phase I

The General Bank of India was set up in the year 1786. Next came Bank of Hindustan and Bengal Bank. The East India Company established Bank of Bengal (1809), Bank of Bombay (1840) and Bank of Madras (1843) as independent units and called it Presidency Banks. These three banks were amalgamated in 1920 and Imperial Bank of India was established which started as private shareholders banks, mostly Europeans shareholders.

In 1865 Allahabad Bank was established and first time exclusively by Indians, Punjab National Bank Ltd. was set up in 1894 with headquarters at Lahore. Between 1906 and 1913, Bank of India, Central Bank of India, Bank of Baroda, Canara Bank, Indian Bank, and Bank of Mysore were set up. Reserve Bank of India came in 1935.

During the first phase the growth was very slow and banks also experienced periodic failures between 1913 and 1948. There were approximately 1100 banks, mostly small. To streamline the functioning and activities of commercial banks, the Government of India came up with The Banking Companies Act, 1949 which was later changed to Banking Regulation Act 1949 as per amending Act of 1965 (Act No. 23 of 1965). Reserve Bank of India was vested with extensive powers for the supervision of banking in india as the Central Banking Authority.

During those days public has lesser confidence in the banks. As an aftermath deposit mobilisation was slow. Abreast of it the savings bank facility provided by the Postal department was comparatively safer. Moreover, funds were largely given to traders.

Phase II

Government took major steps in this Indian Banking Sector Reform after independence. In 1955, it nationalised Imperial Bank of India with extensive banking facilities on a large scale specially in rural and semi-urban areas. It formed State Bank of india to act as the principal agent of RBI and to handle banking transactions of the Union and State Governments all over the country.

Seven banks forming subsidiary of State Bank of India was nationalised in 1960 on 19th July, 1969, major process of nationalisation was carried out. It was the effort of the then Prime Minister of India, Mrs. Indira Gandhi. 14 major commercial banks in the country was nationalised.

Second phase of nationalisation Indian Banking Sector Reform was carried out in 1980 with seven more banks. This step brought 80% of the banking segment in India under Government ownership.

The following are the steps taken by the Government of India to Regulate Banking Institutions in the Country:

- 1949 : Enactment of Banking Regulation Act.
- 1955 : Nationalisation of State Bank of India.
- 1959 : Nationalisation of SBI subsidiaries.
- 1961 : Insurance cover extended to deposits.
- 1969 : Nationalisation of 14 major banks.
- 1971 : Creation of credit guarantee corporation.
- 1975 : Creation of regional rural banks.
- 1980 : Nationalisation of seven banks with deposits over 200 crore.

After the nationalisation of banks, the branches of the public sector bank India rose to approximately 800% in deposits and advances took a huge jump by 11,000%.

Banking in the sunshine of Government ownership gave the public implicit faith and immense confidence about the sustainability of these institutions.

Phase III

This phase has introduced many more products and facilities in the banking sector in its reforms measure. In 1991, under the chairmanship of M Narasimham, a committee was set up by his name which worked for the liberalisation of banking practices.

The country is flooded with foreign banks and their ATM stations. Efforts are being put to give a satisfactory service to customers. Phone banking and net banking is introduced. The entire system became more convenient and swift. Time is given more importance than money.

The financial system of India has shown a great deal of resilience. It is sheltered from any crisis triggered by any external macroeconomics shock as other East Asian Countries suffered. This is all due to a flexible exchange rate regime, the foreign reserves are high, the capital account is not yet fully convertible, and banks and their customers have limited foreign exchange exposure.

Nationalisation of Banks in India

The nationalisation of banks in India took place in 1969 by Mrs. Indira Gandhi the then prime minister. It nationalised 14 banks then. These banks were mostly owned by businessmen and even managed by them.

- Central Bank of India
- Bank of Maharashtra
- Dena Bank
- Punjab National Bank
- Syndicate Bank
- Canara Bank
- Indian Bank
- Indian Overseas Bank
- Bank of Baroda
- Union Bank
- Allahabad Bank
- United Bank of India
- UCO Bank
- Bank of India

Befor the steps of nationalisation of Indian banks, only State Bank of India (SBI) was nationalised. It took place in July 1955 under the SBI Act of 1955. Nationalisation of Seven State Banks of India (formed subsidiary) took place on 19th July, 1960. The State Bank of India is India's largest commercial bank and is ranked one of the top five banks worldwide. It serves 90 million customers through a network of 9,000 branches and it offers -- either directly or through subsidiaries -- a wide range of banking services.

The second phase of nationalisation of Indian banks took place in the year 1980. Seven more banks were nationalised with deposits over 200 crores. Till this year, approximately 80% of the banking segment in India were under Government ownership.

After the nationalisation of banks in India, the branches of the public sector banks rose to approximately 800% in deposits and advances took a huge jump by 11,000%.

- 1955 : Nationalisation of State Bank of India.
- 1959 : Nationalisation of SBI subsidiaries.
- 1969 : Nationalisation of 14 major banks.
- 1980 : Nationalisation of seven banks with deposits over 200 crores.

Scheduled Commercial Banks in India

The commercial banking structure in India consists of:

- Scheduled Commercial Banks in India
- Unscheduled Banks in India

Scheduled Banks in India constitute those banks which have been included in the Second Schedule of Reserve Bank of India(RBI) Act, 1934. RBI in turn includes only those banks in this schedule which satisfy the criteria laid down vide section 42 (6) (a) of the Act.

As on 30th June, 1999, there were 300 scheduled banks in India having a total network of 64,918 branches.The scheduled commercial banks in India comprise of State bank of India and its associates (8), nationalised banks (19), foreign banks (45), private sector banks (32), co-operative banks and regional rural banks.

"Scheduled banks in India" means the State Bank of India constituted under the State Bank of India Act, 1955 (23 of 1955), a subsidiary bank as defined in the State Bank of India (Subsidiary Banks) Act, 1959 (38 of 1959), a corresponding new bank constituted under section 3 of the Banking Companies (Acquisition and Transfer of Undertakings) Act, 1970 (5 of 1970), or under section 3 of the Banking Companies (Acquisition and Transfer of Undertakings) Act, 1980 (40 of 1980), or any other bank being a bank included in the Second Schedule to the Reserve Bank of India Act, 1934 (2 of 1934), but does not include a co-operative bank".

"Non-scheduled bank in India" means a banking company as defined in clause (c) of section 5 of the Banking Regulation Act, 1949 (10 of 1949), which is not a scheduled bank".

The following are the Scheduled Banks in India (Public Sector):

- State Bank of India
- State Bank of Bikaner and Jaipur
- State Bank of Hyderabad
- State Bank of Indore
- State Bank of Mysore

- State Bank of Patiala
- State Bank of Saurashtra
- State Bank of Travancore
- Andhra Bank
- Allahabad Bank
- Bank of Baroda
- Bank of India
- Bank of Maharashtra
- Canara Bank
- Central Bank of India
- Corporation Bank
- Dena Bank
- Indian Overseas Bank
- Indian Bank
- Oriental Bank of Commerce
- Punjab National Bank
- Punjab and Sind Bank
- Syndicate Bank
- Union Bank of India
- United Bank of India
- UCO Bank
- Vijaya Bank

The following are the Scheduled Banks in India (Private Sector):

- Vysya Bank Ltd
- Axis Bank Ltd
- Indusind Bank Ltd
- ICICI Banking Corporation Bank Ltd
- Global Trust Bank Ltd
- HDFC Bank Ltd
- Centurion Bank Ltd
- Bank of Punjab Ltd
- IDBI Bank Ltd

The following are the Scheduled Foreign Banks in India:

- American Express Bank Ltd.

- ANZ Gridlays Bank Plc.
- Bank of America NT & SA
- Bank of Tokyo Ltd.
- Banquc Nationale de Paris
- Barclays Bank Plc
- Citi Bank N.C.
- Deutsche Bank A.G.
- Hongkong and Shanghai Banking Corporation
- Standard Chartered Bank.
- The Chase Manhattan Bank Ltd.
- Dresdner Bank AG.

Banks in India

In India the banks are being segregated in different groups. Each group has their own benefits and limitations in operating in India. Each has their own dedicated target market. Few of them only work in rural sector while others in both rural as well as urban. Many even are only catering in cities. Some are of Indian origin and some are foreign players.

All these details and many more is discussed over here. The banks and its relation with the customers, their mode of operation, the names of banks under different groups and other such useful informations are talked about.

One more section has been taken note of is the upcoming foreign banks in India. The RBI has shown certain interest to involve more of foreign banks than the existing one recently. This step has paved a way for few more foreign banks to start business in India.

Major Banks in India

- ABN-AMRO Bank
- Abu Dhabi Commercial Bank
- American Express Bank
- Andhra Bank
- Allahabad Bank
- Axis Bank (Earlier UTI Bank)
- Bank of Baroda
- Bank of India

- Bank of Maharastra
- Bank of Punjab
- Bank of Rajasthan
- Bank of Ceylon
- BNP Paribas Bank
- Canara Bank
- Catholic Syrian Bank
- Central Bank of India
- Centurion Bank
- China Trust Commercial Bank
- Citi Bank
- City Union Bank
- Corporation Bank
- Dena Bank
- Deutsche Bank
- Development Credit Bank
- Dhanalakshmi Bank
- Federal Bank
- HDFC Bank
- HSBC
- ICICI Bank
- IDBI Bank
- Indian Bank
- Indian Overseas Bank
- IndusInd Bank
- ING Vysya Bank
- Jammu & Kashmir Bank
- JPMorgan Chase Bank
- Karnataka Bank
- Karur Vysya Bank
- Laxmi Vilas Bank
- Oriental Bank of Commerce
- Punjab National Bank
- Punjab & Sind Bank

- Scotia Bank
- South Indian Bank
- Standard Chartered Bank
- State Bank of India (SBI)
- State Bank of Bikaner & Jaipur
- State Bank of Hyderabad
- State Bank of Indore
- State Bank of Mysore
- State Bank of Saurastra
- State Bank of Travancore
- Syndicate Bank
- Taib Bank
- UCO Bank
- Union Bank of India
- United Bank of India
- United Bank Of India
- United Western Bank
- Vijaya Bank

Public Sector Banks in India

Among the Public Sector Banks in India, United Bank of India is one of the 14 major banks which were nationalised on July 19, 1969. Its predecessor, in the Public Sector Banks, the United Bank of India Ltd., was formed in 1950 with the amalgamation of four banks viz. Comilla Banking Corporation Ltd. (1914), Bengal Central Bank Ltd. (1918), Comilla Union Bank Ltd. (1922) and Hooghly Bank Ltd. (1932).

Oriental Bank of Commerce (OBC), a Governmet of India Undertaking offers Domestic, NRI and Commercial banking services. OBC is implementing a GRAMEEN PROJECT in Dehradun District (UP) and Hanumangarh District (Raiasthan) disbursing small loans. This Public Secotor Bank India has implemented 14 point action plan for strengthening of credit delivery to women and has designated 5 branches as specialized branches for women entrepreneurs.

The following are the list of Public Sector Banks in India

- Allahabad Bank
- Andhra Bank

- Bank of Baroda
- Bank of India
- Bank of Maharastra
- Canara Bank
- Central Bank of India
- Corporation Bank
- Dena Bank
- Indian Bank
- Indian Overseas Bank
- Oriental Bank of Commerce
- Punjab & Sind Bank
- Punjab National Bank
- Syndicate Bank
- UCO Bank
- Union Bank of India
- United Bank of India
- Vijaya Bank

List of State Bank of India and its subsidiary, a Public Sector Banks

- State Bank of India
  - State Bank of Bikaner & Jaipur
  - State Bank of Hyderabad
  - State Bank of Indore
  - State Bank of Mysore
  - State Bank of Saurastra
  - State Bank of Travancore

Private Sector Banks in India

Private banking in India was practiced since the begining of banking system in India. The first private bank in India to be set up in Private Sector Banks in India was IndusInd Bank. It is one of the fastest growing Bank Private Sector Banks in India. IDBI ranks the tength largest development bank in the world as Private Banks in India and has promoted a world class institutions in India.

The first Private Bank in India to receive an in principle approval from the Reserve Bank of India was Housing Development Finance

Corporation Limited, to set up a bank in the private sector banks in India as part of the RBI's liberalisation of the Indian Banking Industry. It was incorporated in August 1994 as HDFC Bank Limited with registered office in Mumbai and commenced operations as Scheduled Commercial Bank in January 1995.

ING Vysya, yet another Private Bank of India was incorporated in the year 1930. Bangalore has a pride of place for having the first branch inception in the year 1934. With successive years of patronage and constantly setting new standards in banking, ING Vysya Bank has many credits to its account.

List of Private Banks in India

- Bank of Punjab
- Bank of Rajasthan
- Catholic Syrian Bank
- Centurion Bank
- City Union Bank
- Dhanalakshmi Bank
- Development Credit Bank
- Federal Bank
- HDFC Bank
- ICICI Bank
- IDBI Bank
- IndusInd Bank
- ING Vysya Bank
- Jammu & Kashmir Bank
- Karnataka Bank
- Karur Vysya Bank
- Laxmi Vilas Bank
- South Indian Bank
- United Western Bank
- UTI Bank

Co-Operative Banks in India

The Co operative banks in India started functioning almost 100 years ago. The Cooperative bank is an important constituent of the Indian Financial System, judging by the role assigned to co operative, the expectations the co operative is supposed to fulfil, their number, and the number of offices the cooperative bank operate. Though the co operative movement originated in the West, but the importance of such banks have assumed in India is rarely paralleled anywhere else in the world.

The cooperative banks in India plays an important role even today in rural financing. The businessess of cooperative bank in the urban areas also has increased phenomenally in recent years due to the sharp increase in the number of primary co-operative banks. Co operative Banks in India are registered under the Co-operative Societies Act. The cooperative bank is also regulated by the RBI. They are governed by the Banking Regulations Act 1949 and Banking Laws (Co-operative Societies) Act, 1965.

Cooperative banks in India finance rural areas under:

- Farming
- Cattle
- Milk
- Hatchery
- Personal finance

Cooperative banks in India finance urban areas under:

- Self-employment
- Industries
- Small scale units
- Home finance
- Consumer finance
- Personal finance

Some facts about Cooperative banks in India

- Some cooperative banks in India are more forward than many of the state and private sector banks.
- According to NAFCUB the total deposits & lendings of Cooperative Banks in India is much more than Old Private Sector Banks & also the New Private Sector Banks.
- This exponential growth of Co operative Banks in India is attributed mainly to their much better local reach, personal interaction with customers, their ability to catch the nerve of the local clientele.

Regional Rural Banks in India

Rural banking in India started since the establishment of banking sector in India. Rural Banks in those days mainly focussed upon the agro sector. Regional rural banks in India penetrated every corner of the country and extended a helping hand in the growth process of the country. SBI has 30 Regional Rural Banks in India known as RRBs. The rural banks of SBI is spread in 13 states extending from Kashmir to Karnataka and Himachal Pradesh to North East. The total number of SBIs Regional Rural Banks in India branches is 2349 (16%). Till date in rural banking in India, there are 14,475 rural banks in the country of which 2126 (91%) are located in remote rural areas. Apart from SBI, there are other few banks which functions for the development of the rural areas in India. Few of them are as follows.

Haryana State Cooperative Apex Bank Limited

The Haryana State Cooperative Apex Bank Ltd. commonly called as HARCOBANK plays a vital role in rural banking in the economy of Haryana State and has been providing aids and financing farmers, rural artisans, agricultural labourers, entrepreneurs, etc. in the state and giving service to its depositors.

NABARD

National Bank for Agriculture and Rural Development (NABARD) is a development bank in the sector of Regional Rural Banks in India. It provides and regulates credit and gives service for the promotion and development of rural sectors mainly agriculture, small scale industries, cottage and village industries, handicrafts. It also finance rural crafts and other allied rural economic activities to promote integrated rural development. It helps in securing rural prosperity and its connected matters.

Sindhanur Urban Souharda Co-operative Bank

Sindhanur Urban Souharda Co-operative Bank, popularly known as SUCO BANK is the first of its kind in rural banks of India. The impressive story of its inception is interesting and inspiring for all the youth of this country.

United Bank of India

United Bank of India (UBI) also plays an important role in regional rural banks. It has expanded its branch network in a big way to actively participate in the developmental of the rural and semi-urban areas in conformity with the objectives of nationalisation.

Syndicate Bank

Syndicate Bank was firmly rooted in rural India as rural banking and have a clear vision of future India by understanding the grassroot realities. Its progress has been abreast of the phase of progressive banking in India especially in rural banks.

Upcoming Foreign Banks in India

By 2009 few more names is going to be added in the list of foreign banks in India. This is as an aftermath of the sudden interest shown by Reserve Bank of India paving roadmap for foreign banks in India greater freedom in India. Among them is the world's best private bank by EuroMoney magazine, Switzerland's UBS.

The following are the list of foreign banks going to set up business in India

- Royal Bank of Scotland
- Switzerland's UBS
- US-based GE Capital
- Credit Suisse Group
- Industrial and Commercial Bank of China

Merrill Lynch is having a joint venture in Indian investment banking space -- DSP Merrill Lynch. Goldman Sachs holds stakes in Kotak Mahindra arms. GE Capital is also having a wide presence in consumer finance through GE Capital India.

India's GDP is seen growing at a robust pace of around 7% over the next few years, throwing up opportunities for the banking sector to profit from.

The credit of banks has risen by over 25% in 2004-05 and the growth momentum is expected to continue over the next four to five years. Participation in the growth curve of the Indian economy in the next four years will provide foreign banks a launch pad for greater business expansion when they get more freedom after April 2009.

Banking Services in India

With years, banks are also adding services to their customers. The Indian banking industry is passing through a phase of customers market. The customers have more choices in choosing their banks. A competition has been established within the banks operating in India.

With stiff competition and advancement of technology, the services provided by banks has become more easy and convenient. The past days are witness to an hour wait before withdrawing cash from accounts or a cheque from north of the country being cleared in one month in the south. This section of banking deals with the latest discovery in the banking instruments along with the polished version of their old systems.

Bank Account

Open bank account - the most common and first service of the banking sector. There are different types of bank account in Indian banking sector. The bank accounts are as follows:

- Bank Savings Account - Bank Savings Account can be opened for eligible person / persons and certain organisations / agencies (as advised by Reserve Bank of India (RBI) from time to time)
- Bank Current Account - Bank Current Account can be opened by individuals / partnership firms / Private and Public Limited Companies / HUFs / Specified Associates / Societies / Trusts, etc.
- Bank Term Deposits Account - Bank Term Deposits Account can be opened by individuals / partnership firms / Private and Public Limited Companies / HUFs/ Specified Associates / Societies / Trusts, etc.
- Bank Account Online - With the advancement of technology, the major banks in the public and private sector has faciliated their customer to open bank account online. Bank account online is registered through a PC with an internet connection. The advent of bank account online has saved both the cost of operation for banks as well as the time taken in opening an account.

Note :- A minor account can be opened but jointly with a guardian and only the guardian would is allowed to operate the account.

General Procedure to Open an Account

- The Bank will provide you with details of various types of accounts that you may open with the Bank.
- You can have your choice on what type of account would best suit you, based on your needs and requirements
- The Bank will, prior to opening an account, require documentation and information as prescribed by the "Know

Your Customer" (KYC) guidelines issued by RBI and or such other norms or procedures adopted by the Bank prior to opening the account.

- The due diligence process that the Bank would follow, will involve providing documentation verifying your identity, verifying your address, and information onyour occupation or business and source of funds. As part of the due diligence process the Bank may also require an introduction from a person acceptable to the Bank if they so deem necessary and will need your recent photographs.
- The Bank is required by law to obtain Permanent Account Number (PAN) or General Index Register (GIR) Number or, where you do not possess such registration, declaration in Form No. 60 or 61 as specified under the Income Tax Rules.
- In the event that the account opening process is likely to take longer than normal, the Bank will inform you of the revised timeline.
- You can also call your branch or the executive for any queries that you may have and the branch / executive will revert on the query at the earliest.
- The Bank will provide you with the account opening forms and other relevant material to enable you open the account. Bank personnel will advise you on the complete details of information that would be required by the Bank for the verification process.
- The Bank reserves the right, at its sole discretion, to open any account and at such terms as the Bank may prescribe from time to time

Plastic Money

Credit cards in India is gaining ground. A number of banks in India are encouraging people to use credit card. The concept of credit card was used in 1950 with the launch of charge cards in USA by Diners Club and American Express. Credit card however became more popular with use of magnetic strip in 1970.

Credit card in India became popular with the introduction of foreign banks in the country.

Credit cards are financial instruments, which can be used more than once to borrow money or buy products and services on credit. Basically banks, retail stores and other businesses issue these.

Global Player in Credit Card Market

MasterCard

MasterCard is a product of MasterCard International and along with VISA are distributed by financial institutions around the world. Cardholders borrow money against a line of credit and pay it back with interest if the balance is carried over from month to month.

Its products are issued by 23,000 financial institutions in 220 countries and territories. In 1998, it had almost 700 million cards in circulation, whose users spent $650 billion in more than 16.2 million locations.

VISA Card

VISA cards is a product of VISA USA and along with MasterCard is distributed by financial institutions around the world. A VISA cardholder borrows money against a credit line and repays the money with interest if the balance is carried over from month to month in a revolving line of credit. Nearly 600 million cards carry one of the VISA brands and more than 14 million locations accept VISA cards.

American Express

The world's favorite card is American Express Credit Card. More than 57 million cards are in circulation and growing and it is still growing further. Around US $ 123 billion was spent last year through American Express Cards and it is poised to be the world's No. 1 card in the near future. In a regressive US economy last year, the total amount spent on American Express cards rose by 4 percent. American Express cards are very popular in the U.S., Canada, Europe and Asia and are used widely in the retail and everyday expenses segment.

Diners Club International

Diners Club is the world's No. 1 Charge Card. Diners Club cardholders reside all over the world and the Diners Card is a alltime favourite for corporates. There are more than 8 million Diners Club cardholders. They are affluent and are frequent travelers in premier businesses and institutions, including Fortune 500 companies and leading global corporations.

JCB Cards

The JCB Card has a merchant network of 10.93 million in approximately 189 countries. It is supported by over 320 financial institutions worldwide and serves more than 48 million cardholders in eighteen countries world wide. The JCB philosophy of "identify the customer's needs and please the customer with Service from the Heart" is paying rich dividends as their customers spend US$43 billion annually on their JCB cards.

Debit Card

Debit cards, also known as check cards look like credit cards or ATM cards (automated teller machine card). It operate like cash or a personal check. Debit cards are different from credit cards. Credit card is a way to "pay later," whereas debit card is a way to "pay now." When we use a debit card, our money is quickly deducted from the bank account.

Debit cards are accepted at many locations, including grocery stores, retail stores, gasoline stations, and restaurants. Its an alternative to carrying a checkbook or cash.

With debit card, we use our own money and not the issuer's money.

In India almost all the banks issue debit card to its account holders.

Features of Debit Card

- Obtaining a debit card is often easier than obtaining a credit card.
- Using a debit card instead of writing checks saves you from showing identification or giving out personal information at the time of the transaction.
- Using a debit card frees you from carrying cash or a checkbook.
- Using a debit card means you no longer have to stock up on traveler's checks or cash when you travel.
- Debit cards may be more readily accepted by merchants than checks, especially in other states or countries wherever your card brand is accepted.
- The debit card is a quick, "pay now" product, giving you no grace period.
- Using a debit card may mean you have less protection than with a credit card purchase for items which are never delivered, are defective, or were misrepresented. But, as with credit cards, you may dispute unauthorized charges or other mistakes within 60 days. You should contact the card issuer if a problem cannot be resolved with the merchant.

- Returning goods or canceling services purchased with a debit card is treated as if the purchase were made with cash or a check.

Tips for responsible use of Debit Card

- If your card is lost or stolen, report the loss immediately to your financial institution.
- If you suspect your card is being fraudulently used, report it immediately to your financial institution.
- Hold on to your receipts from your debit card transactions. A thief may get your name and debit card number from a receipt and order goods by mail or over the telephone. Your card does not have to be missing in order for it to be misused.
- If you have a PIN number, memorize it. Do not keep your PIN number with your card. Also, don't choose a PIN number that a smart thief could figure out, such as your phone number or birthday.
- Never give your PIN number to anyone. Keep your PIN private.
- Always know how much money you have available in your account. Don't forget that your debit card may allow you to access money that you have set aside to cover a check which has not cleared your bank yet.
- Keep your receipts in one place -- for easy retrieval and better oversight of your bank account.

Loans

Banks in India with the way of development have become easy to apply in loan market. The following loans are given by almost all the banks in the country:

- Personal Loan
- Car Loan or Auto Loan
- Loan against Shares
- Home Loan
- Education Loan or Student Loan

In Personal Loan, one can get a sanctioned loan amount between Rs 25,000 to 10,00,000 depending upon the profile of person applying for the loan. SBI, ICICI, HDFC, HSBC are some of the leading banks which deals in Personal Loan.

Almost all the banks have jumped into the market of car loan which is also sometimes termed as auto loan. It is one of the fast moving financial product of banks. Car loan / auto loan are sanctioned to the extent of 85% upon the ex-showroom price of the car with some simple paper works and a small amount of processing fee. Loan against shares is very easy to get because liquid guarantee is involved in it.

Home loan is the latest craze in the banking sector with the development of the infrastructure. Now people are moving to township outside the city. More number of townships are coming up to meet the demand of 'house for all'. The RBI has also liberalised the interest rates of home loan inorder to match the repayment capability of even middle class people. Almost all banks are dealing in home loan. Again SBI, ICICI, HDFC, HSBC are leading.

The educational loan, rather to be termed as student loan, is a good banking product for the mass. Students with certain academic brilliance, studying at recognised colleges/universities in India and abroad are generally given education loan / student loan so as to meet the expenses on tuition fee/ maintenance cost/books and other equipment.

Money Transfer

Beside lending and depositing money, banks also carry money from one corner of the globe to another. This act of banks is known as transfer of money. This activity is termed as remittance business. Banks generally issue Demand Drafts, Banker's Cheques, Money Orders or other such instruments for transferring the money. This is a type of Telegraphic Transfer or Tele Cash Orders.

It has been only a couple of years that banks have jumped into the money transfer businessess in India. The international money transfer market grew 9.3% from 2003 to 2004 i.e. from US$213 bn. to US$233 bn. in 2004. Economists say that the market of money transfer will further grow at a cumulative 10.1% average growth rate through 2008.

With the use of high technology and varieties of product it seems that "Free" money transfers will become commonplace. We will see more bundling of tailored money services by banks and non-traditional entrants that will include "free" money transfers. Many banks will even use money transfer services as loss-leaders inorder to generate account openings and cross-sell opportunities. The price evolution of money transfer products for banks will be similar to that of consumer bill pay-the product is worth giving away as an account acquisition tool to win overall market share and establish banking relationships.

ATM money transfer card products have had terrible bank adoption rates since being introduced in the last three to four years. Remittees who are highly educated and have been already been exposed to ATM technology in receiving countries tend to have an interest in this product. Money transfer to India is one of the most important part played by the banks. This service provide peace of mind to either the NRIs or to the visitors to India. Many Indian banks have ATM'S (automatic teller machine), enable to draw foreign currency in India.

By 2007, we will see a good percent of all foreign-born households doing some level of online banking. First-mover banks will start having a window of opportunity to include online transfer functionality within the next couple of years, which currently frequents traditional money transmitters such as Western Union. There is a terrific opportunity for banks and non-banks to offer more robust global inter-institutional funds transfer services online. More than half of Western Union's customers today are already banked, and most do not have an alternative product marketed by their bank that is painless, quick, and cost-effective. That will change as banks offer transfer services through their online channel.

Money Transfer to India

Apart from banks few financial institutions and online portals gives services of money transfer to India. Some of them are as under:

- Western Union Money Transfer
- Union Money Transfer
- IKobo Money Transfer
- Cash2india.com
- Remit2india
- Samachar Money Transfer
- Timesofmoney.com
- Wells Fergo International Money Transfer
- Travellers Express
- Money Gram International

Visa Money Transfer

Visa has recently introduced the 'Visa Money Transfer' option for its savings and current account holder of any bank with a visa debit card. This facility helps its customer to transfer funds from his bank account to any visa card, either debit or credit within India.

A Visa Money Transfer is of similar kind, in many respects, to the third-party fund transfer option given by some banks to its account holders through e-cheque, but this is restricted to only visa cardholders.

How to transfer money?

- Log on to your bank account through your respective bank websites.
- Fill the beneficiary details like visa card numbers, name, address and then specify the amount that needs to be transferred. For bank account specify the visa card number and credit card number for paying credit card bill.
- Click on to VISA Transfer Payments button.
- Transfer immediately or on schedule date. Your account will be debited according to the date mentioned.

Notable points of Visa Money Transfer

- The time taken for money transfers could be the same or even more than that of a demand draft i.e. two or three days or even more.
- Currently there are no charges but limits has been set by certain banks on the current transfers.
- It is available in 150 cities across the country now.
- The transferred amount can neither be changed nor stopped once it is initiated.

The Banking System

Almost 80% of the business are still controlled by Public Sector Banks (PSBs). PSBs are still dominating the commercial banking system. Shares of the leading PSBs are already listed on the stock exchanges.

The RBI has given licences to new private sector banks as part of the liberalisation process. The RBI has also been granting licences to industrial houses. Many banks are successfully running in the retail and consumer segments but are yet to deliver services to industrial finance, retail trade, small business and agricultural finance.

The PSBs will play an important role in the industry due to its number of branches and foreign banks facing the constrait of limited number of branches. Hence, in order to achieve an efficient banking system, the onus is on the Government to encourage the PSBs to be run on professional lines.

Development Finance Institutions

FIs's access to SLR funds reduced. Now they have to approach the capital market for debt and equity funds.

Convertibility clause no longer obligatory for assistance to corporates sanctioned by term-lending institutions.

Capital adequacy norms extended to financial institutions.

DFIs such as IDBI and ICICI have entered other segments of financial services such as commercial banking, asset management and insurance through separate ventures. The move to universal banking has started.

Non-banking Finance Companies

In the case of new NBFCs seeking registration with the RBI, the requirement of minimum net owned funds, has been raised to Rs.2 crores.

Until recently, the money market in India was narrow and circumscribed by tight regulations over interest rates and participants. The secondary market was underdeveloped and lacked liquidity. Several measures have been initiated and include new money market instruments, strengthening of existing instruments and setting up of the Discount and Finance House of India (DFHI).

The RBI conducts its sales of dated securities and treasury bills through its open market operations (OMO) window. Primary dealers bid for these securities and also trade in them. The DFHI is the principal agency for developing a secondary market for money market instruments and Government of India treasury bills. The RBI has introduced a liquidity adjustment facility (LAF) in which liquidity is injected through reverse repo auctions and liquidity is sucked out through repo auctions.

On account of the substantial issue of government debt, the gilt-edged market occupies an important position in the financial set- up. The Securities Trading Corporation of India (STCI), which started operations in June 1994 has a mandate to develop the secondary market in government securities.

Long-term debt market: The development of a long-term debt market is crucial to the financing of infrastructure. After bringing some order to the equity market, the SEBI has now decided to concentrate on the development of the debt market. Stamp duty is being withdrawn at the time of dematerialisation of debt instruments in order to encourage paperless trading.

The Capital Market

The number of shareholders in India is estimated at 25 million. However, only an estimated two lakh persons actively trade in stocks. There has been a dramatic improvement in the country's stock market trading infrastructure during the last few years.

Expectations are that India will be an attractive emerging market with tremendous potential. Unfortunately, during recent times the stock markets have been constrained by some unsavoury developments, which has led to retail investors deserting the stock markets.

Mutual Funds

The mutual funds industry is now regulated under the SEBI (Mutual Funds) Regulations, 1996 and amendments thereto. With the issuance of SEBI guidelines, the industry had a framework for the establishment of many more players, both Indian and foreign players.

The Unit Trust of India remains easily the biggest mutual fund controlling a corpus of nearly Rs.70,000 crores, but its share is going down. The biggest shock to the mutual fund industry during recent times was the insecurity generated in the minds of investors regarding the US 64 scheme. With the growth in the securities markets and tax advantages granted for investment in mutual fund units, mutual funds started becoming popular.

The foreign owned AMCs are the ones which are now setting the pace for the industry. They are introducing new products, setting new standards of customer service, improving disclosure standards and experimenting with new types of distribution.

The insurance industry is the latest to be thrown open to competition from the private sector including foreign players. Foreign companies can only enter joint ventures with Indian companies, with participation restricted to 26 per cent of equity. It is too early to conclude whether the erstwhile public sector monopolies will successfully be able to face up to the competition posed by the new players, but it can be expected that the customer will gain from improved service.

The new players will need to bring in innovative products as well as fresh ideas on marketing and distribution, in order to improve the low per capita insurance coverage. Good regulation will, of course, be essential.

Overall Approach to Reforms

The last ten years have seen major improvements in the working of various financial market participants. The government and the regulatory authorities have followed a step-by-step approach, not a big bang one. The entry of foreign players has assisted in the introduction of international practices and systems. Technology developments have improved customer service. Some gaps however remain (for example: lack of an inter-bank interest rate benchmark, an active corporate debt market and a developed derivatives market). On the whole, the cumulative effect of the developments since 1991 has been quite encouraging. An indication of the strength of the reformed Indian financial system can be seen from the way India was not affected by the Southeast Asian crisis.

However, financial liberalisation alone will not ensure stable economic growth. Some tough decisions still need to be taken. Without fiscal control, financial stability cannot be ensured. The fate of the Fiscal Responsibility Bill remains unknown and high fiscal deficits continue. In the case of financial institutions, the political and legal structures hve to ensure that borrowers repay on time the loans they have taken. The phenomenon of rich industrialists and bankrupt companies continues. Further, frauds cannot be totally prevented, even with the best of regulation. However, punishment has to follow crime, which is often not the case in India.

Reserve Bank of India (RBI)

Kindly Take Note : Reserve Bank of India (RBI) is the central bank of the country and is different from Central Bank of India.

The central bank of the country is the Reserve Bank of India (RBI). It was established in April 1935 with a share capital of Rs. 5 crores on the basis of the recommendations of the Hilton Young Commission. The share capital was divided into shares of Rs. 100 each fully paid which was entirely owned by private shareholders in the begining. The Government held shares of nominal value of Rs. 2,20,000.

Reserve Bank of India was nationalised in the year 1949. The general superintendence and direction of the Bank is entrusted to Central Board of Directors of 20 members, the Governor and four Deputy Governors, one Government official from the Ministry of Finance, ten nominated Directors by the Government to give representation to important elements in the economic life of the country, and four nominated Directors by the Central Government to represent the four local Boards with the headquarters at Mumbai, Kolkata, Chennai and New Delhi.

Local Boards consist of five members each Central Government appointed for a term of four years to represent territorial and economic interests and the interests of co-operative and indigenous banks.

The Reserve Bank of India Act, 1934 was commenced on April 1, 1935. The Act, 1934 (II of 1934) provides the statutory basis of the functioning of the Bank.

The Bank was constituted for the need of following:

- To regulate the issue of banknotes
- To maintain reserves with a view to securing monetary stability and
- To operate the credit and currency system of the country to its advantage.

Functions of Reserve Bank of India

The Reserve Bank of India Act of 1934 entrust all the important functions of a central bank the Reserve Bank of India.

Bank of Issue

Under Section 22 of the Reserve Bank of India Act, the Bank has the sole right to issue bank notes of all denominations. The distribution of one rupee notes and coins and small coins all over the country is undertaken by the Reserve Bank as agent of the Government. The Reserve Bank has a separate Issue Department which is entrusted with the issue of currency notes. The assets and liabilities of the Issue Department are kept separate from those of the Banking Department. Originally, the assets of the Issue Department were to consist of not less than two-fifths of gold coin, gold bullion or sterling securities provided the amount of gold was not less than Rs. 40 crores in value. The remaining three-fifths of the assets might be held in rupee coins, Government of India rupee securities, eligible bills of exchange and promissory notes payable in India. Due to the exigencies of the Second World War and the post-was period, these provisions were considerably modified. Since 1957, the Reserve Bank of India is required to maintain gold and foreign exchange reserves of Ra. 200 crores, of which at least Rs. 115 crores should be in gold. The system as it exists today is known as the minimum reserve system.

Banker to Government

The second important function of the Reserve Bank of India is to act as Government banker, agent and adviser. The Reserve Bank is agent of Central Government and of all State Governments in India excepting that of Jammu and Kashmir. The Reserve Bank has the obligation to transact Government business, via. to keep the cash balances as deposits free of interest, to receive and to make payments on behalf of the Government and to carry out their exchange remittances and other banking operations. The Reserve Bank of India helps the Government - both the Union and the States to float new loans and to manage public debt. The Bank makes ways and means advances to the Governments for 90 days. It makes loans and advances to the States and local authorities. It acts as adviser to the Government on all monetary and banking matters.

Bankers' Bank and Lender of the Last Resort

The Reserve Bank of India acts as the bankers' bank. According to the provisions of the Banking Companies Act of 1949, every scheduled bank was required to maintain with the Reserve Bank a cash balance equivalent to 5% of its demand liabilites and 2 per cent of its time liabilities in India.

By an amendment of 1962, the distinction between demand and time liabilities was abolished and banks have been asked to keep cash reserves equal to 3 per cent of their aggregate deposit liabilities. The minimum cash requirements can be changed by the Reserve Bank of India.

The scheduled banks can borrow from the Reserve Bank of India on the basis of eligible securities or get financial accommodation in times of need or stringency by rediscounting bills of exchange. Since commercial banks can always expect the Reserve Bank of India to come to their help in times of banking crisis the Reserve Bank becomes not only the banker's bank but also the lender of the last resort.

Controller of Credit

The Reserve Bank of India is the controller of credit i.e. it has the power to influence the volume of credit created by banks in India.

It can do so through changing the Bank rate or through open market operations. According to the Banking Regulation Act of 1949, the Reserve Bank of India can ask any particular bank or the whole banking system not to lend to particular groups or persons on the basis of certain types of securities. Since 1956, selective controls of credit are increasingly being used by the Reserve Bank. The Reserve Bank of India is armed with many more powers to control the Indian money market.

Every bank has to get a licence from the Reserve Bank of India to do banking business within India, the licence can be cancelled by the Reserve Bank of certain stipulated conditions are not fulfilled. Every bank will have to get the permission of the Reserve Bank before it can open a new branch.

Each scheduled bank must send a weekly return to the Reserve Bank showing, in detail, its assets and liabilities. This power of the Bank to call for information is also intended to give it effective control of the credit system. The Reserve Bank has also the power to inspect the accounts of any commercial bank.

As supereme banking authority in the country, the Reserve Bank of India, therefore, has the following powers:

(a) It holds the cash reserves of all the scheduled banks.

(b) It controls the credit operations of banks through quantitative and qualitative controls.

(c) It controls the banking system through the system of licensing, inspection and calling for information.

(d) It acts as the lender of the last resort by providing rediscount facilities to scheduled banks.

Custodian of Foreign Reserves

The Reserve Bank of India has the responsibility to maintain the official rate of exchange. According to the Reserve Bank of India Act of 1934, the Bank was required to buy and sell at fixed rates any amount of sterling in lots of not less than Rs. 10,000.

The rate of exchange fixed was Re. 1 = sh. 6d. Since 1935 the Bank was able to maintain the exchange rate fixed at lsh.6d. though there were periods of extreme pressure in favour of or against the rupee. After India became a member of the International Monetary Fund in 1946, the Reserve Bank has the responsibility of maintaining fixed exchange rates with all other member countries of the I.M.F.

Besides maintaining the rate of exchange of the rupee, the Reserve Bank has to act as the custodian of India's reserve of international currencies. The vast sterling balances were acquired and managed by the Bank. Further, the RBI has the responsibility of administering the exchange controls of the country.

Supervisory Functions

In addition to its traditional central banking functions, the Reserve bank has certain non-monetary functions of the nature of supervision of banks and promotion of sound banking in India. The Reserve Bank Act, 1934, and the Banking Regulation Act, 1949 have given the RBI wide powers of supervision and control over commercial and co-operative banks, relating to licensing and establishments, branch expansion, liquidity of their assets, management and methods of working, amalgamation, reconstruction, and liquidation. The RBI is authorised to carry out periodical inspections of the banks and to call for returns and necessary information from them. The nationalisation of 14 major Indian scheduled banks in July 1969 has imposed new responsibilities on the RBI for directing the growth of banking and credit policies towards more rapid development of the economy and realisation of certain desired social objectives. The supervisory functions of the RBI have helped a great deal in improving the standard of banking in India to develop on sound lines and to improve the methods of their operation.

Promotional Functions

With economic growth assuming a new urgency since Independence, the range of the Reserve Bank's functions has steadily widened. The Bank now performs a varietyof developmental and promotional functions, which, at one time, were regarded as outside the normal scope of central banking. The Reserve Bank was asked to promote banking habit, extend banking facilities to rural and semi-urban areas, and establish and promote new specialised financing agencies. Accordingly, the Reserve Bank has helped in the setting up of the IFCI and the SFC; it set up the Deposit Insurance Corporation in 1962, the Unit Trust of India in 1964, the Industrial Development Bank of India also in 1964, the Agricultural Refinance Corporation of India in 1963 and the Industrial Reconstruction Corporation of India in 1972. These institutions were set up directly or indirectly by the Reserve Bank to promote saving habit and to mobilise savings, and to provide industrial finance as well as agricultural finance. As far back as 1935, the Reserve Bank of India set up the Agricultural Credit Department to provide agricultural credit.

But only since 1951 the Bank's role in this field has become extremely important. The Bank has developed the co-operative credit movement to encourage saving, to eliminate moneylenders from the villages and to route its short term credit to agriculture. The RBI has set up the Agricultural Refinance and Development Corporation to provide long-term finance to farmers.

Classification of RBIs Functions

The monetary functions also known as the central banking functions of the RBI are related to control and regulation of money and credit, i.e., issue of currency, control of bank credit, control of foreign exchange operations, banker to the Government and to the money market. Monetary functions of the RBI are significant as they control and regulate the volume of money and credit in the country.

Equally important, however, are the non-monetary functions of the RBI in the context of India's economic backwardness. The supervisory function of the RBI may be regarded as a non-monetary function (though many consider this a monetary function).

The promotion of sound banking in India is an important goal of the RBI, the RBI has been given wide and drastic powers, under the Banking Regulation Act of 1949 - these powers relate to licencing of banks, branch expansion, liquidity of their assets, management and methods of working, inspection, amalgamation, reconstruction and liquidation. Under the RBI's supervision and inspection, the working of banks has greatly improved.

Commercial banks have developed into financially and operationally sound and viable units. The RBI's powers of supervision have now been extended to non-banking financial intermediaries. Since independence, particularly after its nationalisation 1949, the RBI has followed the promotional functions vigorously and has been responsible for strong financial support to industrial and agricultural development in the country.

Industrial Development Bank of India Ltd. (IDBI)

Industrial Development Bank of India (IDBI) is the tength largest bank in the world in terms of development.

The National Stock Exchange (NSE), The National Securities Depository Services Ltd. (NSDL), Stock Holding Corporation of India (SHCIL) are some of the institutions which has been built by IDBI. IDBI is a strategic investor in a plethora of institutions which have revolutionized the Indian Financial Markets.

IDBI Bank, promoted by IDBI Group started in November 1995 with a branch at Indore with an equity capital base of Rs. 1000 million.

Main Functions of IDBI

IDBI is vested with the responsibility of co-ordinating the working of institutions engaged in financing, promoting and developing industries. It has evolved an appropriate mechanism for this purpose. IDBI also undertakes/supports wide-ranging promotional activities including entrepreneurship development programmes for new entrepreneurs, provision of consultancy services for small and medium enterprises, upgradation of technology and programmes for economic upliftment of the underprivileged.

IDBI's Role as a Catalyst

IDBI's role as a catalyst to industrial development encompasses a wide spectrum of activities. IDBI can finance all types of industrial concerns covered under the provisions of the IDBI Act. With over three decades of service to the Indian industry, IDBI has grown substantially in terms of size of operations and portfolio.

Developmental Activities of IDBI

Promotional Activities

In fulfilment of its developmental role, the Bank continues to perform a wide range of promotional activities relating to developmental programmes for new entrepreneurs, consultancy services for small and medium enterprises and programmes designed for accredited voluntary agencies for the economic upliftment of the underprivileged. These include entrepreneurship development, self-employment and wage employment in the industrial sector for the weaker sections of society through voluntary agencies, support to Science and Technology Entrepreneurs' Parks, Energy Conservation, Common Quality Testing Centres for small industries.

Technical Consultancy Organisations

With a view to making available at a reasonable cost, consultancy and advisory services to entrepreneurs, particularly to new and small entrepreneurs, IDBI, in collaboration with other All-India Financial Institutions, has set up a network of Technical Consultancy Organisations (TCOs) covering the entire country. TCOs offer diversified services to small and medium enterprises in the selection, formulation and appraisal of projects, their implementation and review.

Entrepreneurship Development Institute

Realising that entrepreneurship development is the key to industrial development, IDBI played a prime role in setting up of the

Entrepreneurship Development Institute of India for fostering entrepreneurship in the country. It has also established similar institutes in Bihar, Orissa, Madhya Pradesh and Uttar Pradesh. IDBI also extends financial support to various organisations in conducting studies or surveys of relevance to industrial development.

Easy Banking

This section is fully dedicated to the Tech Banking. A decade before, it was tough to belief that banking secctor will be at a finger tip. Now its possible. A mobile hand set with a connection is the only instrument needed to make a gateway to your banking transaction, the latest innovation of technology.

Apart from the Mobile Banking, including of SMS Banking, Net Banking and ATMs are the major steps taken by the banks in India towards modernisation. With all these devises and systems, there is a complete freedom to experience. Check your account, transfer your fund, make payments and what more, do anything of everything what has been followed in physical banking since ages. But this time no standing for hours in front of cash counter and no time boundation in withdrawing your own money.

Indian Banks Association

The Indian Banks Association (IBA) was formed on the 26th September, 1946 with 22 members. Today IBA has more than 156 members comprising of Public Sector banks, Private Sector banks, Foreign banks having offices in India, Urban Co-operative banks, Developmental financial institutions, Federations, merchant banks, mutual funds, housing finance corporations, etc.

The Functioning of IBA

- To promote sound and progressive banking principles and practices.
- To render assistance and to provide common services to members.
- To organise co-ordination and co-operation on procedural, legal, technical, administrative and professional matters.
- To collect, classify and circulate statistical and other information.
- To pool together expertise towards common purposes such as reduction in costs, increase in efficiency, productivity and improve systems, procedures and banking practices.

- To project good public image of banking through publicity and public relations.
- To encourage sports and cultural activities among bank employees.

The Organisational Structure of IBA

The Managing Committee manages the affairs, business and funds of IBA. The managing Committee is elected by the Ordinary members of the Association, and is the highest management and policy making body of the Association.

The Chairman of the Association heads upon the working of the Association. He provides guidelines to the Association. The administrative head of IBA is the Chief Executive of IBA. He is also the Secretary to the Managing Committee. He leads a team of executives, officers and other staff members.

IBA constitutes standing committees/task forces/ small groups/ committees of experts from member banks for the examining of various aspects relating to industry level issues to get solutions.

Recommendations of these groups/committees, are communicated to members with the approval of the managing committee or taken up with the concerned authorities for action.

Proxy Banking In India

Indian villages were miles away from mutual funds, insurance and even equity trading. Thanks to Internet Kiosk and the ATM duo which has made it possible for rural India. This kiosk has been set up by ICICI Bank in partnership with network n-Logue Communications in remote villages of Southern part of the country. This is known as Proxi Banking. With the help of fibre optic cables, this kiosk works on wireless in local loop technology.

2

Regional Rural Banks

What are They

RRBs are state sponsored, regionally based and rural oriented commercial banks envisaged to combine simultaneously the desirable qualities of both co-operative banks and commercial banks. RRBs, being an important segment of the Rural Financial Institutions in the country, have carved out a special place for themselves in terms of geographical coverage, clientele outreach, business volume and contributions for development of rural economy. RRBs are focusing their attention on the attainment of sustainable viability, improved customer services, new and innovative loan products and diversified business portfolio. RRBs are at par with the scheduled commercial banks in respect of priority sector lending, investment avenues and credit discipline and transparency.

While the performance of many RRBs improved significantly, the performance of some of them remains far from being satisfactory in view of their tardy business growth and lack of operational viability.

How they are Different from Commercial Banks

Though RRBs are basically scheduled commercial Banks they differ from the commercial banks in the following respects:

- The area of operation of an RRB is limited to a particular region comprising one or more districts of a State.
- RRBs grant direct loans and advances specifically to weaker sections of the rural areas for productive purpose

They are to provide credit to agriculturists and others in the rural areas at the lower lending rate than any other agency in the rural area. To facilitate this various concessions have been provided to them by the sponsoring bank, as well as the Reserve Bank of India. These concessions take the form of lower rate of interest on refinance by RBI, refinance facilities by NABARD, lower cash ratio, lower SLR, lower rate of interest from the sponsoring banks, managerial and staff assistance from the sponsoring banks and reimbursement of expenses on staff training.

How they Came into Existence

Although the co-operative and commercial banks had an impressive record in terms of geographical coverage and disbursement of credit, it was observed that the vast majority of the poor were generally deprived of credit and other banking facilities. In order to provide access to low-cost banking facilities to the poor, a new set-up of banks, viz. RRBs, was established in the country to meet exclusively the needs of the weaker sections of the rural population, as institutions which "combine the local feel and the familiarity with rural problems which the cooperatives possess and the degree of business organization, ability to mobilize deposits, access to central money markets and modernized outlook which the commercial banks have".

The Govt. of India, in July 1975, appointed a Working Group to study in depth the problem of devising alternative agencies to provide institutional credit to the rural people in the context of steps then initiated under the 20 Point Economic Programme. The Working Group identified various weaknesses of the co-operative credit agencies and the commercial banks and felt that these institutions would not be able to fill the regional and functional gaps in the rural credit system within a reasonable period of time. The Group therefore recommended a new type of institution which combines-

- Local feel and familiarity with rural possess problems which co-operative banks.
- Degree of business organization ability to mobilise deposit, access to money market and modernised outlook which commercial banks have.

Thus, it was envisaged to combine desirable qualities of co-operative banks and commercial banks in RRB's at the same time, it was emphasised that the role of RRB's would be to supplement and not supplant the other institutional agencies already existing in the field.

The Government of India promulgated the Regional Rural Banks Ordinance on 26th September 1975, which was later replaced by the

Regional Rural Bank Act 1976. The preamble to the Act states the objective to develop rural economy by providing credit and facilities for the development of agriculture, trade, commerce, industry and other productive activities in the rural areas, particularly to small and marginal farmers, agricultural labourers, artisans and small entrepreneurs.

The RRB Act empowers the Central Govt. to open the banks from time to time at places where it may consider it necessary. A Regional Rural Bank is jointly owned by the Govt. of India, the Government of concerned state and public sector bank, which sponsored it. The authorised capital of each bank is Rs. 1 crores (subsequently raised 5 Crores) with paid-up capital Rs.25 Lacs (subsequently increased to Rs.1 Crore) which is held by them in the proportion of 50, 15 and 35 per cent respectively. Each bank carries the banking business within the local limits specified by the Govt. notification.

Progress of RRBs

These banks, which at the outset adopted lower scales of compensation for their staff than their sponsor banks, were specially mandated to lend to weaker sections at rates of interest with a concessional element. They could initially manage to lend at concessional rates because of their access to subsidised refinance from their sponsor banks and NABARD.

But the RRBs were crippled soon enough by several factors among which was a new compensation policy in pursuance of which they had to pay their employees on par with those of their sponsor banks. Their character as low cost institutions specially designed to serve rural areas was thus lost irretrievably. They were also adversely affected by the problems of mounting overdues and uneasy industrial relations.

Other deficiencies of RRBs are as under:

According to Narasimham Committee, RRBs have low earning capacity. They have not been able to earn much profits in view of their policy of providing low cost loans

According to RBI, recovery position of RRBs is not satisfactory. There are a large number of defaulters.

Their cost of operation has been high on account of the increase in the salary scales of the employees of these banks in line with the salary structure of the employees of commercial banks. In most cases these banks followed the same methods of operation and procedures as followed by commercial banks. Therefore these procedures have not found favour with the rural masses.

In many cases banks have not been located at the right place. For instance the sponsoring banks are also running their branches in the same areas where RRBs are operating

Reconstruction of RRBs

Government of India have to be take up reconstruction/ recapitalisation of the RRBs to sustain their viability and progress. Government of India started making recurring annual budgetary allocations for this purpose.

Impact of Restructuring Programme on RRBs

Recapitalisation and other restructuring measures have had a very positive impact on the performance of RRBs. A tremendous awareness has been created and all concerned are now alive to the reality that the future of RRBs depends upon their successfully competing with other banking organisations. For this purpose, efficiency, productivity and profitability have been given their due importance. There is now a greater awareness among the sponsor banks themselves as they have become more responsive to the problems of RRBs.

On the financial front, the performance of RRBs though actually improved in the years immediately following the first phase of recapitalisation i.e. in 1995-96 and 1996-97, it was overshadowed due to the introduction of prudential norms of Asset Classification, Income Recognition and Provisioning for the RRBs. The RRBs' financial performance came in the limelight in 1997-98 when RRBs as a group earned profit for the first time since their establishment.

During 2001-02, as many as 167 RRBs earned profit of Rs.699.92 crore as against only 32 RRBs earning profit of Rs.29 crore during 1994-95. On the other hand, the losses incurred by the loss incurring RRBs reduced from Rs.423 crore (164 RRBs) to Rs.92.05 crore (29 RRBs) during the same period.

The RRBs as a group made a profit of Rs.73 crore for the first time during 1997-98 and improved the same further to Rs.601 crore and to Rs.608 crore during the last two years i.e. 2000-01 and 2001-2002.

The viability based categorisation of RRBs as on 31 March 2002 shows that out of 196 RRBs, 86 RRBs have wiped off their accumulated losses and in a way attained a sustainable viability whereas 89 other RRBs have achieved a turn around and attained a current viability status leaving only 29 RRBs which continued to incur losses.

The genuine credit needs of the borrowers are being met by RRBs in their respective area of operations. The total loans disbursed by RRBs have increased from Rs.1440 crore in 1993-94 to Rs.10571 crore in 2001-02. The total Outstanding Advances of RRBs stood at Rs.18629 crore as on 31 March 2002 as against Rs.5253 crore as on 31 March 1994.

The recovery performance of RRBs have shown a consistent improvement from around 40% in 1991-92 to 70 % during the year 2001-02. The NPAs of RRBs have also been declining in percentage terms and stood at 16% as on 31 March 2002 as against 43% as on 31 March 1996 when the norms were first made applicable to the RRBs.

Terms of Reference of Working Group on RRBs

To review the progress in dispensation of rural credit especially through RRBs since their inception.

To examine the legal, regulatory and policy framework of RRBs with particular reference to determine their effectiveness in meeting the complete banking needs of rural households and rural economy.

To make detailed recommendations in regard to legal, regulatory, supervisory, institutional and technological dimensions for making RRBs an effective instrument for development and growth of the rural economy.

The group has submitted its report during August 2002, and has suggested amendments to several provisions of the Act.

The relevant provisions relate to Preamble of the Act, licence to RRBs, capital structure and share capital, devolution of some powers of the Finance Ministry to Reserve Bank of India, corporate governance, supervisory authority, appointment of auditors, recovery of dues and penalties. The committee has classified the RRBs (regional rural banks) into four categories. The group says, "this categorisation of RRBs into A, B, C and D should be the basis for providing flexibility in ownership options. The adoption of the concept of a "sponsor institution" has been recommended with its prescribed minimum level of shareholding at 51 per cent so as "to ensure adequate commitment as well as powers for the sponsor institution."

In the category A fall the top class RRBs, i.e. those RRBs which have no accumulated loss and which reported profits for the past three consecutive years; in category B fall those RRBs which posted profits for the past three consecutive years and their accumulated losses have not caused erosion of public deposits; in the category C are those which reported loss in one or more of the last three years and have accumulated losses that have caused erosion in the value of their assets not in excess of 10 per cent of their total deposits as on March 31, 2002 and in the category D have been put all those RRBs which have reported losses in one or more in the last three years and have accumulated loss causing erosion of the value of their assets in excess of 10 per cent of their total deposits.

After having made the classifications, the committee has suggested that category A RRBs should be allowed to access capital market. The Union Government stake in these RRBs should be reduced to 33 per cent and the State Government's stake in them too may be purchased by the sponsoring bank.

In the category B RRBs, sponsoring banks, according to the committee, must hold majority stake and thus control. Before the Union Government disinvests 17 per cent of its stake in these RRBs, the three shareholders should inject fresh capital to wipe out the past losses.

The RRB Act needs to be amended to facilitate the sponsor institution pick up the state government stake of 15 per cent (total paid up capital of an RRB is Rs. one crore). The committee argues for sponsor banks holding 35 per cent stake in RRBs to sell off to another as a part of the revamp. "In the post-capital issue scenario as well, the shareholding of the sponsor institution may continue to be at a minimum of 51 per cent though the proportionate share of the Central Government and State Government may come down," the working group adds.

These categories of RRBs may be upgraded to category A. The State Government shares in these RRBs may be purchased by sponsoring bank.

For the category C RRBs, the committee has opposed the change in the ownership pattern. The amalgamation of these RRBs with other suitable RRBs has also been suggested.

The committee has suggested liquidation of the majority of the category D RRBs, conceding that some of these perpetually losing RRBs may have to be allowed to continue in public interest.

In such cases, the Union and the State Government concerned must acquire the ownership and work out appropriate policies for their functioning. The Union and State Governments might be required to provide financial support.

The salary of those employed in the RRBs, according to the committee, should be determined by the respective boards with prior approval of the sponsoring banks and in determining so the boards should pay due regard to the standard norms relating to work performance, financial position, paying capacity and the sustainable viability of the RRB concerned.

The working group is in favour of slapping capital adequacy and licensing norms on RRBs. "The capital adequacy norms may be introduced in a phased manner... starting with 5 per cent of outstanding risk weighted assets effective April 1, 2003, to be enhanced by one percentage point every year to bring it at par with that for commercial banks," the group lays down. It wants to make licensing mandatory for RRBs under the Banking Regulation Act, 1949. As of now they draw legitimacy from the RRB Act alone.

"The existing RRBs or those created out of amalgamation of two or more existing RRBs may continue doing banking business during the pendency of consideration of their application for license by RBI and they would have to cease business if a license is refused to them." The group is in favour of RBI continuing as the regulator with a separate "Supervisory Authority" in place of NABARD to oversee functioning of RRBs.

The Local Area Banks

The Local Area Bank Scheme was introduced in August 1996 pursuant to the announcement of the then Finance Minister.

In his budget speech, the Finance Minister referred to the setting up of new private local banks with jurisdiction over two or three contiguous districts. He observed that this would enable the mobilization of rural savings by local institutions and make them available for investments in the local areas. The Local Area Banks (LABs) were expected to bridge the gap in credit availability and strengthen the institutional credit framework in the rural and semi-urban areas.

Following this, guidelines for setting up of LABs in the private sector were announced by the Reserve Bank of India (RBI) on 24th August 1996.

Over a period of about five and a half years, as many as 227 applications for establishment of LABs in the private sector had been received by the RBI of which 214 applications were rejected while 'in-principle' approvals for establishment of 10 LABs were issued and 3 applications are under examination. However, due to the inability of the promoters to fulfill the conditions stipulated in the 'in-principle' approvals, 4 such approvals were withdrawn.

5 banks were licensed under Section 22 of the Banking Regulation Act 1949. Of these, only 4 LABs are functioning at present. 1 application is pending.

Status of LABs Functioning

Only four LABs are functioning at present. These are, Coastal Local Area Bank Ltd. established on 27th December 1999 with an area of operation comprising three contiguous districts viz. Krishna, Guntur and West Godavari with its head office at Vijayawada (Andhra Pradesh), Capital Local Area Bank Ltd. established on 14th January 2000 with its area of operation comprising three districts viz. Jalandhar, Kapurthala and Hoshiarpur with its head office at Phagwara (Punjab), South Gujarat Local Area Bank Ltd., established on 3rd October 2000 with an area of operation comprising three contiguous districts viz. Navsari, Surat and Bharuch with its head office at Navsari (Gujarat),

Krishna Bhima Samruddhi Local Area Bank Ltd.established on 28th February 2001 with an area of operation comprising three contiguous districts of Mahbubnagar in Andhra Pradesh and Raichur and Gulbarga in the state of Karnataka with its head office at Mahbubnagar(Andhra Pradesh). The licence of Vinayak Local Area Bank Ltd., Sikar (Rajastan) established on 21st October 2000 was cancelled by Reserve Bank on 16th January 2002 as major irregularities were noted in its functioning.

Branch Licensing

The LABs were allowed to open branches in only one urban centre per District and rest of the branches were allowed to be opened in the rural and semi urban centers subject to requisite clearance in respect of rural branches from the District Consultative Committee for the concerned districts.

Scheduling of LABs

The LABs could be included in the Second Schedule of the Reserve Bank of India Act, 1934 subject to the fulfillment of the eligibility criteria laid down in Section 42(6) of the said Act ibid.

Regulatory Jurisdiction

The regulatory responsibility over the LABs vests with Rural Planning and Credit Department (RPCD) of the RBI. The RPCD issues licence for these banks as per provisions of Section 22 of the Banking Regulation Act, 1949 and grants permission for opening of branches at new places of business as per the provisions of Section 23 of the Act ibid. T

he financial health of the LABs is monitored through off-site returns and other statements required to be submitted by these banks. The appointment of the CEO and the Chairman of the LAB requires clearance of the RBI as per the provisions of Section 10B of the Banking Regulation Act, 1949 read with Section 35B of the Act ibid. The remuneration of the CEO also requires prior approval of the RBI.

The composition of the Board of these banks is to be in accord with the provisions of Section 10A of the Banking Regulation Act, 1949. As LABs are commercial banks in the private sector, banking policies as applicable to commercial banks are made applicable to them except where these pertain to areas of business which LABs are not permitted to undertake.

Supervision over LABs

Supervision over LABs lies with the Department of Banking Supervision (DBS). During the first year of its operation, the LAB is subjected to quarterly on-site supervisory monitoring visits. The quarterly visits cover areas such as examination of loans and investments, treasury functions, internal checks and controls so as to ensure that the affairs of the bank are not being conducted in a manner detrimental to the interests of the depositors.

Thereafter, the LAB is covered under Annual Financial Inspection (AFI) Programme of DBS. This covers areas such as management functions, functioning of Board of the bank and constitution of various committees of the Board, internal control system, internal audit and inspection, information system, deposit, advance and investment portfolio, NPAs, profitability, capital adequacy and maintenance of statutory norms as CRR and SLR.

An analysis about the functioning of LABs and about the report of the Review Group appointed by RBI in 2002 to study and make recommendations on the LAB Scheme are discussed in the next article.

Report of the Review Group for Local Area Bank Scheme

As no comprehensive review of the scheme had been made since the issuance of guidelines in 1996, the RBI appointed a Review Group in July 2002 under chairmanship of Mr.G.Ramachandran former finance secretary to study and make recommendations on the LAB Scheme.

Kisan Credit Card (KCC) Scheme

Genesis

Hon'ble Union Finance Minister announced in his budget speech for 1998-99 that NABARD would formulate a Model scheme for issue of Kisan Credit Cards to farmers, on the basis of their land holdings, for uniform adoption by banks, so that the farmers may use them to readily purchase agricultural inputs such as seeds, fertilisers, pesticides, etc. and also draw cash for their production needs'.

NABARD formulated a Model Kisan Credit Card Scheme in consultation with major banks. Model Scheme circulated by RBI to commercial banks and by NABARD to Cooperative banks and RRBs in August 1998, with instructions to introduce the same in their respective area of operation.

Objectives

As a pioneering credit delivery innovation, Kisan Credit Card Scheme aims at provision of adequate and timely support from the banking system to the farmers for their cultivation needs including purchase of inputs in a flexible and cost effective manner.

Contents of Credit Card

Beneficiaries covered under the Scheme are issued with a credit card and a pass book or a credit card cum pass book incorporating the name, address, particulars of land holding, borrowing limit, validity period, a passport size photograph of holder etc., which may serve both as an identity card and facilitate recording of transactions on an ongoing basis.

Borrower is required to produce the card cum pass book whenever he/she operates the account.

Benefits of the Scheme to the Banks

Reduction in work load for branch staff by avoidance of repeat appraisal and processing of loan papers under Kisan Credit Card Scheme.

Minimum paper work and simplification of documentation for drawal of funds from the bank.

Improvement in recycling of funds and better recovery of loans. Reduction in transaction cost to the banks.

Better Banker - Client relationships.

Refinance Support for ST(SAO) Loans disbursed under KCC Scheme

Operational Guidelines

SCBs/DCCBs and RRBs were advised operational guidelines governing provision of refinance for their ST(SAO) disbursements under the KCC Scheme vide Circular letter No. NB.PCD(OPR)/662/ A137(Spl.)/99-2000 dt.26.05.99 and Circular letter No. NB.PCD(OPR)/ 662-A/A137(Spl.)/99-2000 dt. 26.05.99 respectively. The same are summarised below: instructions on computation of Demand, Collection and Balance (DCB) position, maintenance of Non-overdue Cover (NODC), financing of small/marginal farmers, etc, conveyed in circular letter No.NB.PCD(OPR)/5980/A.135/90-91 dated 17 December 1990 addressed to RCS and in circular letter No.NB.PCD(OPR)/1271/ 334/ 95-96 dated 02 November 1995 addressed to RRBs will also be, mutatis mutandis, applicable for advances made under the KCC Scheme by SCBs/DCCBs and RRBs respectively. although under the KCC Scheme, production credit for SAO, advances for allied activities, non-farm activities and consumption purposes can be covered, only the production credit for SAO is eligible for refinance from NABARD under the ST(SAO) credit limits. Banks required to maintain separate details of sanctions and accounts for operations on credit limits for SAO purposes under the KCC Scheme to facilitate submission of drawal applications for obtaining refinance from NABARD in respect of eligible loans and reporting such loans in the monthly NODC statements for ST(SAO) loans and advances.

Short-term loans outstanding for financing ancillary activities relating to crop production such as maintenance of agricultural machinery/implements, electricity charges, etc. under the KCC Scheme also eligible for refinance from NABARD under ST(SAO) credit limits.

Coverage of Farmers - Future Strategy

Banks, vide our Circular letter No.NB.PCD(KCC)/29/ 2001-02 dated 10 April 2001, requested to draw up an action plan immediately in consultation with our Regional Office concerned, based on their past performance and experience in implementing the scheme, to ensure the coverage of all the eligible agricultural farmers under the KCC Scheme within the next three years i.e. by 31 March 2004.

Banks to ensure that targets fixed for 2001-02, 2002-03 and 2003-04 include new agricultural farmers likely to become eligible for their KC cards after 31 March 2001 also.

Targets fixed for issue of KC Cards be disaggregated month-wise and branch/PACS-wise to facilitate close monitoring of progress vis-a-vis target and also advised to RO concerned.

In order to ensure achievement of the targets so fixed, banks requested to follow strategies suggested by NABARD from time to time. Towards this end, banks to launch a campaign approach to accelerate pace of implementation of the Scheme. Following specific steps may be taken by the banks:

Conduct of Sensitisation/training programmes for the officers of controlling offices of banks, branch managers and field level functionaries as also district level functions for distribution of cards.

Holding Banker-Farmers' Meets, as part of the Kharif 2001 campaign, in each block to identify the ground level constraints in the smooth implementation of the Scheme and to initiate remedial measures therefor.

Use of VVV Clubs fora for propagation of the scheme.

Placement of hoardings/banners etc. at prominent places, such as branch premises, Panchayat buildings, Mandis, etc.

Use of audio-video media, bringing out KCC literature in local language to create better awareness about KCC Scheme among farmers.

Issue of plastic/laminated cards to serve as Identity Cards.

Monitoring of progress in implementation of the Scheme in Board meetings as also through various state/ district and block level fora with the participation of Government functionaries, bankers, farmers etc.

Progress in implementation of the Scheme

Since launching in August 1998, around 2.38 crore Kisan Credit Cards issued upto 31 March 2002 by Cooperative Banks, Regional Rural Banks and Commercial Banks put together. Scheme implemented in all States and Union Territories (except Chandigarh, Daman & Diu and Dadra & Nagar Haveli) with all Cooperative Banks, RRBs and Commercial Banks participating. Agency-wise/State-wise progress in issue of cards by all banks during 2001-02 and since inception of Scheme.

Agency-wise KC Cards issued upto 31 March 2003 (since inception) (No. of cards)

Year	Cooperative Banks	RRBs	Commercial Banks	Total
1998-99	155353	6421	445451	607225
1999-00	3594869	173301	1365911	5134081
2000-01	5614445	648324	2389588	8652357
2001-02	5435859	833629	3071046	9340534
2002-03	4578923	963950	2067219*	7610092
Total	19379449	2625625	9339215	31344289

(*) data for commercial banks upto 31 December 2002.

Micro Finance in India-An Overview

Micro-finance by NGO - SEWA and the Shri Mahila SEWA Sahakari Bank Ltd.

Other Modules under Project Banking Theory & Practice

Research studies conducted by NABARD during the early eighties showed that despite having an extremely wide network of rural bank branches which implemented specific poverty alleviation programmes that sought creation of self-employment opportunities through bank credit for almost two decades, a very large number of the poorest of the poor continued to remain outside the fold of the formal banking system.

These studies gave signals that the existing banking policies, systems and procedures, and deposit and loan products were perhaps not most suited to meet the immediate needs of the very poor. What they really needed was a better access to these services and products, rather than cheap subsidised credit.

Unique Features of Credit needs of Rural Poor

The priority of the rural poor was for consumption credit, savings, production credit and insurance, in that order.

Consumption needs included credit for short periods for emergent needs.

The dividing line between consumption credit and production credit for the poor was gossamery. Consumption requirements were met by the informal sources at exploitative interest rates, as the poor borrowers were unable to offer to the banks any security for the small consumption loans.

Main constraint faced by banks in extending credit in small doses to poor borrowers was the high transaction cost in financing large numbers in small quantities.

The same constraint applied to provision of other financial services like small savings, where very small savers scattered in the rural areas were to be harnessed.

The Alternate Model - Micro Finance & its Easy Accessibility

Against this background, a need was felt for alternative policies, systems and procedures, savings and loan products, other complementary services, and new delivery mechanisms, which would fulfill the requirements of the poorest, especially of the women members of such households. The emphasis therefore was on improving the access of the poor to microFinance (mF) rather than just micro-credit. As a village based network of bank branches already existed, it focused not on creating alternate organisations, but on finding ways and means to improve the access of the poor to existing banking network. The rural and semi-urban banking network in India includes about 33,000 branches of scheduled commercial banks, 14,500 branches of Regional Rural Banks and 92,000 Primary Agricultural Cooperative Societies.

Many research studies, done in-house as well as sponsored to professional institutions, and some action research projects funded out of the Research and Development Fund of NABARD, led it to develop the Self Help Group [SHG] - Bank linkage model as the core strategy that could be used by the banking system in India for increasing their outreach to the poorest of the poor who were hitherto getting by-passed by them. The strategy involved forming small, cohesive and participative groups of the poor, encouraging them to pool their thrift regularly and using the pooled thrift to make small interest bearing loans to members, and in the process learning the nuances of financial discipline. Subsequently, bank credit also becomes available to the Group, to augment its resources for lending to its members. It needs to be emphasised that NABARD sees the promotion and bank linking of SHGs not as a credit programme but as part of an overall arrangement for providing financial services to the poor in a sustainable manner and also an empowerment process for the members of these SHGs. NABARD, however, also took a conscious decision to experiment with other successful strategies such as replicating Grameen.

Starting with a NABARD led limited scale Pilot Project (with the support of the Central Bank of the country, i.e., Reserve Bank of India) in 1992 that aimed at promoting and financing 500 SHGs across the entire country, the SHG- bank linkage strategy has come a long way. The strategy includes financing of SHGs promoted by external facilitators like NGOs and government agencies, as also promotion of SHGs by banks themselves and financing SHGs indirectly where NGOs and similar organisations act as financial intermediaries as well.

Research Studies and Action research projects by NABARD resulted in evolution of the 'Self Help Groups (SHGs)- bank linkage model' as an appropriate mechanism. Other delivery modes include replication of Grameen, networking of NGOs, federations of SHGs, cooperatives, etc.

Against the back cloth of different structures, diverse legal framework and varied approaches, the need for a national policy framework arose.

Task Force on Micro Finance

A High level Task Force on microFinance was constituted under the Chairmanship of Mr. Y. C. Nanda, Managing Director, NABARD. MicroFinance was defined by the Task Force as "provision of thrift, credit and other financial services and products of very small amounts to the poor in rural, semi-urban or urban areas for enabling them to raise their income levels and improve living standards".

Capacity Building Initiatives

Sensitisation of senior executives of commercial banks and Chairmen of RRBs have been taken up by NABARD.

Under the direct training programme for staff of banks/ NGOs, over 25,000 field level functionaries have already been trained by NABARD.

NABARD provides training inputs on SHG financing to training establishments of participating banks, to help them to internalise the training requirements at their level.

NABARD gives technical support to banks to evolve suitable intermediate structures like Farmers' Clubs (Vikas Volunteer Vahini

Programme of the National Bank) to increase the outreach of their branches in promotion and linking SHGs

NABARD supports and helps banking institutions (especially RRBs) to take on the role of Self Help Promoting Institutions (SHPIs)

Support to Governments

Necessary assistance is provided to the governments by NABARD for dovetailing mF practices with the poverty alleviation programmes

NABARD also encourages the association of Panchayati Raj Institutions (PRIs) in adopting group processes for maximisation of empowerment.

Alternate Micro Finance Practices

The NGOs and other local bodies at village, block and district levels in the North Eastern States are encouraged to take up alternative micro-credit delivery mechanisms through direct funding.

Formation and operation of SHG Federations is supported and encouraged by NABARD. Similarly, networking of NGOs is also encouraged.

Policy and Regulatory Initiatives

The recommendations of the Task Force on microFinance are being followed up and implemented, to spawn a supportive and conducive policy mechanism for sustained growth of mF initiatives in India. These steps include facilitating emergence of standards for Micro Finance in India, Supporting graduation of Micro Finance - NGOs to pure Micro Finance Institutions, etc..

Coordinating Micro Finance Efforts in India

NABARD coordinates the mF activities in India at international/ national/state/district levels. These include organising international/ national Workshops, Seminars, etc for experience sharing, Organising National and State level Meets of Bankers and NGOs, etc..

Monitoring and Review

Block/district/state level review meetings are organised and/or organised by NABARD. The relative documentation and data base is also carried out by NABARD. In addition, periodical Monitoring studies are conducted through NABARD/Bank Officers.

3

Managing Challenges in Banking Industry

Financial System is the most important institutional and functional vehicle for economic transformation of any country. Banking sector is reckoned as a hub and barometer of the financial system. As a pillar of the economy, this sector plays a predominant role in the economic development of the country. The geographical pervasiveness of the bank coupled with the range and depth of their services make the system an indispensable medium in every day transactions. The virtual monopoly of banks in 'Payment Mechanism' touches the lives of millions of people every day and every where. Thus the banking sector has been playing a significant role as growth facilitator.

The Changing Paradigm of Banking

Change is the only constant factor in this dynamic world and banking is not an exception. The changes staring in the face of bankers relates to the fundamental way of banking-which is undergoing rapid transformation in the world of today, in response to the forces of completion productivity and efficiency of operations, reduced operating margins better asset/liability management, risk management, any time and any where banking. The major challenge faced by banks today is to protect the falling margins due to the impact of competition. Another significant impact of banks today is the technology issue. There is an imperative need for not mere technology up gradation but also its integration with the general way of functioning of banks to give them an edge in respect of services provided to optimizing the use of funds and building up MIS for decision making and better management of assets and liabilities and risk assumed which in turns have a direct impact on the balance sheet of banks as a whole. Word over, technology has demonstrated potential to change methods of selling marketing, advertising, designing, pricing and distributing financial products of an electronic, self-service product delivery channel. All these changes call for a new, more dynamic, aggressive and challenging work culture to meet the demands of customer relationships, product differentiation, brand values, reputation, corporate governance and regulatory prescriptions.

Challenges Facing Indian Banking

The main challenges facing by Indian banking are the role of financial instrumentation in different phases of the business cycle, the emerging compulsions of the new prudential norms and benchmarking the Indian financial system against international standards and best practices. The need for introduction of new technology in the banking and the importance of skill building and intellectual capital formation in the banking industry are also equal important.

Financial Intermediation

Till recently the role of banks in the economy was perceived to be 'catalysts' of mobilizing resource requirement for growth. This view has undergone a change and banks are no longer viewed as passive mobilizer of funds, Efficiency in the financial intermediation is the ability of the financial institution to intermediate between savers and investors, to set economic prices for capital and allocate resources among completing demands is now emphasized. In the wake of the recent emphasized in the economy the intermediation role assumes even greater relevance. By virtue of their experience and superior credit assessment of the investment proposals banks should play a significant role in identifying and nurturing growth impulse in the commodity and service producing sector in the economy.

Market Discipline

Transparency and disclosure norms are assuming greater importance in the emerging environment. Banks are now required to be more responsive and accountable to the investors. Banks move to disclose in their balance sheets information on maturity profiles of assets and liabilities, lending to sensitive sectors, movements in NPAs, besides providing information on capital, provisions, shareholdings of the government, value of investment in India and abroad, and other operating and profitability indicators. They also have to make a disclosure of total investments made in equity shares, units of mutual funds, bonds and debentures and aggregate advances against shares in their notes to balance sheet. Efforts are on to set up a credit information bureau to collect and share information on borrowers and improve the credit appraisal of banks and financial institutions.

Adopting International Standards

The fallout of Asian crisis and the impetus given to the strengthening of domestic financial systems has resulted in a more by the regulators to set up universally acceptable standards and codes for benchmarking financial systems. RBI has also set-up an advisory group to draw a road map for implementation of appropriate standards and codes in light of existing levels of compliance, cross country experience and the existing legal and institutional infrastructure. In view of the vast diversity in the size, an asset liability profiles of the banks it becomes very difficult for a few of them to meet the new benchmark of global standards. Each bank has to draw it own strategy to move towards this direction.

Technology Banking

Innovation in technology and world-wide revolution in information and communication technology are perceived to be the catalyst of productivity growth. The relationship between IT and Banking is fundamentally symbiotic. It is expected to reduce costs, increase volumes and facilitate customized products. Technology adoption is a dire necessity for the public sector banks to complete with new generation private sector and foreign banks. It is a 'compulsion' rather than a 'choice'. Retention of existing customer is the primary concern of majority of the banks today.

The major challenge for banks is to fall in line with the emerging scenario and adopting the require technology to provide stake-of-the-art services to the customers. Introduction of on-line, inter-connected automatic teller machines (ATM), telephone banking, on-line bill payment and Internet banking are some of the high tech facilities. Banks have to provide in order to survive in the competitive scenario. Technology should ultimate results in better customer service, low cost and quick delivery.

Rural Banking

Having committed 75% of their branches network to serving rural and semi-urban population, public sector banks have to adopt a financial emerging approach to rural banking.

Human Resource Development in Banks

T he core function of HRD in the banking industry is to facilitate performance improvement, measured not only in terms of certain financial indicators of operational efficiency but also in terms of quality of financial services provided. The skill level, attitude and knowledge of the personnel play an important role in determining the competitiveness of a bank. Banks have to understand that the capital and technology-considered to be the most important pillars of banking-are replicable, but not human capital, which needs to be viewed as a valuable resource for the achievement of competitive advantage.

The primary concern of the bank should be to bring in proper integration of human resource management strategies with the business strategies. It should faster cohesive team work and create commitment to improve the efficiency of its human capital. More than operational skills today's banking call for these 'soft skills' to attend the needs and requirement of the customers at the counter. The need to adopt global best practices to financial sector regulation and supervision and adopt them to the domestic environment, places a premium skills and expertise of the bank human resources.

E-Banking and Value Added Services

Electronic banking can offer customers an enhanced range of services at a very low cost. ATMs are expensive to own but are a much cheaper way of processing withdrawals than over the counter. The distribution infrastructure for mobile phone banking is already in existence. Electronic Banking promises to extend low-cost virtual bank accounts to a large number of currently un-banked individuals worldwide. Change is being driven by falling costs of technology, by competition and by the ability of electronic banking solutions to offer customers an enhanced range of services at a very low cost.

Electronic Banking Technology

There are a number of options facing institutions thinking about investing in electronic banking for the mass market. This article attempts to provide a detailed comparison of the different technical options. The options include the following.

Personal Digital Assistants (PDAs)

An increasing number of financial institutions are introducing personal digital assistants (PDAs). PDAs are small hand-held computers that can run specialized programmes to manage MFI and client records.

Automated Teller Machines (ATMs)

ATMs can be fully functional teller machines that accept deposits, dispense cash and can be programmed with other functions. Or they can be cash dispensers only. ATMs are expensive to own and operate but offer the financial institution a much cheaper way of processing a large volume of withdrawals than through over-the-counter operations.

Magstripe Cards

Debit cards, often based around magnetic stripe technology, allow customers online access to their accounts through a network of POS (point-of-sale) devices and ATMs. The principle advantages quoted by proponents of magstripe cards are low price and the requirement that transactions are performed online.

Smart Cards

Smart cards have a machine-readable chip embedded in the card. This chip is able to store detailed transaction records offline and perform transactions without a link to the customer's account. In order to do this, value is stored on the chip by the customer and is periodically reloaded, over the counter, through ATM machines or through POS devices.

The principle advantages quoted by proponents of the smart card are security and offline functionality. Biometric security allows a cardholder's picture and fingerprints to be stored on the card and used to identify the user.

Euro card, Master Card and Visa

They are currently introducing a new standard (called EMV) whereby all Visa, Master Card and Euro card branded cards will be issued with a magstripe and a smart chip. Whilst this offers security advantages, it could significantly increase the cost of any mass market solution that relies upon the Visa or Master Card distribution network.

Mobile Phone Banking

The phenomenal expansion of mobile phone networks in Africa and other parts of the world provides an opportunity to operate virtual bank accounts through mobile phones, either through menu-driven systems or through SMS (short message service, or text messaging) technology which is already being used by millions. This option has the significant advantage that the distribution infrastructure is already in existence – through millions of mobile phones.

The Customer Perspective – The Value Proposition

An electronic banking solution must provide sufficient value to persuade the customer to move away from cash. However, cash is an incredibly versatile medium of exchange. It is universally recognized as a store of value, it is accessible, portable and divisible. The Significant factors that are valued by the customer include features, accessibility of the service, affordability and ease of use.

An Introduction to Internet Banking

Internet banking, sometimes called online banking, is an outgrowth of PC banking. Internet banking uses the Internet as the delivery channel by which to conduct banking activity, for example, transferring funds, paying bills, viewing checking and savings account balances, paying mortgages, and purchasing financial instruments and certificates of deposit.

An Internet banking customer accesses his or her accounts from a browser— software that runs Internet banking programs resident on the bank's World Wide Web server, not on the user's PC. Net Banker defines a " true Internet bank" as one that provides account balances and some transactional capabilities to retail customers over the World Wide Web. Internet banks are also known as virtual, cyber, net, interactive, or web banks.

To date, more banks have established an advertising presence on the Internet— primarily in the form of informational or interactive web sites—than have created transactional web sites. However, a number of Banks that do not yet offer transactional Internet banking services have indicated on their web sites that they will offer such banking activities in the future.

Although Internet banks offer many of the same services as do traditional brick-and-mortar Banks, analysts view Internet banking as a means of retaining increasingly sophisticated customers, of developing a new customer base, and of capturing a greater share of depositor assets. A typical Internet bank site specifies the types of transactions offered and provides information about account security. Because Internet banks generally have lower operational and transactional costs than do traditional brick-and-mortar banks, they are often able to offer low-cost checking and high-yield Certificates of deposit.

Internet banking is not limited to a physical site; some Internet banks exist without physical branches, for example, Telebank

(Arlington, Virginia) and Banknet (UK). Further, in some cases, web banks are not restricted to conducting transactions within national borders and have the ability to make transactions involving large amounts of assets instantaneously. According to industry analysts, electronic banking provides a variety of attractive possibilities for remote account access, including:

- Availability of inquiry and transaction services around the clock;
- worldwide connectivity;
- Easy access to transaction data, both recent and historical; and
- " Direct customer control of international movement of funds without intermediation of financial institutions in customer's jurisdiction."

Internet banking is the technology that allows banking customers to do the things they would normally do at their banks from comfort of home with a connection to internet. In the year 2000 an estimated 14 million American banked online according to per internet and American life. By 2004 some 53 million Americans were performing online banking transactions.

Consumer Behaviour Aspects and Promotion of Banking Services

Consumer behaviour is very complex phenomenon, which is considered primarily in marketing decisions. It has been rightly said *"Understand, you do not understand, you will not understand, you cannot understand all your customers but still you have to do your best to understand them."*

In consumer behavour this is very difficult to make a uniform theory that may suggest that a particular individual or group will behave in a particular manner. Consumer behaviour is dynamic and to be studied regularly. Increasing awareness, living standards and urbanization has led to increase in the changing preferences and the same has forced the marketers to change their product features, packaging styles, distribution channels and so on. There is a famous saying the "Success has a simple formula-Do your best and people must like it".

Similarly, for marketers the advice is-offer the best and customers must like it'. Identical products always have their life cycle the product life cycle suggests that there is a level of maturity of the product and after that no more consumers can be attracted for that. The case is very same with preferences of consumers that they always like some innovative and different products to use. The study of consumer behaviour is compulsory to know about likes and dislikes of consumers from time to time so that the products and services can be offered accordingly.

Customers have their own unique needs, demands and preferences in a particular segment. Marketers have to study customers in particular segment. Really interesting it is, the study of consumer behaviour can make it possible that after observing and examining the behaviour of consumer a marketer can present his product in such a way that the product can capture the market. However it was very difficult to sell that product earlier. Consumer behaviour indeed gives every possible answer to the complex questions concerned with consumer's buying reasons.

The following diagramme will tell about the all marketing decisions taken in services industry or banking services. These all are essential decisions which are concerned are essential ingredients of services marketing mix. The analysis has been done in the context of banking services. When customer is treated as the king of the market, the study of consumer behaviour becomes more important for marketing decisions. There is no doubt that the behaviour is the base of marketing decisions.

Banks are defined as the *"Organizations, which accepts deposits from public and give loans from the general public."* In the present time they are over and above this definition. Banks are providing innovative services with innovates styles. ATMs, Credit cards and Internet banking have changed the quality of delivery of services of banks. Banking services are growing with many new additions such as money transfers, Bankassurance, NRI services and so on. Promotion of service has been a challenging task. Banking services being of a sophisticated nature should be promoted carefully, clearly and innovatively.

Mass Media Advertising: Most Preferred mode for marketing of Banking Services

Mass media advertising includes TV commercials and advertising in national level newspapers which have a wide coverage. Advertising in these has made maximum people aware about the offerings of the banks and established most of the bank names as big brands. In a recent survey ICICI Bank has been considered as the most popular banks in private sector. The use of umbrella branding works well in promotion of banking services. Different types of advertisement campaigns have been seen in form of TV commercials and as print ad in newspapers. Print ads mainly focus on corporate image advertising of banks as well as a new offering of the bank such as increase in interest rate on deposits or decrease in the interest rates in loans and so on.

TV commercials mainly focused on corporate advertising, where banking service is promoted as a whole rather than a particular product of banks.

Themes and Appeals Used in TV Commercials of Banking

Advertising appeal is the method used to draw the attention of consumers and to influence their feelings toward the product, service, or cause. There are hundreds of different appeals that can be used as the foundation for advertising messages. These are the central idea of an ad which has been used to catch the attraction of customer by heart. The theme of a commercial strikes a person in depth and forces him/her to act in the desired manner. Generally advertising appeals are broken into two categories: rational appeals and emotional appeals.

Personal Selling is being very much popular and effective for private banks in India. It is concerned with face to face meeting with the customer and making the presentation of the service offering to the prospect and making the person customer of the bank. This process has its own advantages and disadvantages. Banks may have some complex service offer which may include so many charges and facilities of different types.

The biggest advantage of personal selling in banking services is that the salesperson can make the prospect well understood about the product. Further customers may prefer it because they need not to go anywhere the sales person comes to them. But there is certain limitation also people usually do not give their time to meet and talk on issue. It also does not become cost effective if the sales are not closed in a handsome number. Banks are going to be societal now and taking care of environment the plantation Bank of Baroda and Punjab National Bank is the examples of the same.

Consumers are always emotional about the Brands doing social and national services. Banks wants to win the faith of the customers and also wants to come out from their typical financial image. Societal marketing really helps to attain this objective. Sales promotional has become popular due to the popularity of the usage of debit and credit cards. The offers are also given to the customers for registering and transacting with internet banking.

For example recently HDFC bank has come with the offer where a flip book light is free on opening an account and a DVD of famous movie on shopping with Debit Card. Further there are lots of other schemes also giving discount and other gifts on different types of purchase on debit and credit card of the bank.

The corporation/Brands such as Indiatimes shooping, Barista, Mudra Pure Glod, Ayush Therapy Centre, VLCC Slimming Beauty Fitness, Welhome, Dr. Batra's Multispeciality Hospitals, Javed Habib, Gini & Jony, Vishal Mega mart, Dominos and Book my Show have clubbed with the bank to provide this promotion to the customers. However the sales promotion has its nature that it is always for a particular time being.

The purpose of sales promotion is to enhance the sales in particular time duration. The sales promotion offers are redesigned frequently for effective promotion in sales. Consumers feel happy when they get something extra then the regular utility. Sales promotion offers really attract customers.

In present time the most popular tool for promotion of banking services has become Internet Marketing of services. E-Advertising is being very much popular. In city areas of India, people use internet so frequently. Studies tell that they use internet mostly for checking their mails, finding results and educations and research purposes.

The e-advertising of banking services not only promote the services by giving offers but it also interacts with the person and a potential customer can purchase the product with the help of this.

However internet advertising in pop ups irritates the internet users but advertisements done on home page of any website such as email service provider is useful and customers get knowledge about the new banking services and promotions. When they see something in front of their eyes they can remember it much.

In brief of the study, this can be concluded that consumer behaviour is the base of all marketing activities and promotional strategies are also the part of marketing so they are also designed by considering all the aspects of consumer's behaviour.

Indian Banking and Finance – A Paradigm Shift

Banking Industry in India has travelled a long path to assume its present status. It has undergone a major structural transformation after the independence including the assumption of social banking. The success in transformation has been achieved by overcoming hurdles and impediments, stresses and strains. Thus, the development in the banking industry covers the activities of money lenders with their limited resources and of large scale operations by banks with huge resources and diversified activities.

Oldest System of Banking

The oldest banking institutions consisted of indigenous banks, money lenders, nidhis etc. They played significant role in the development of banking by meeting the needs of business people and others in the local area. Generally, they charge exorbitant rates of interest by exploiting mercilessly illiterate and ignorant villagers and have limited resources. They could not survive successfully in the changing environment of highly technical and business development. They also lost their importance in the rural areas because of competition spread by the Co-operative Banks, Regional Rural Banks and the growing social and political consciousness amongst rural masses.

Modern Banking System

The earliest banking system played a significant role till the Mughal period. Their importance is reduced during the British period as they could not make much use of their services on account of difference in language and style. In order to meet their financial requirements and banking assistance, the English agency houses started their own banking business in Calcutta and Bombay. This was the beginning of the modern banking system in India. So, the history of modern banking in India dates back to the last quarter of 18th Century.

The earliest European Bank was started by the English agency houses along with their trading activities in 1710 in the name of Bank of Hindustan. This was followed by setting up of the Bengal Bank in 1984, General Bank of India in 1786 etc.

However, all these banks failed sooner or later due to various reasons. In order to meet the needs of the foreign rulers, a number of quasi banking institutions were established. They included Presidency Bank of Bengal (1806), Presidency Bank of Madras (1840) and the Presidency Bank of Calcutta and later by 1921 these three banks were amalgamated to constitute one bank called Imperial Bank of India.

Joint Stock Banks

The enactment of Joint Stock Companies Act in 1850 was the milestone to incorporate the concept of "limited liability" into corporate sector under the organized system which was recognized in the year 1857. In 1860, the principle of limited liability was applied to joint stock banks.

From 1860 till the end of the 19th Century, several joint stock banks were established and they were Oudh Commercial Bank in 1881 followed by the Punjab National Bank in 1895 and People's Bank in 1901.

The Swadesi movement gave impetus to the starting of Indian banks like Bank of India in 1906, Bank of Baroda Ltd., in 1908 and Central Bank of India in 1911 and several of these banks failed on account of the serious bank crisis in 1913-17 and this situation continued till the Second World War.

Establishment of Reserve Bank of India

The Hilton Young Commission in 1926 recommended the establishment of a separate bank in the country known as Reserve Bank of India. So a bill was introduced in the Legislative Assembly in 1933 which led to the establishment of Reserve Bank in 1935.

After the establishment of Reserve Bank of India, the Imperial Bank was authorized to function as a sole agent of the Reserve Bank of India at all places in India where the Reserve Bank had no branches.

Banking System During Post Independence Period

The post independence period has massive growth of the Indian banking system. The first step taken in this direction was nationalization of the Reserve Bank of India in 1948. It changed the outlook of the Reserve Bank by giving them the status of monitoring authority to regulate and control the socio-economic activities laid down by the government.

In order to have sound and balanced growth of banking business in the country, the Reserve Bank of India Act, 1949 was passed to have control of the Reserve bank over the banking industry. In 1955, the Imperial Bank of India was nationalized under the name of State Bank of India.

The scheme of social control was initiated by the government in the year 1967. Followed by it, the government nationalized 14 major banks which held a deposit of around Rs. 50 crores on 19th July 1969 and 6 more banks which held deposit of around Rs. 200 crores on 15th April 1980. This process was done to ensure more equitable of purposeful distribution of the credit.

Specialized Financial Institution

Besides the above developments, financial institutions for meeting the specialized needs were established. They include Industrial Development Bank of India (IDBI), Industrial Credit and Investment Bank of India for meeting the long – term financial needs of the large scale operations. Similarly for meeting the requirements of the Small Scale Industries (SSIs), State Financial Corporation (SFC), Small Industries Development (SIDC) and Small Industries Development Bank of India (SIDBI) have been established.

The National Bank for Agriculture and Rural Development (NABARD), Land Development Bank (LDB), Regional Rural Bank (RRB) etc. have been established for taking care of the credit needs of agriculture. Export Import Bank of India, Export Credit Guarantee Corporation of India take care of export and import needs. Two important financial institutions, National Housing Bank and Discount and Financial House of India Ltd., have been established to take care of the housing finance and money market instruments respectively.

The above said institutions meet mainly the credit needs of various segments of the country. Some other institutions, Life Insurance Corporation of India and Unit Trust of India are essentially engaged in investing the money in corporate, quasi-government and Government securities.

These developments have brought up Indian banking system in comparison to other banking set up in the world.

Changing Corporate Environment

The Indian Business environment has altered radically since 1991 with the changes in the economic policies and introduction of new institutional mechanisms of economic liberalization and financial sector reforms. They paved the way for the growth of various business houses on competitive strength. Moreover, the arrival of the internet and e-commerce in India has altogether changed the business landscapes, this enabled them to expand beyond the frontiers of the country.

Accordingly, the expectation and requirement of the business houses are more and the banks are required to act as financial super market with an inside range of products at a lower transaction cost. This scenario forced the banking industry to take up the operations in a large scale manner and facing the competition brought by new private sector banks equipped with latest technology.

Reforms and Consolidations

There was a time when the banking system was not well regulated and also security to customers was also not assured. After independence, it was necessary to mobilize adequate resource for development, to reduce inequalities between region and group. So the government of India decided to nationalize the banks and it was done under the control of the Reserve Bank of India which assured safety and security to its customers.

As a result of change in credit policy, they maintain close touch with state government in order to get the best out of the money system. They are at the disposal of crores of rupees from the government as additional resources. With these resources, the banks have created export cell, Small Industry Advisory panels and opportunities have been offered to unemployed technical graduates and other educated people, women entrepreneurs and of late financial assistance are given to the worthy students to pressure their education.

Moreover branches have been opened in rural areas and offer financial assistance along with advice and guidance on several critical problems which transforms the life of rural people. But the nationalization of banks is critical on the ground that social control of banks was hardly satisfactory. The Reserve Bank of India has secured enormous control over the banking systems and the banks faced that the allocation was also not sound and the gap was filled by the well managed private sector banks on sound footing both economically and technically.

But in the wake of contemporary changes in the world economy and other domestic crisis like adverse balance of payments, increasing fiscal deficits etc., our country too embarked upon economic reforms.

As banking sector represents a part of the financial sector, it is necessary to have effective provision of services to meet the economic challenges for the faster economic growth. To meet the adverse situation in banking, Several committees have been appointed to suggest certain measures to overcome the weakness of the banking sector in India and they have suggested banking sector reforms including M&As in the banking industry as a measure to strengthen the ability of the banks. The various committees and their suggestions are:

The Narasimham Committee 1991 And 1999

As the prevailing trend in the global level is merger and acquisition for various reasons, the Narasimham Committee suggested mergers among strong banks both in the public sector and private sector, developmental financial institutions and non-banking financial companies. Such merger needs to be based on synergies, location and business specific complementary and must make second commercial sense. Further, committee desired that ensure mergers to be managerial, it should yield benefits to staff and branch network nationalization. It should lead to the emergence of a strong bank by way of increased capital base and with organizational strength.

The Khan Committee 1997

The committee was appointed to study harmonization of roles of commercial banks and financial institutions. It recommended that banks and developmental financial institutions should be permitted to explore and enter into gainful merger.

Further, the committee not only recommended merger between banks but also between banks and development financial institution, between strong and weak banks and between two strong banks and development financial institution.

Verma Committee 1998

The Verma Committee in its report observed and recommended that merger should take into account synergies and complementaries of merging units and to provide opportunities for pooling of strengths, lead to overall reduction of cost.

Operations with increases competitive ability, operational efficiency and better positioning and longer market share in business. So it recommended mergers only between strong banks that lead to cost reduction and increase in business and profit.

Rationale of Banking Sector Reforms

Banking sector reforms were introduced to remove the deficiencies in the banking sector and to improve the performance to comply with the required standards. Since 1991, the banking sector was facing the following problems:

* Highly regulated by the Reserve Bank of India;
* Eroded productivity and efficiency of public sector banks;
* Continuous loss borne by public sector banks;
* Increasing NPAs;
* Deteriorated portfolio quality;
* Poor customer service;

* Obsolete work technology;
* Inability to meet the competitive environment.

Consolidation Process in India

The Banking Regulation Act provided for the voluntary Amalgamations of Banks before 1960. But in 1960, the failure of Palai Central Bank and Laxmi Bank led to loss of confidence in the banking system as a whole. There were instances of the private sector banks having low capital base and were mostly operating with other money hard to be rescued or closed down.

For instance, against the total deposit of Rs.2750 crores at the end of December, 1968, the Paid-up capital of private banks was only Rs.28.50 crores i.e., more than 1% only. But after that, the Act was amended by adding section 45 allow for compulsory amalgamations wherever possible in order to strengthen the banking system by eliminating small and weak banks.

Under these circumstances, mergers were initiated to avoid the losses to depositors and maintain confidence in the banking system. In 1961, the Banking Companies (Amendment) Act empowered the Reserve Bank of India to formulate and carryout a scheme for the reconstruction and compulsory amalgamation of sales of standard banks with well managed ones.

Consequently, out of the 42 banks, 22 were amalgamated with other banks. After 1969, the banks had a faster branch expansion and spread throughout the country. This growth had resulted in surfacing of several internal deficiencies in the system. It affected customer service badly, work technology remained stagnant and the "transaction cost" went on increasing over the years.

Inspite of positions of achievements and meeting various socio-economic goals, the banking system in India during 1980s, has experienced several problems mainly related to the profitability and inability of banks.

The recent trend of merger and acquisition in India is in the form of restructuring through consolidation to face likely competition from the foreign companies which opened their office as a result of liberalization.

Between 1988 and 1992, the banking industry experienced 121 amalgamations and mergers in addition to 37 take overs. So it was felt that the needs of hour that public sector banks are in the dire need of restructuring and enable them to become efficient by closing down the enviable banks.

But from 1991 onwards, the number of merger and take over activities in India got increased. Mergers in the year 1988 were about 25% in India, which increased to 50% in 1999. In 2000s, the state of bank merger reveals that most of the private sector banks like Times Bank, Bank of Madura, Bharat Overseas Bank, Ganesh Bank of Kurunwad, Lord Krishna Bank and United Western Bank merged with strong banks from the private sector.

Conclusion

In the last six decades since independence, Banking system in India has evolved through four distinct stages as under:

1. Foundatation stage from 1050s, 1960s and the 1969;
2. Expansion stage mid 1960's i.e. 1969 to 1984;
3. Consolidation stage from 1985 to 1990; and
4. Reform stage from 1991 onwards.

To conclude, it is understood that the move from old to new business environment has created the demands on Indian bank like enhanced work flow, full customer access to banking transactions through electronic mode etc. In the emerging scenario of fierce competition backed by twin force of deregulation and technology, the degree of competition in the Indian financial Sector has increased to unprecedented level.

Hence the operational efficiency of banks has achieved immense significance for their survival in the present scenario through relevant mode like merger and acquisition, amalgamation and take-over.

4

Insurance Sector

Insurance

Insurance is the equitable transfer of the risk of a potential loss, from one entity to another, in exchange for a premium. Insurer is the company that sells the insurance policy and schemes. Insurance rate is a factor used to determine the amount, called the premium, to be charged for a certain amount of insurance coverage. Risk management or insurance as the practice of appraising and controlling risk, has evolved as a hot career option in the post-liberalization era in India. As a result, not only insurance agents but also marketers and actuaries are in great demand in the insurance sector.

Insurance Companies deal in two main areas - Life insurance and General insurance. With the liberalization and opening up of this field several companies have come up in the field of Life insurance and general insurance.

Insurance Agents: Agents are not on the payrolls of the insurance company. The insurance agents get a fixed commission on each policy they (insurance-agent) manage to sell

Eligibility and Process: People who wish to become insurance agents are required to undergo 100 hours of training by the respective insurance company. Once the training is complete, the candidate is eligible to appear for an online examination conducted by the Insurance Regulatory Development Authority (IRDA) with at least 50 per cent marks set for qualifying.

Composite Agent—is the one who sells both life and general insurance policies. One has to put in 100 hours promoting life insurance products assuming that you are a general insurance agent. A life insurance agent, before appearing for another exam, has to dedicate 50 hours towards promoting general insurance products. A composite agent has to appear for another test also (conducted by the IRDA).

The agent is supposed to renew his license after three years, by putting in another 25 hours (and 50 hours for composite insurance agent) of training. An agent can register under a development officer in any insurance company. The training institutes are accredited by the IRDA and the insurance Company merely sponsors its agents. An agent works with the Development Officer in the insurance Company and the credit for the policy of the insurance agents goes to the Development Officers within the organization. Nevertheless, this job is as good as freelancing. Secondly, the insurance companies also provide incentive schemes for the insurance agents from time to time.

Surveyors, Loss Adjusters and Assessors are technically qualified professionals who perform the job of assessing the losses, according to their qualifications and experience. They work as 'consultants' for the company. A surveyor with a background in mechanical engineering assesses industrial accidents. Here the surveyor would investigate, evaluate, assess, adjust and determine the liability, negotiate and then finally submit a report.

A surveyor must hold either a fellowship or associateship from one of the following

- The Institute of Insurance surveyors and Adjusters (IISA), Mumbai
- A degree or diploma in architecture from a recognized university or institute
- Fellowship or Associateship from the Institute of Chartered Accountants or Costs and Works Accountants
- A degree or diploma from a recognized institute of engineering or a degree or diploma in naval architecture.
- They have to apply to the IRDA for a license that further categorizes them as Class A, B, C, or D. A surveyor, loss adjuster or assessor is the only specialized link between the insurers and the insured.

Insurance & Actuarials

The opening up of the Insurance sector to private enterprises will usher in a new phase in this century old sector.

In 1950, with the enactment of the Insurance Act, the entire business of life insurance was nationalised. The central office of LIC was set up in Mumbai with seven zonal offices. The head office was responsible for formulation of policies and the zonal offices for coordinating with and supervising divisional offices. The LIC operates through almost a hundred divisional offices and nearly 2000 branch offices located across the country and in some locations abroad.

Insurance companies deal in 3 main areas, life insurance, health insurance, property and accident insurance. Companies may specialise in one or all the three types of insurance coverage. While LIC deals with insurance of life, the General Insurance Company (GIC) is another insurance firm concerned with motor, marine, personal accident and fire insurance.

Both LIC and GIC have branches all over the country. GIC has four subsidiaries - Oriental Insurance, United India Insurance, New India Assurance and National Insurance, netting business in India and in over thirty locations abroad.

Insurance Underwriters

Significant Points: Most large insurance companies prefer college graduates who have a degree in business administration or finance with courses in accounting; however, a bachelor's degree in any field—plus courses in business law and accounting—may be sufficient to qualify.

Continuing education is necessary for advancement.

Employment is expected to grow more slowly than average as the continuing spread of underwriting software increases worker productivity. Job opportunities should be best for those with a background in finance and strong computer and communication skills.

Nature of the Work: Insurance companies protect individuals and organizations from financial loss by assuming billions of dollars in risk each year. Underwriters are needed to identify and calculate the risk of loss from policyholders, establish appropriate premium rates and write policies that cover this risk. An insurance company may lose business to competitors if the underwriter appraises risks too conservatively, or it may have to pay excessive claims if the underwriting actions are too liberal.

With the aid of computers, underwriters analyze information in insurance applications to determine whether a risk is acceptable and will not result in a loss. Applications often are supplemented with reports from loss-control consultants, medical reports, reports from data vendors and actuarial studies. Underwriters then must decide whether to issue the policy and, if so, the appropriate premium to charge. In making this determination, underwriters serve as the main link between the insurance carrier and the insurance agent. On occasion, they accompany sales agents to make presentations to prospective clients.

Technology plays an important role in an underwriter's job. Underwriters use computer applications called "smart systems" to manage risks more efficiently and accurately. These systems automatically analyze and rate insurance applications, recommend acceptance or denial of the risk and adjust the premium rate in accordance with the risk. With these systems, underwriters are better equipped to make sound decisions and avoid excessive losses.

The Internet also has affected the work of underwriters. Many insurance carriers' computer systems are now linked to different databases on the Internet that allow immediate access to information—such as driving records—necessary in determining a potential client's risk. This kind of access reduces the amount of time and paperwork necessary for an underwriter to complete a risk assessment.

Most underwriters specialize in one of three major categories of insurance: life, health and property and casualty. Life and health insurance underwriters may further specialize in group or individual policies.

Property and casualty underwriters usually specialize in either commercial or personal insurance and then by type of risk insured, as in fire, homeowners', automobile, marine, or liability insurance, or workers' compensation. In cases where casualty companies provide insurance through a single "package" policy covering various types of risks, the underwriter must be familiar with different lines of insurance. For business insurance, the underwriter often must be able to evaluate the firm's entire operation in appraising its application for insurance.

An increasing proportion of insurance sales, particularly in life and health insurance, is being made through group contracts. A standard group policy insures everyone in a specified group through a single contract at a standard premium rate. The group underwriter analyzes the overall composition of the group to ensure that the total risk is not excessive. Another type of group policy provides members of a group—a labour union, for example—with individual policies reflecting their needs. These usually are casualty policies, such as those covering automobiles. The casualty underwriter analyzes the application of each group member and makes individual appraisals. Some group underwriters meet with union or employer representatives to discuss the types of policies available to their group.

Working Conditions: Underwriters have desk jobs that require no unusual physical activity. Their offices usually are comfortable and pleasant. Although underwriters typically work a standard 40-hour week, more are working longer hours due to the downsizing of many insurance companies. Most underwriters are based in a home or regional branch office, but they occasionally attend meetings away from home for several days. Construction and marine underwriters frequently travel to inspect worksites and assess risks.

Training, Other Qualifications and Advancement: For entry-level underwriting jobs, most large insurance companies prefer college graduates who have a degree in business administration or finance with courses or experience in accounting. However, a bachelor's degree in almost any field—plus courses in business law and accounting—provides a good general background and may be sufficient to qualify an individual. Because computers are an integral part of most underwriters' jobs, computer skills are essential.

New employees usually start as underwriter trainees or assistant underwriters. They may help collect information on applicants and evaluate routine applications under the supervision of an experienced risk analyst. Property and casualty trainees study claims files to become familiar with factors associated with certain types of losses. Many larger insurers offer work-study training programmes, lasting from a few months to a year. As trainees gain experience, they are assigned policy applications that are more complex and cover greater risks. Analyzing and processing these applications efficiently requires the use of computers.

Underwriting can be a satisfying career for people who enjoy analyzing information and paying attention to detail. In addition, underwriters must possess good judgment in order to make sound decisions. Excellent communication and interpersonal skills also are essential, as much of the underwriter's work involves dealing with agents and other insurance professionals.

Continuing education is necessary for advancement. Insurance companies usually pay tuition for underwriting courses that their trainees complete; some also offer salary incentives. Independent-study programmes for experienced property and casualty underwriters are available as well. The Insurance Institute of America offers both a programme called "Introduction to Underwriting" for beginning underwriters and the specialty designation of Associate in Commercial Underwriting (ACU), a formal step in developing a career in underwriting business insurance policies. Those interested in developing a career underwriting personal insurance policies may earn the Associate in Personal Insurance (API) designation. To earn either the ACU or API designation, underwriters complete a series of courses and examinations that generally last 1 to 2 years.

The American Institute for Chartered Property Casualty Underwriters (AICPCU) awards the Chartered Property and Casualty Underwriter (CPCU) designation, the final stage of development for an underwriter. Earning the CPCU designation requires passing 10 exams, meeting a requirement of at least 3 years of insurance experience and abiding by the AICPCU's code of professional ethics. Exams cover risk management; insurance operations and regulations, business and insurance law and financial management and financial institutions. In conjunction with the Insurance Institute of America, the AICPCU offers 22 insurance-related educational programmes, including associate designation programmes in claims underwriting, risk management and reinsurance. The American College offers the Chartered Life Underwriter (CLU) designation and the Registered Health Underwriter (RHU) designation for all life and health insurance professionals.

Experienced underwriters who complete courses of study may advance to senior underwriter or underwriting manager positions. Some underwriting managers are promoted to senior managerial jobs. Some employers require a master's degree to achieve this level. Other underwriters are attracted to the earnings potential of sales and, therefore, obtain State licenses to sell insurance and related financial products as agents or brokers.

Employment: Insurance underwriters held about 101,000 jobs in 2004. Approximately 2 out of 3 underwriters work for insurance carriers. Most of the remaining underwriters work in insurance agencies or for organizations that offer insurance services to insurance companies and policyholders. A small number of underwriters work in agencies owned and operated by banks, mortgage companies and real estate firms.

Most underwriters are based in the insurance company's home office, but some, mainly in the property and casualty area, work out of regional branch offices of the insurance company. These underwriters usually have the authority to underwrite most risks and determine an appropriate rating without consulting the home office.

Job Outlook: Employment of underwriters is expected to grow more slowly than average for all occupations through 2014. Underwriting software will continue to make workers more productive; however, because computer software does not do away with the need for human skills, employment will increase as economic and population growth result in increased insurance needs by businesses and individuals. Job opportunities should be best for those with a background in finance and strong computer and communication skills.

In addition to openings arising from some job growth, openings will be created by the need to replace underwriters who transfer to another job or leave the occupation. Insurance carriers always are assessing new risks and offering policies to meet changing circumstances.

Underwriters are needed particularly in the area of product development, where they assess risks and set the premiums for new lines of insurance. One new line of insurance being offered by life insurance carriers that may provide job opportunities for underwriters is long-term care insurance.

Demand for underwriters also is expected to improve as insurance carriers try to restore profitability to make up for an unusually large number of underwriting losses in recent years. As the carriers' returns on their investments have declined, insurers are placing more emphasis on underwriting to generate revenues. This renewed interest in underwriting should result in job opportunities for underwriters. Because insurance is considered a necessity for people and businesses, there will always be a need for underwriters—a profession that is less subject to recession and layoffs than other fields.

Earnings: Median annual earnings of insurance underwriters were $48,550 in May 2004. The middle 50 percent earned between $37,490 and $65,450 a year. The lowest 10 percent earned less than $30,410, while the highest 10 percent earned more than $86,110. Median annual earnings of underwriters working with insurance carriers were $49,280, while earnings of these in agencies, brokerages and other insurance related activities were $46,750.

Insurance companies usually provide better-than-average benefits, including retirement plans and employer-financed group life and health insurance.

Claims Investigators

Significant Points: Adjusters and examiners investigate insurance claims, negotiate settlements and authorize payments; appraisers assess the cost or value of an insured item; investigators deal with claims about which there is a question of liability and where fraud or criminal activity is suspected.

Licensing and continuing education requirements vary by State. College graduates have the best opportunities; competition will be keen for jobs as investigators, because this occupation attracts many qualified people.

Nature of the Work: Individuals and businesses purchase insurance policies to protect against monetary losses. In the event of a loss, policyholders submit claims, or requests for payment, seeking compensation for their loss. Adjusters, appraisers, examiners and investigators work primarily for property and casualty insurance companies, for whom they handle a wide variety of claims alleging property damage, liability, or bodily injury.

Their main role is to investigate the claims, negotiate settlements and authorize payments to claimants, all the while mindful not to violate the claimant's rights under Federal and State privacy laws. They must determine whether the customer's insurance policy covers the loss and how much of the loss should be paid to the claimant. Although many adjusters, appraisers, examiners and investigators have overlapping functions and may even perform the same job, the insurance industry generally assigns specific roles to each of these claims workers.

Adjusters plan and schedule the work required to process a claim that would follow, for example, an automobile accident or damage to one's home caused by a storm. They investigate claims by interviewing the claimant and witnesses, consulting police and hospital records and inspecting property damage to determine the extent of the company's liability. Adjusters may consult with other professionals, such as accountants, architects, construction workers, engineers, lawyers and physicians, who can offer a more expert evaluation of a claim. The information gathered, including photographs and written or audio-taped or video-taped statements, is set down in a report that is then used to evaluate the associated claim. When the policyholder's claim is legitimate, the claims adjuster negotiates with the claimant and settles the claim. When claims are contested, adjusters will work with attorneys and expert witnesses to defend the insurer's position.

Many companies centralize claims adjustment in a claims centre, where the cost of repair is determined and a check is issued immediately. More complex cases, usually involving bodily injury, are referred to senior adjusters. Some adjusters work with multiple types of insurance; however, most specialize in homeowner claims, business losses, automotive damage, or workers' compensation.

Claimants can opt not to rely on the services of their insurance company's adjuster and may instead choose to hire a public adjuster. These workers assist clients in preparing and presenting claims to insurance companies and in trying to negotiate a fair settlement. They perform the same services as adjusters who work directly for companies; however, they work in the best interests of the client, rather than the insurance company.

Claims examiners within property and casualty insurance firms may have duties similar to those of an adjuster, but often their primary job is to review the claims submitted in order to ensure that proper guidelines have been followed. They may assist adjusters with complex and complicated claims or when a disaster suddenly greatly increases the volume of claims. Most claims examiners work for life or health insurance companies. In health insurance companies, examiners review health-related claims to see whether costs are reasonable on the basis of the diagnosis.

The examiners are provided with guides that supply information on the average period of disability, the expected treatments and the average hospital stay, for patients with the various ailments for which a claim may be submitted.

Examiners check claim applications for completeness and accuracy, interview medical specialists and consult policy files to verify the information reported in a claim. Examiners will then either authorize the appropriate payment or refer the claim to an investigator for a more thorough review. Claims examiners usually specialize in group or individual insurance plans and in hospital, dental, or prescription drug claims.

In life insurance, claims examiners review the causes of death, particularly in the case of an accident, because most life insurance policies pay additional benefits if a death is accidental. Claims examiners also may review new applications for life insurance to make sure that the applicants have no serious illnesses that would make them a high risk to insure and thus disqualify them from obtaining insurance.

Another occupation that plays an important role in the accurate settlement of claims is that of the *appraiser*, whose role is to assess the cost or value of an insured item. The majority of appraisers employed by insurance companies and independent adjusting firms are *auto damage appraisers*. These appraisers inspect damaged vehicles after an accident and estimate the cost of repairs. This information is then relayed to the adjuster, who incorporates the appraisal into the settlement. Auto damage appraisers are valued by insurance companies because they can provide an unbiased judgment of repair costs. Otherwise, the companies would have to rely on auto mechanics' estimates, which might be unreasonably high.

Many claims adjusters and auto damage appraisers are equipped with laptop computers from which they can download the necessary forms and files from insurance company databases. Many adjusters and appraisers use digital cameras, which allow photographs of the damage to be sent to the company via the Internet. Many also input information about the damage directly into their computers, where software programmes produce estimates of damage on standard forms. These new technologies allow for faster and more efficient processing of claims.

When adjusters or examiners suspect fraud, they refer the claim to an investigator. *Insurance investigators* in an insurance company's special investigative unit handle claims in which the company suspects fraudulent or criminal activity, such as arson, falsified workers' disability claims, staged accidents, or unnecessary medical treatments. The severity of insurance fraud cases can vary greatly, from claimants simply overstating the damage to a vehicle to complicated fraud rings responsible for many claimants and supported by dishonest doctors, lawyers and even insurance personnel.

Investigators usually start with a database search to obtain background information on claimants and witnesses. Investigators can access certain personal information and identify Social Security numbers, aliases, driver's license numbers, addresses, phone numbers, criminal records and past claims histories to establish whether a claimant has ever attempted insurance fraud. Then, investigators may visit claimants and witnesses to obtain a recorded statement, take photographs and inspect facilities, such as doctors' offices, to determine whether the doctors have a proper license. Investigators often consult with legal counsel and can be expert witnesses in court cases.

Often, investigators also perform surveillance work. For example, in a case involving fraudulent workers' compensation claims, an investigator may covertly observe the claimant for several days or even weeks. If the investigator observes the subject performing an activity that is ruled out by injuries stated in a workers' compensation claim, the investigator will take video or still photographs to document the activity and report it to the insurance company.

Working Conditions: Working environments of claims adjusters, appraisers, examiners and investigators vary greatly. Most claims examiners employed by life and health insurance companies work a standard 5-day, 40-hour week in a typical office environment. Many claims adjusters and auto damage appraisers, however, often work outside the office, inspecting damaged buildings and automobiles. Adjusters who inspect damaged buildings must be wary of potential hazards such as collapsed roofs and floors, as well as weakened structures.

In general, adjusters are able to arrange their work schedules to accommodate evening and weekend appointments with clients. This accommodation sometimes results in adjusters working irregular schedules or more than 40 hours a week, especially when they have a lot of claims to investigate. Some report to the office every morning to get their assignments, while others simply call in from home and spend their days travelling to claim sites. New technology, such as laptop computers and cellular telephones, is making telecommuting easier for claims adjusters and auto damage appraisers. Many adjusters work inside their office only a few hours a week, while others conduct their business entirely out of their home and automobile.

Occasionally, experienced adjusters must be away from home for days—for example, when they travel to the scene of a disaster such as a tornado, hurricane, or flood—to work with local adjusters and government officials. Adjusters often are called to work in the event of such emergencies and may have to work 50 or 60 hours a week until all claims are resolved.

Insurance investigators often work irregular hours because of the need to conduct surveillance and contact people who are not available during normal working hours. Early morning, evening and weekend work is common. Some days, investigators will spend all day in the office, searching databases, making telephone calls and writing reports. Other times, they may be away, performing surveillance activities or interviewing witnesses. Some of the work can involve confrontation with claimants and others involved in a case, so the job can be stressful and dangerous.

Training, Other Qualifications and Advancement: Training and entry requirements vary widely for claims adjusters, appraisers, examiners and investigators. Although many in these occupations do not have a college degree, most companies prefer to hire college graduates. No specific college major is recommended, but a variety of backgrounds can be an asset. A claims adjuster who, for example, has a business or an accounting background might specialize in claims of financial loss due to strikes, breakdowns of equipment, or damage to merchandise.

College training in architecture or engineering is helpful in adjusting industrial claims, such as those involving damage from fires or other accidents. Some claims adjusters and examiners apply expertise acquired through specialized professional training to adjust claims. A legal background can be beneficial to someone handling workers' compensation and product liability cases. A medical background is useful for those examiners working on medical and life insurance claims.

Because they often work closely with claimants, witnesses and other insurance professionals, claims adjusters and examiners must be able to communicate effectively with others. Knowledge of computer applications also is extremely helpful. In addition, a valid driver's license and a good driving record are required for workers for whom travel is an important aspect of their job. Some companies require applicants to pass a series of written aptitude tests designed to measure their communication, analytical and general mathematical skills.

Licensing requirements for these workers vary by State. Some States have very few requirements, while others require either the completion of pre-licensing education or a satisfactory score on a licensing exam. Fulfilling the requirements for earning a voluntary professional designation may, in some cases, be substituted for completing the exam. In some States, claims adjusters employed by insurance companies can work under the company license and need not become licensed themselves. Separate or additional requirements may apply for public adjusters. For example, some States require public adjusters to file a surety bond.

Continuing education in claims is very important for claims adjusters, appraisers, examiners and investigators, because Federal and State laws and court decisions affect how claims are handled or who is covered by insurance policies. Also, examiners working on life and health claims must be familiar with new medical procedures and prescription drugs. Some States that require licensing also require a certain number of continuing education credits per year in order to renew the license. These credits can be obtained from a number of sources.

Many companies offer training sessions to inform their employees of industry changes. A number of schools and associations give courses and seminars on various topics having to with claims. Correspondence courses via the Internet are making long-distance learning possible. Workers also can earn continuing education credits by writing articles for claims publications or by giving lectures and presentations. In addition, numerous adjusters and examiners choose to earn professional certifications and designations for independent recognition of their professional expertise. Although requirements for these designations vary, many entail at least 5 to 10 years of experience in the claims field and the successful completion of an examination; in addition, a certain number of continuing education credits must be earned each year to retain the designation.

For auto damage appraiser jobs, insurance companies and independent adjusting firms typically prefer to hire persons with experience as an estimator for, or manager of, an auto body repair shop. An appraiser must know how to repair vehicles in order to identify and estimate damage and technical skills are essential. While auto damage appraisers do not require a college education, most companies prefer to hire persons with formal training.

Many vocational colleges offer 2-year programmes in auto body repair on how to estimate and repair damaged vehicles. Some States require auto damage appraisers to be licensed and certification also may be required or preferred. Basic computer skills are an important qualification for many auto damage appraiser positions. As with adjusters and examiners, continuing education is important because of the continual introduction of new car models and repair techniques.

Most insurance companies prefer to hire former law enforcement officers or private investigators as insurance investigators. Many experienced claims adjusters or examiners also become investigators. Licensing requirements vary among States. Most employers look for individuals with ingenuity who are persistent and assertive. Investigators should not be afraid of confrontation, should communicate well and should be able to think on their feet. Good interviewing and interrogation skills also are important and usually are acquired in earlier careers in law enforcement.

Beginning claims adjusters, appraisers, examiners and investigators work on small claims under the supervision of an experienced worker. As they learn more about claims investigation and settlement, they are assigned larger, more complex claims. Trainees are promoted as they demonstrate competence in handling assignments and progress in their coursework.

Employees who demonstrate competence in claims work or administrative skills may be promoted to more responsible managerial or administrative jobs. Similarly, claims investigators may rise to supervisor or manager of the investigations department. Once they achieve a certain level of expertise, many choose to start their own independent adjusting or auto damage appraising firms.

Employment: Adjusters, appraisers, examiners and investigators held about 263,000 jobs in 2004. Only 5 percent of these jobs were held by auto damage insurance appraisers. Insurance carriers, agencies, brokerages and related industries, such as private claims adjusting companies, employed more than 8 out of 10 claims adjusters, appraisers, examiners and investigators. Relatively few adjusters, appraisers, examiners and investigators were self-employed.

Job Outlook: Employment of claims adjusters, appraisers, examiners and investigators is expected to grow about as fast as average for all occupations over the 2004–14 period. College graduates have the best opportunities. Numerous job openings also will result from the need to replace workers who transfer to other occupations or leave the labour force.

Many insurance carriers are downsizing their claims staff in an effort to contain costs. Larger companies are relying more on customer service representatives in call centres to handle the recording of the necessary details of the claim, allowing adjusters to spend more of their time investigating claims. New technology is reducing the amount of time it takes for an adjuster to complete a claim, thereby increasing the number of claims that one adjuster can handle.

However, as long as more insurance policies are being sold to accommodate a growing population, there will be a need for adjusters, appraisers, examiners and investigators. Further, as the elderly population increases, there will be a greater need for health care, resulting in more health insurance claims.

Despite recent gains in productivity resulting from technological advances, these jobs are not easily automated. Adjusters still are needed to contact policyholders, inspect damaged property and consult with experts.

Although the number of claims in litigation and the number and complexity of insurance fraud cases are expected to increase over the next decade, demand for insurance investigators is not expected to grow significantly, because technology such as the Internet, which reduces the amount of time it takes to perform background checks, will allow investigators to handle more cases. Competition for investigator jobs will remain keen because the occupation attracts many qualified people, including retirees from law enforcement and military careers, as well as experienced claims adjusters and examiners who choose to get their investigator license.

As with claims adjusters, examiners and investigators, employment of auto damage appraisers should grow about as fast as the average for all occupations. Insurance companies and agents continue to sell growing numbers of auto insurance policies, leading to more claims being filed that require the attention of an auto damage appraiser.

The work of this occupation is not easily automated, because most appraisals require an onsite inspection. However, employment growth will be limited by downsizing in the insurance industry and by the implementation of new technology that is making auto damage appraisers more efficient. In addition, some insurance companies are opening their own repair facilities, which may reduce the need for auto damage appraisers.

Earnings: Earnings of claims adjusters, appraisers, examiners and investigators vary significantly. Median annual earnings were $44,220 in May 2004. The middle 50 percent earned between $33,900 and $57,410. The lowest 10 percent earned less than $27,220 and the highest 10 percent earned more than $72,620.

Many claims adjusters, especially those who work for insurance companies, receive additional bonuses or benefits as part of their job. Adjusters often are furnished a laptop computer, a cellular telephone and a company car or are reimbursed for the use of their own vehicle for business purposes.

Median annual earnings of auto damage insurance appraisers were $45,330 in May 2004. The middle 50 percent earned between $37,210 and $54,280. The lowest 10 percent earned less than $29,550 and the highest 10 percent earned more than $63,220.

Insurance Sales Agents

Significant Points: Agents increasingly offer comprehensive financial planning services, including retirement and estate planning; as a result, in addition to offering insurance policies, agents sell mutual funds, annuities and securities.

Agents must obtain a license in the States where they plan to do their selling.

Despite slower than average growth, job opportunities should be good for college graduates who have sales ability, excellent interpersonal skills and expertise in a wide range of insurance and financial services.

Successful agents often have high earnings, but many beginning agents fail to earn enough from commissions to meet their income goals and eventually transfer to other careers.

Nature of the Work: Most people have their first contact with an insurance company through an insurance sales agent. These workers help individuals, families and businesses select insurance policies that provide the best protection for their lives, health and property. Insurance sales agents who work exclusively for one insurance company are referred to as captive agents. Independent insurance agents, or brokers, represent several companies and place insurance policies for their clients with the company that offers the best rate and coverage. In either case, agents prepare reports, maintain records, seek out new clients and, in the event of a loss, help policyholders settle their insurance claims. Increasingly, some are also offering their clients financial analysis or advice on ways the clients can minimize risk.

Insurance sales agents, commonly referred to as "producers" in the insurance industry, sell one or more types of insurance, such as property and casualty, life, health, disability and long-term care. Property and casualty insurance agents sell policies that protect individuals and businesses from financial loss resulting from automobile accidents, fire, theft, storms and other events that can damage property. For businesses, property and casualty insurance can also cover injured workers' compensation, product liability claims, or medical malpractice claims.

Life insurance agents specialize in selling policies that pay beneficiaries when a policyholder dies. Depending on the policyholder's circumstances, a cash-value policy can be designed to provide retirement income, funds for the education of children, or other benefits.

Life insurance agents also sell annuities that promise a retirement income. Health insurance agents sell health insurance policies that cover the costs of medical care and loss of income due to illness or injury. They also may sell dental insurance and short-term and long-term-disability insurance policies.

An increasing number of insurance sales agents are offering comprehensive financial planning services to their clients, such as retirement planning, estate planning, or assistance in setting up pension plans for businesses. As a result, many insurance agents are involved in "cross-selling" or "total account development." Besides offering insurance, these agents may become licensed to sell mutual funds, variable annuities and other securities. This practice is most common with life insurance agents who already sell annuities; however, property and casualty agents also sell financial products.

Technology has greatly affected the insurance agency, making it much more efficient and giving the agent the ability to take on more clients. Agents' computers are now linked directly to the insurance carriers via the Internet, making the tasks of obtaining price quotes and processing applications and service requests faster and easier. Computers also allow agents to be better informed about new products that the insurance carriers may be offering.

The growth of the Internet in the insurance industry is gradually altering the relationship between agent and client. In the past, agents devoted much of their time to marketing and selling products to new clients, a practice that is now changing. Increasingly, clients are obtaining insurance quotes from a company's Web site and then contacting the company directly to purchase policies. This interaction gives the client a more active role in selecting a policy at the best price, while reducing the amount of time agents spend actively seeking new clients. Because insurance sales agents also obtain many new accounts through referrals, it is important that they maintain regular contact with their clients to ensure that the clients' financial needs are being met. Developing a satisfied clientele that will recommend an agent's services to other potential customers is a key to success in this field.

Increasing competition in the insurance industry has spurred carriers and agents to find new ways to keep their clients satisfied. One solution is to increase the use of call centres, which usually are accessible to clients 24 hours a day, 7 days a week. Insurance carriers and sales agents also are hiring customer service representatives to handle routine tasks such as answering questions, making changes in policies, processing claims and selling more products to clients. The opportunity to cross-sell new products to clients will help agents' businesses grow. The use of call centres also allows agents to concentrate their efforts on seeking out new clients and maintaining relationships with old ones.

Working Conditions: Most insurance sales agents are based in small offices, from which they contact clients and provide information on the policies they sell. However, much of their time may be spent outside their offices, travelling locally to meet with clients, close sales, or investigate claims. Agents usually determine their own hours of work and often schedule evening and weekend appointments for the convenience of clients. Although most agents work a 40-hour week, some work 60 hours a week or longer. Commercial sales agents, in particular, may meet with clients during business hours and then spend evenings doing paperwork and preparing presentations to prospective clients.

Training, Other Qualifications and Advancement: For insurance sales agent jobs, most companies and independent agencies prefer to hire college graduates—especially those who have majored in business or economics. High school graduates are occasionally hired if they have proven sales ability or have been successful in other types of work. In fact, many entrants to insurance sales agent jobs transfer from other occupations. In selling commercial insurance, technical experience in a particular field can help sell policies to those in the same profession. As a result, new agents tend to be older than entrants in many other occupations.

College training may help agents grasp the technical aspects of insurance policies and the fundamentals and procedures of selling insurance. Many colleges and universities offer courses in insurance and a few schools offer a bachelor's degree in the field. College courses in finance, mathematics, accounting, economics, business law, marketing and business administration enable insurance sales agents to understand how social and economic conditions relate to the insurance industry. Courses in psychology, sociology and public speaking can prove useful in improving sales techniques. In addition, because computers provide instantaneous information on a wide variety of financial products and greatly improve agents' efficiency, familiarity with computers and popular software packages has become very important.

Insurance sales agents must obtain a license in the States where they plan to do their selling. Separate licenses are required for agents to sell life and health insurance and property and casualty insurance. In most States, licenses are issued only to applicants who complete specified pre-licensing courses and who pass State examinations covering insurance fundamentals and State insurance laws. The insurance industry is increasingly moving toward uniform State licensing standards and reciprocal licensing, allowing agents who earn a license in one State to become licensed in other States upon passing the appropriate courses and examination.

A number of organizations offer professional designation programmes that certify one's expertise in specialties such as life, health and property and casualty insurance, as well as financial consulting. For example, The National Alliance for Education and Research offers a wide variety of courses in health, life and property and casualty insurance for independent insurance agents. Although voluntary, such programmes assure clients and employers that an agent has a thorough understanding of the relevant specialty. Agents are usually required to complete a specified number of hours of continuing education to retain their designation.

Employers also are placing greater emphasis on continuing professional education as the diversity of financial products sold by insurance agents increases. It is important for insurance agents to keep up to date on issues concerning clients. Changes in tax laws, government benefits programmes and other State and Federal regulations can affect the insurance needs of clients and the way in which agents conduct business.

Agents can enhance their selling skills and broaden their knowledge of insurance and other financial services by taking courses at colleges and universities and by attending institutes, conferences and seminars sponsored by insurance organizations. Most State licensing authorities also have mandatory continuing education requirements focusing on insurance laws, consumer protection and the technical details of various insurance policies.

As the demand for financial products and financial planning increases, many insurance agents are choosing to gain the proper licensing and certification to sell securities and other financial products. Doing so, however, requires substantial study and passing an additional examination—either the Series 6 or Series 7 licensing exam, both of which are administered by the National Association of Securities Dealers (NASD). The Series 6 exam is for individuals who wish to sell only mutual funds and variable annuities, whereas the Series 7 exam is the main NASD series license that qualifies agents as general securities sales representatives.

In addition, to further demonstrate competency in the area of financial planning, many agents find it worthwhile to earn the certified financial planner or chartered financial consultant designation. The Certified Financial Planner credential issued by the Certified Financial Planner Board of Standards, requires relevant experience, completion of education requirements, passing a comprehensive examination and adherence to an enforceable code of ethics. The CFP exams test the candidate's knowledge of the financial planning process, insurance and risk management, employee benefits planning, taxes and retirement planning and investment and estate planning. The Chartered Financial Consultant (ChFC) designation, issued by the American College in Bryn Mawr, Pennsylvania, which requires experience and the completion of an eight-course programme of study. The CFP and ChFC designation and other professional designations have continuing education requirements.

Insurance sales agents should be flexible, enthusiastic, confident, disciplined, hard working and willing to solve problems. They should communicate effectively and inspire customer confidence. Because they usually work without supervision, sales agents must be able to plan their time well and have the initiative to locate new clients.

An insurance sales agent who shows ability and leadership may become a sales manager in a local office. A few advance to agency superintendent or executive positions. However, many who have built up a good clientele prefer to remain in sales work. Some—particularly in the property and casualty field—establish their own independent agencies or brokerage firms.

Employment: Insurance sales agents held about 400,000 jobs in 2004. Most insurance sales agents employed in wage and salary positions work for insurance agencies and brokerages. A decreasing number work directly for insurance carriers. Although most insurance agents specialize in life and health insurance or property and casualty insurance, a growing number of "multiline" agents sell all lines of insurance. A small number of agents work for banks and securities brokerages as a result of the increasing integration of finance and insurance industries. Approximately 1 out of 4 insurance sales agents is self-employed.

Insurance sales agents are employed throughout the country, but most work in or near large urban centres. Some are employed in the headquarters of insurance companies, but the majority work out of local offices or independent agencies.

Job Outlook: Although employment of insurance sales agents is expected to grow more slowly than average for all occupations through 2014, opportunities will be favourable for college graduates who have sales ability, excellent interpersonal skills and expertise in a wide range of insurance and financial services. Multilingual agents also should be in high demand because they can serve a wider range of customers.

Insurance language tends to be quite technical, so it is important for insurance sales agents to have a firm understanding of relevant technical and legal terms. Many beginning agents fail to earn enough from commissions to meet their income goals and eventually transfer to other careers. Most job openings are likely to result from the need to replace agents who leave the occupation or retire. A large number of agents are expected to retire over the next decade.

Future demand for insurance sales agents depends largely on the volume of sales of insurance and other financial products. Sales of health insurance and long-term-care insurance are expected to rise sharply as the population ages. In addition, a growing population will increase demand for insurance for automobiles, homes and high-priced valuables and equipment. As new businesses emerge and existing firms expand their insurance coverage, sales of commercial insurance also should increase, including coverage such as product liability, workers' compensation, employee benefits and pollution liability insurance. Employment of agents will not keep up with the rising level of insurance sales, however. Many insurance carriers are trying to contain costs. As a result, many are shedding their captive agents—those agents working directly for insurance carriers—and are relying more on independent agents or direct marketing through the mail, by phone, or on the Internet.

Agents who incorporate new technology into their existing businesses will remain competitive. Agents who use the Internet to market their products will reach a broader client base and expand their businesses, but because most clients value their relationship with their agent, the Internet should not threaten jobs, given that many individuals still prefer discussing their policies directly with their agents, rather than through a computer. Also, the automation of policy and claims processing is allowing insurance agents to take on more clients.

Agents may face increased competition from traditional securities brokers and bankers as they begin to sell insurance policies. Because of increasing consolidation among insurance companies, banks and brokerage firms and due to increasing demands from clients for more comprehensive financial planning, insurance sales agents will need to expand the products and services they offer.

Agents who offer better customer service also will remain competitive. Call centres are another important way carriers and agents are offering better service to customers, because such centres provide greater access to their policies and more prompt services.

Insurance and investments are becoming more complex and many people and businesses lack the time and expertise to buy insurance without the advice of an agent. Moreover, most individuals and businesses consider insurance a necessity, regardless of economic conditions. Therefore, agents are not likely to face unemployment because of a recession.

Earnings: The median annual earnings of wage and salary insurance sales agents were $41,720 in May 2004. The middle 50 percent earned between $29,980 and $66,160. The lowest 10 percent had earnings of $23,170 or less, while the highest 10 percent earned more than $108,800. Median annual earnings in May 2004 in the two industries employing the largest number of insurance sales agents were $42,010 for insurance carriers and $41,840 for agencies, brokerages and other insurance related activities.

Many independent agents are paid by commission only, whereas sales workers who are employees of an agency or an insurance carrier may be paid in one of three ways—salary only, salary plus commission, or salary plus bonus. In general, commissions are the most common form of compensation, especially for experienced agents. The amount of the commission depends on the type and amount of insurance sold and on whether the transaction is a new policy or a renewal. Bonuses usually are awarded when agents meet their sales goals or when an agency meets its profit goals.

Some agents involved with financial planning receive a fee for their services, rather than a commission. Company-paid benefits to insurance sales agents usually include continuing education, training to qualify for licensing, group insurance plans, office space and clerical support services. Some companies also may pay for automobile and transportation expenses, attendance at conventions and meetings, promotion and marketing expenses and retirement plans. Independent agents working for insurance agencies receive fewer benefits, but their commissions may be higher to help them pay for marketing and other expenses.

Insurance Broker

Insurance brokers are independent advisers, helping clients to choose the insurance product or products most appropriate to their present and/or future needs. Also known as intermediaries, they are the link between insurance companies and customers. Brokers use their knowledge and experience to assess a client's risk profile and find appropriate policies from over several hundred insurers in the industry, searching for the most comprehensive cover at the most competitive price.

Brokers deal with a great range of cases, from simple ones, such as car insurance, where an immediate quotation can be given, to relatively complex cases. In the case of commercial insurance, they may need to provide reports to insurance underwriters, carry out surveys and negotiate with underwriters for cover. This is a highly regulated industry and insurance brokers are required to put the interests of their client first. They may also help clients resolve claims, processing paperwork and negotiating settlements with the insurer. This can lead into a specialised role as a claims broker.

Entry Level: People join broking firms with a variety of different academic backgrounds. Many organisations prefer two A levels/three H grades plus two GCSEs/S grades (A-C/1-3) in English and maths, although there are no formal entry requirements for insurance brokers. Greater emphasis is placed on individual characteristics, particularly communication.

If you choose to take a degree, one of the following subjects might increase your chances: accounting/finance, business/management, economics, mathematics or statistics.

Making the Grade: Training is usually undertaken on the job, with trainees working under the supervision of a senior broker or team leader. Large brokers have structured training schemes, giving new entrants experience of different areas of work over a period of 18 months to two years. Working as a Lloyd's broker requires passing the Lloyd's Introductory Test within 15 months of starting work. Study can be undertaken in-house or by public courses.

The Chartered Insurance Institute (CII) and British Insurance Brokers Association run courses in insurance broking and other relevant subjects, such as information technology and marketing, some of which may be linked to qualifications at NVQ/SVQ Levels 2 and 3. The CII courses have been carefully designed to provide insurance brokers with a recognised qualification - from the most basic level through to Fellowship of the Institute. Studying is provided through day release, evening classes or distance learning.

The Institute of Financial Services provides additional qualifications, including the Certificate of Regulated General Insurance. As a your career develops, progression might be possible into a managerial position, managing a team of brokers or even several branches of a division.

Personal Qualities: Personal attributes are important for a career in insurance broking. Some employers prefer applicants to be more mature with relevant experience, as this is a service driven industry.

To succeed as an insurance broker, you must be scrupulously honest and discreet, both with clients and with other professionals. You would need excellent communication and IT skills, together with the ability to gather and absorb information quickly.

You must be numerate in order to understand and work with statistics and you must keep up to date with changes in the insurance market.

Looking Ahead: Broking firms vary widely in size and type. The largest brokers tend to be international companies, negotiating cover on a global basis. Their clients can range from individuals to small businesses, right up to multinational companies with global offices and assets worth millions of pounds.

The larger brokers generally have different divisions with teams specialising in different risks, including commercial property, marine, aviation, political risks and casualty. Smaller brokers often require a more general knowledge of products and services, enabling them to act as a surveyor, loss adjuster, underwriter, negotiator and sales adviser. Some also service dedicated sectors, such as charities or the public sector.

Insurance broking can be quite a volatile sector of employment, evolving constantly through acquisitions and mergers. Legislative developments and changes in the economy can place specialist brokers in high demand, particularly in areas like political risk, construction, claims and commercial property insurance.

Currently, there is a greater need for specialisation and technical competence, creating better opportunities for graduates with the required skills.

Employment with the larger brokers tends to be centred near investment institutions in the larger cities, although brokers are also employed in regional offices. Smaller practices are spread countrywide. Prospects are good for those keen to advance, although competition for graduate placements can be high.

Insurance Agent

Insurance agents sell insurance packages to the public. They visit potential clients in their homes to sell life assurance and general or fire insurance policies. They collect premium payments as they fall due and deal with any enquiries.

Work Activities: Insurance provides a service to customers who wish to be protected from loss caused by events such as fire, theft, accident or illness. The customer pays a regular premium and receives a written policy that sets out the conditions under which an insurance company pays compensation.

Insurance agents sell insurance packages direct to the public. They operate as home service agents, direct selling representatives or financial advisers. Home service agents visit potential clients in their homes to sell general or fire insurance packages. The agent identifies the client's insurance needs, explains policy terms and conditions and tries to sell a policy. The agent collects premium payments as they fall due and deals with any queries. Financial advisers must be registered by their companies with the Financial Services Authority to sell life assurance or other financial packages. Direct selling representatives sell packages by telephone or post or through call-centre operations.

An insurance agent may also act as a new business or agency inspector linking an insurance company with brokers, estate agents and building societies who also promote and sell their policies.

Personal Qualities and Skills: To become an agent you would usually have experience of office based insurance work. Knowledge of insurance is mostly gained on the job. Skills of persuasion are important as most agents depend on commission to supplement their salaries.

Inspectors have experience of work in an insurance office and must obtain the Chartered Insurance Institute's (CII) Associateship qualification as they also need to be knowledgeable about financial planning, estate duty and taxation. Financial advisers must pass the Financial Planning Certificate examinations of the CII.

Pay and Opportunities: Salaries vary widely and some agents work on commission only or basic pay plus commission. The pay rates given below are approximate. Insurance agents with relevant qualifications earn in the range of £16,500 - £18,500 a year, rising to £30,000 - £39,500. Higher earners can make around £43,000 a year.

Working hours may be during the day, in the evening and at weekends to meet clients' needs. Employers are life assurance companies throughout the UK. Some agents are self-employed.

The following information is sourced from government statistics. The government's definition of types of job is slightly different to that used in this programme. For this type of job, the most relevant Government-defined occupation is 'Finance and investment analysts/ advisers'.

In 2001 there were 10,400 people working as 'Finance and investment analysts/advisers' in Scotland. 48 in every 10,000 employees working in Scotland were employed as 'Finance and investment analysts/advisers'.

Entry Routes and Training: You can enter the insurance business from a wide variety of backgrounds. Most employers prefer to recruit older applicants with relevant work experience, in particular in office based insurance work. Graduates of all types enter the industry, but it is also open to non-graduates.

Degrees in Finance are available. Some Business Studies degree courses offer options in insurance. Some institutions offer degree courses in Financial Management or Money, Banking and Finance.

The Chartered Institute of Insurance (CII) offers qualifications in general insurance. These include the Introductory Award in Insurance, Certificate in Insurance, Diploma in Insurance, Advanced Diploma in Insurance and the Fellowship of the CII. These can be studied by day or block release classes, evening classes or through distance learning.

There is an SVQ Insurance General and Intermediaries at level 3.

Qualifications: A good standard of literacy and numeracy are needed for this career. Standard Grades in English and Maths are an advantage. It is usual to have some experience, for example, in office based insurance work.

Adult Opportunities: Most insurance agents and direct selling staff are at least in their mid-to-late 30s. Applicants with relevant experience, for example, in office-based insurance work, have an advantage.

Previous retail experience, either shop-based, by telephone or door-to-door is advantageous. Other customer service work experience, especially dealing with financial products, is useful.

- 20% of people in occupations such as insurance sales adviser are self-employed.
- 9% work part-time.
- 13% have flexible hours.

Insurance Claims Inspector

Insurance claims inspectors are employed by insurance underwriters to investigate claims made by policy holders. They check that each claim is covered by the terms and conditions of the policy and investigate the cause of loss or damage.

Work Activities: Insurance provides a service to customers who wish to be protected from loss caused by events such as fire, theft, accident or illness. The customer pays a regular premium and receives a written policy that sets out the conditions under which an insurance company pays compensation.

Insurance claims assessors, sometimes known as claims inspectors or officials, work for insurance underwriters and are responsible for investigating claims submitted by policyholders. They check that each claim is covered by the terms and conditions of the policy and investigate the cause of loss or damage. The assessor might have to interview claimants who will be upset, shocked or distressed, especially if death or injury are involved. Consequently the assessor must be tactful, sympathetic and patient.

The assessor may need to inspect damaged buildings or vehicles in order to gather the evidence needed to determine a settlement. They may find evidence in more complicated cases by talking to solicitors, the police and eye-witnesses. In straightforward claims, agreement between an insurance company and a claimant may be reached quickly.

However, even after they have decided whether the insurance company should pay out, it can take a long time to decide what the settlement sum should be. Throughout their investigations, assessors must be aware that the claim could be fraudulent.

Very complicated claims require the intervention of an independent loss adjuster who acts as an intermediary between insurer and claimant. A loss adjuster performs the same function as an insurance claims assessor but is employed by a company of loss adjusters rather than an insurance company.

Claims are submitted as a result of personal accident, loss of goods in transit, theft, loss of profits, fire, flood and storm damage. Large scale disasters such as floods generate a huge number of claims, all requiring prompt attention. Some insurance firms and many assessors and loss adjusters specialise in a particular type of insurance such as aviation, motor or marine.

Personal Qualities and Skills: To be a claims assessor you need to be thorough and methodical. Communication skills are essential as assessors advise and interview claimants and negotiate appropriate settlements. Integrity and trustworthiness are necessary to win the confidence of claimants. When interviewing claimants who are upset, shocked or distressed you must show tact, sympathy and patience.

Pay and Opportunities: The pay rates given below are approximate. Insurance claims inspectors earn in the range of £18,000 - £23,000 a year, rising to around £30,500 - £43,000. Higher earners can make around £65,000 a year. Other benefits may include low-rate mortgages, medical insurance and life and pension cover.

Assessors usually work 35 hours Monday to Friday. Occasional evening/weekend work may be required.

Opportunities occur with insurance companies throughout the UK. The following information is sourced from government statistics. The government's definition of types of job is slightly different to that used in this programme. For this type of job, the most relevant Government-defined occupation is 'Estimators, valuers and assessors'.

In 2001 there were 4,600 people working as 'Estimators, valuers and assessors' in Scotland. 21 in every 10,000 employees working in Scotland were employed as 'Estimators, valuers and assessors'.

Entry Routes and Training: Insurance claims assessors may study for the professional examinations of the Chartered Insurance Institute or the Chartered Institute of Loss Adjusters. Many prospective assessors start training after Highers or Higher National Certificate/ Higher National Diploma qualifications and, with these qualifications, you can register for the Chartered Insurance Institute's Advanced Diploma qualifications and become an Associate member of the CII.

Most employers also recruit graduates from a wide range of academic subjects.

Degrees in insurance studies are available. Some degree and HND/HNC Business Studies courses include insurance options.

A number of Insurance SVQs are available at levels 2 and 3. Modern Apprenticeships, leading to SVQ level 3, may be available in your area.

Qualifications: There are no set entry requirements for this job, as requirements vary from employer to employer. Entry is possible at several levels.

For direct entry to the Chartered Insurance Institute (CII) Advanced Diploma qualification the minimum requirement is 3 Highers (A-C) plus Standard Grades in 2 other subjects, including English and Maths. Applicants with appropriate equivalent qualifications are also considered.

Entry to the Diploma in Insurance requires 4 Standard Grades or equivalent qualifications if you are under 21 years of age.

Entry to this job is also common for those with higher qualifications such as Higher National Certificates/Higher National Diplomas or degrees.

Adult Opportunities: A background in financial or business-related work is an advantage. A clean current driving licence is usually necessary.

Suitable applicants aged 21 or over may do a college or university Access course. No formal qualifications are required to enter an Access course, but you should check individual course details. They lead to relevant degree/HND courses.

Some employers recruit graduates with a business-related (including insurance) or numerate degree.

The Chartered Insurance Institute (CII) may relax the usual academic entrance requirements for adults who wish to take their exams.

Distance learning is available from the CII for professional qualifications.

- 8% of people in occupations such as insurance claims inspector work part-time.
- 22% have flexible hours.

Insurance Loss Adjuster

Insurance loss adjusters are responsible for investigating claims submitted by policy holders. They usually become involved in complicated claims and act as a negotiator between insurers and claimants.

Work Activities: Insurance provides a service to customers who wish to be protected from loss caused by events such as fire, theft, accident or illness. The customer pays a regular premium and receives a written policy that sets out the conditions under which an insurance company pays compensation.

Insurance loss adjusters investigate claims submitted by policyholders as a result of personal accident, loss of goods in transit, theft, fire, flood and storm damage. They usually become involved in the investigation of particularly complicated claims and act as an intermediary between insurers and claimants. A large-scale incident such as a flood may generate a sudden rush of claims, all requiring prompt action. Many loss adjusters specialise in a particular type of insurance, such as property or motor insurance, for example.

Loss adjusters check that the terms and conditions of the policy cover each claim and investigate the cause of loss or damage. They may occasionally need to interview claimants who are distressed or upset. A loss adjuster presents a report to insurers who then agree a suitable settlement with the claimant. Should either party dispute the findings of the report, negotiations continue until a settlement is reached.

If a loss adjuster suspects a claim is fraudulent, they may have to carry out a further detailed investigation. In some cases this might require the involvement of the police, private investigators and, in exceptional cases, forensic experts.

Personal Qualities and Skills: You'll need to be tactful, sympathetic and patient to work as a loss adjuster. You must also be thorough, observant and methodical. Communication skills are important as you will advise and interview claimants and negotiate settlements. Integrity is important and loss adjusters should also be fair and unbiased when dealing with claims.

Good written skills are necessary for report writing. A basic knowledge of accounts and book-keeping is also helpful.

Pay and Opportunities: Salaries for loss adjusters depend on qualifications and experience. The pay rates given below are approximate. Loss adjusters earn in the range of £18,000 - £23,000 a year, rising to around £30,500 - £43,000. Higher earners can make around £65,000 a year.

Loss adjusters usually work 35 hours, Monday to Friday, but often work late and at weekends in response to call-outs.

Employment is with specialist loss adjusting firms throughout the UK. Some work independently as consultants. Work in other countries is possible.

The following information is sourced from government statistics. The government's definition of types of job is slightly different to that used in this programme. For this type of job, the most relevant Government-defined occupation is 'Estimators, valuers and assessors'.

In 2001 there were 4,600 people working as 'Estimators, valuers and assessors' in Scotland. 21 in every 10,000 employees working in Scotland were employed as 'Estimators, valuers and assessors'.

Entry Routes and Training: If you are registering as a student member of the Chartered Institute of Loss Adjusters (CILA), you will need to have a professional qualification in a relevant subject. Examples are insurance, accountancy, law, engineering or surveying. You'll also need to have two years' experience with a firm of chartered loss adjusters before being eligible to sit the Institute's examinations.

The majority of entrants have professional qualifications and relevant work experience, although some do enter directly from school or college with Highers (or equivalent) or a degree. To enter without a relevant qualification you would generally begin work with a company of loss adjusters and study for the qualifications of the Chartered Insurance Institute (CII). Students who pass the CII's examinations may go on to study for the CILA's qualifications.

Training is usually provided on the job. Those with professional qualifications take three to four years to study for CILA's examinations. But it can take up to six or seven years to qualify. Subjects include principles and practice of insurance in connection to loss adjusting, property claims, accident and liability claims and commercial claims.

It is also possible to start working in an insurance company as a clerk and study for further qualifications. Once these have been gained, you may move onto a loss adjusting firm.

A number of Insurance SVQs are available at levels 2 and 3.

Qualifications: For direct entry to the Chartered Insurance Institute (CII) Associateship examinations, the minimum requirement is 3 Highers plus 2 Standard Grades. English is required at either level.

Entry to this job is also common for those with higher qualifications such as Higher National Diplomas or degrees.

Applicants with relevant equivalent qualifications are also considered. Candidates with a professional qualification in a relevant subject such as Accountancy, Law or Engineering may register directly with the Chartered Institute of Loss Adjusters.

Adult Opportunities: Applicants with a background in surveying, engineering, law or accountancy plus professional qualifications have an advantage.

Previous experience in insurance, for example, in administration, is useful. A clean current driving licence is often necessary.

Relevant distance learning courses are available from The Chartered Insurance Institute (CII), which may relax the normal academic requirements for adults who wish to take their exams.

- 11% of people in occupations such as insurance loss adjuster are self-employed.
- 8% work part-time.
- 22% have flexible hours.

Insurance Surveyor

Insurance surveyors provide underwriters with detailed technical reports on the risks involved in a request for insurance cover. Reports outline any aspects which might affect the insurance premium.

Work Activities: Insurance provides a service to customers who wish to be protected from loss caused by events such as fire, theft, accident or illness. The customer pays a regular premium and receives a written policy that sets out the conditions under which an insurance company pays compensation.

Most insurance surveyors work for insurance companies, providing underwriters with detailed technical reports on the risks involved in a particular request for insurance cover. Surveyors normally inspect premises to obtain information on factors such as the construction of buildings or the work processes that take place in a location. They may also look at factors such as the condition of machinery, the possibility of fire or flood damage and the current extent of safety precautions.

An insurance surveyor's report outlines any aspects that may affect the insurance premium charged by an underwriter. A surveyor's report may also suggest ways in which risks can be minimised and unsatisfactory factors improved. This could involve installing smoke detectors and sprinkler systems in case of fire and burglar alarms in case of theft. The insurance surveyor recommends whether insurers should accept any risk and offer insurance cover and whether any conditions should be attached to that cover. Surveyors can specialise in different areas, for example engineering or liability.

Personal Qualities and Skills: As an insurance surveyor you'll need good information gathering and report writing skills. You need a methodical approach to work and a high level of technical expertise. Insurance surveyors need to have a current driving licence.

Pay and Opportunities: Salaries for insurance surveyors vary depending on qualifications and experience. The pay rates given below are approximate. Insurance surveyors earn in the range of £24,000 - £32,500 a year, rising to £45,000 - £72,500 a year. Higher earners can make around £105,000 a year Surveyors normally work 35 hours Monday to Friday. However, depending on the post, they may work flexible hours, evenings and weekends.

Opportunities occur with insurance companies throughout the UK and with specialist engineering insurance companies. There may be opportunities to work in other countries, for example, for a UK insurer. The following information is sourced from government statistics. The government's definition of types of job is slightly different to that used in this programme. For this type of job, the most relevant Government-defined occupation is 'Estimators, valuers and assessors'.

In 2001 there were 4,600 people working as 'Estimators, valuers and assessors' in Scotland. 21 in every 10,000 employees working in Scotland were employed as 'Estimators, valuers and assessors'.

Entry Routes and Training: Insurance surveyors are often appointed from the ranks of experienced insurance staff who have developed an interest in this field.

Insurance surveyors are qualify as an Associate of the Chartered Insurance Institute (ACII), by studying for the Advanced Diploma in Insurance. This can be through day or block release, evening classes or by distance learning.

The Institute of Risk Management offers the Certificate and Diploma in Risk Management through distance learning. Employers also recruit graduates, particularly if your degree is in science or engineering. There are a number of degrees and postgraduate courses in risk management available. An SVQ in Insurance General and Intermediaries is available at level 3.

Modern Apprenticeships, leading to SVQ level 3, may be available in your area.

Qualifications: It is usual to have experience in a related area, for example in insurance underwriting, engineering, architecture or science. Most employers would prefer candidates to have at least 3 Highers and 2 Standard Grades, including English and Maths, or equivalent qualifications.

Many employers prefer to recruit those who have a degree. No specific degree subject is required, but degrees in science or technology, insurance or risk management may be particularly helpful. Candidates who hope to specialise in engineering surveying may have to have an engineering degree. To enter a degree course you need to have a minimum of 3 Highers and 2 Standard Grades, including English and maths. Many courses will ask for higher entry qualifications than the minimum.

Adult Opportunities: Entry is unlikely before the age of about 25. Many insurance surveyors are recruited internally from staff in underwriting departments. Adults with qualifications such as those in engineering, civil engineering, architecture or science can enter specialist areas of insurance surveying.

Suitable applicants aged 21 or over may do a college or university Access course. No formal qualifications are required to enter an Access course, but you should check individual course details. They lead to relevant degree/HND courses.

Some employers recruit graduates, especially those with a science, engineering or other numerate degree.

The Chartered Insurance Institute may relax the usual academic entrance requirement for adults who wish to take their exams.

- 7% of people in occupations such as insurance surveyor are self-employed.
- 8% work part-time.
- 22% have flexible hours.

5

Online Banking

Online banking (or Internet banking) allows customers to conduct financial transactions on a secure website operated by their retail or virtual bank, credit union or building society.

Features

Online banking solutions have many features and capabilities in common, but traditionally also have some that are application specific. The common features fall broadly into several categories

- Transactional (e.g., performing a financial transaction such as an account to account transfer, paying a bill, wire transfer... and applications... apply for a loan, new account, etc.)
    - o Electronic bill presentment and payment-EBPP
    - o Funds transfer between a customer's own checking and savings accounts, or to another customer's account
    - o Investment purchase or sale
    - o Loan applications and transactions, such as repayments of enrollments
- Non-transactional (e.g., online statements, check links, cobrowsing, chat)
    - o Bank statements
- Financial Institution Administration-
- Support of multiple users having varying levels of authority
- Transaction approval process
- Wire transfer.

Features commonly unique to Internet banking include;

Personal financial management support, such as importing data into personal accounting software. Some online banking platforms support account aggregation to allow the customers to monitor all of their accounts in one place whether they are with their main bank or with other institutions.

History

The precursor for the modern home online banking services were the distance banking services over electronic media from the early '80s. The term online became popular in the late '80s and referred to the use of a terminal, keyboard and TV (or monitor) to access the banking system using a phone line. 'Home banking' can also refer to the use of a numeric keypad to send tones down a phone line with instructions to the bank. Online services started in New York in 1981 when four of the city's major banks (Citibank, Chase Manhattan, Chemical and Manufacturers Hanover) offered home banking services using the videotex system. Because of the commercial failure of videotex these banking services never became popular except in France where the use of videotex (Minitel) was subsidised by the telecom provider and the UK, where the Prestel system was used.

The UK's first home online banking services was set up by Bank of Scotland for customers of the Nottingham Building Society (NBS) in 1983. The system used was based on the UK's Prestel system and used a computer, such as the BBC Micro, or keyboard (Tandata Td1400) connected to the telephone system and television set. The system (known as 'Homelink') allowed on-line viewing of statements, bank transfers and bill payments. In order to make bank transfers and bill payments, a written instruction giving details of the intended recipient had to be sent to the NBS who set the details up on the Homelink system. Typical recipients were gas, electricity and telephone companies and accounts with other banks. Details of payments to be made were input into the NBS system by the account holder via Prestel. A cheque was then sent by NBS to the payee and an advice giving details of the payment was sent to the account holder. BACS was later used to transfer the payment directly.

Stanford Federal Credit Union was the first financial institution to offer online internet banking services to all of its members in Oct, 1994. Today, many banks are internet only banks. Unlike their predecessors, these internet only banks do not maintain brick and mortar bank branches. Instead, they typically differentiate themselves by offering better interest rates and online banking features.

Security

Protection through single password authentication, as is the case in most secure Internet shopping sites, is not considered secure enough for personal online banking applications in some countries. Basically there exist two different security methods for online banking.

- The PIN/TAN system where the PIN represents a password, used for the login and TANs representing one-time passwords to authenticate transactions. TANs can be distributed in different ways, the most popular one is to send a list of TANs to the online banking user by postal letter. The most secure way of using TANs is to generate them by need using a security token. These token generated TANs depend on the time and a unique secret, stored in the security token (this is called two-factor authentication or 2FA). Usually online banking with PIN/TAN is done via a web browser using SSL secured connections, so that there is no additional encryption needed.
- Signature based online banking where all transactions are signed and encrypted digitally. The Keys for the signature generation and encryption can be stored on smartcards or any memory medium, depending on the concrete implementation.

Attacks

Most of the attacks on online banking used today are based on deceiving the user to steal login data and valid TANs. Two well known examples for those attacks are phishing and pharming. Cross-site scripting and keylogger/Trojan horses can also be used to steal login information. A method to attack signature based online banking methods is to manipulate the used software in a way, that correct transactions are shown on the screen and faked transactions are signed in the background.

A recent FDIC Technology Incident Report, compiled from suspicious activity reports banks file quarterly, lists 536 cases of computer intrusion, with an average loss per incident of $30,000. That adds up to a nearly $16-million loss in the second quarter of 2007. Computer intrusions increased by 150 between the first quarter of 2007 and the second. In 80 of the cases, the source of the intrusion is unknown but it occurred during online banking, the report states.

The most recent kind of attack is the so-called Man in the Browser attack, where a Trojan horses permits a remote attacker to modify the destination account number and also the amount.

Countermeasures

There exist several countermeasures which try to avoid attacks. Digital certificates are used against phishing and pharming, the use of class-3 card readers is a measure to avoid manipulation of transactions by the software in signature based online banking variants. To protect their systems against Trojan horses, users should use virus scanners and be careful with downloaded software or e-mail attachments. In 2001 the FFIEC issued guidance for multifactor authentication (MFA) and then required to be in place by the end of 2006.

Internet Banking (E-Banking)

Internet banking (or E-banking) means any user with a personal computer and a browser can get connected to his bank-s website to perform any of the virtual banking functions. In internet banking system the bank has a centralized database that is web-enabled. All the services that the bank has permitted on the internet are displayed in menu. Any service can be selected and further interaction is dictated by the nature of service. The traditional branch model of bank is now giving place to an alternative delivery channels with ATM network. Once the branch offices of bank are interconnected through terrestrial or satellite links, there would be no physical identity for any branch. It would a borderless entity permitting anytime, anywhere and anyhow banking. The network which connects the various locations and gives connectivity to the central office within the organization is called intranet. These networks are limited to organizations for which they are set up. SWIFT is a live example of intranet application.

Internet Banking in India

The Reserve Bank of India constituted a working group on Internet Banking. The group divided the internet banking products in India into 3 types based on the levels of access granted. They are:

i) Information Only System: General purpose information like interest rates, branch location, bank products and their features, loan and deposit calculations are provided in the banks website. There exist facilities for downloading various types of application forms. The communication is normally done through e-mail. There is no interaction between the customer and bank's application system. No identification of the customer is done. In this system, there is no possibility of any unauthorized person getting into production systems of the bank through internet.

ii) Electronic Information Transfer System: The system provides customer-specific information in the form of account balances, transaction details, and statement of accounts. The information is still largely of the 'read only' format. Identification and authentication of the customer is through password. The information is fetched from the bank's application system either in batch mode or off-line. The application systems cannot directly access through the internet.

iii) Fully Electronic Transactional System: This system allows bi-directional capabilities. Transactions can be submitted by the customer for online update. This system requires high degree of security and control. In this environment, web server and application systems are linked over secure infrastructure. It comprises technology covering computerization, networking and security, inter-bank payment gateway and legal infrastructure.

Automated Teller Machine (ATM)

ATM is designed to perform the most important function of bank. It is operated by plastic card with its special features. The plastic card is replacing cheque, personal attendance of the customer, banking hours restrictions and paper based verification. There are debit cards. ATMs used as spring board for Electronic Fund Transfer. ATM itself can provide information about customers account and also receive instructions from customers-ATM cardholders. An ATM is an Electronic Fund Transfer terminal capable of handling cash deposits, transfer between accounts, balance enquiries, cash withdrawals and pay bills. It may be on-line or Off-line. The on-line ATN enables the customer to avail banking facilities from anywhere. In off-line the facilities are confined to that particular ATM assigned. Any customer possessing ATM card issued by the Shared Payment Network System can go to any ATM linked to Shared Payment Networks and perform his transactions.

Credit Cards/Debit Cards

The Credit Card holder is empowered to spend wherever and whenever he wants with his Credit Card within the limits fixed by his bank. Credit Card is a post paid card. Debit Card, on the other hand, is a prepaid card with some stored value. Every time a person uses this card, the Internet Banking house gets money transferred to its account from the bank of the buyer.

The buyers account is debited with the exact amount of purchases. An individual has to open an account with the issuing bank which gives debit card with a Personal Identification Number (PIN). When he makes a purchase, he enters his PIN on shops PIN pad. When the card is slurped through the electronic terminal, it dials the acquiring bank system- either Master Card or VISA that validates the PIN and finds out from the issuing bank whether to accept or decline the transactions. The customer can never overspend because the system rejects any transaction which exceeds the balance in his account. The bank never faces a default because the amount spent is debited immediately from the customers account.

Smart Card

Banks are adding chips to their current magnetic stripe cards to enhance security and offer new service, called Smart Cards. Smart Cards allow thousands of times of information storable on magnetic stripe cards. In addition, these cards are highly secure, more reliable and perform multiple functions. They hold a large amount of personal information, from medical and health history to personal banking and personal preferences.

You can avail the following services through E-Banking.

Bill Payment Service

You can facilitate payment of electricity and telephone bills, mobile phone, credit card and insurance premium bills as each bank has tie-ups with various utility companies, service providers and insurance companies, across the country. To pay your bills, all you need to do is complete a simple one-time registration for each biller. You can also set up standing instructions online to pay your recurring bills, automatically. Generally, the bank does not charge customers for online bill payment.

Fund Transfer

You can transfer any amount from one account to another of the same or any another bank. Customers can send money anywhere in India. Once you login to your account, you need to mention the payees's account number, his bank and the branch. The transfer will take place in a day or so, whereas in a traditional method, it takes about three working days. ICICI Bank says that online bill payment service and fund transfer facility have been their most popular online services.

Credit Card Customers

With Internet banking, customers can not only pay their credit card bills online but also get a loan on their cards. If you lose your credit card, you can report lost card online.

Railway Pass

This is something that would interest all the aam janta. Indian Railways has tied up with ICICI bank and you can now make your railway pass for local trains online. The pass will be delivered to you at your doorstep. But the facility is limited to Mumbai, Thane, Nashik, Surat and Pune.

Investing Through Internet Banking

You can now open an FD online through funds transfer. Now investors with interlinked demat account and bank account can easily trade in the stock market and the amount will be automatically debited from their respective bank accounts and the shares will be credited in their demat account. Moreover, some banks even give you the facility to purchase mutual funds directly from the online banking system.

Nowadays, most leading banks offer both online banking and demat account. However if you have your demat account with independent share brokers, then you need to sign a special form, which will link your two accounts.

Recharging Your Prepaid Phone

Now just top-up your prepaid mobile cards by logging in to Internet banking. By just selecting your operator's name, entering your mobile number and the amount for recharge, your phone is again back in action within few minutes.

Shopping

With a range of all kind of products, you can shop online and the payment is also made conveniently through your account. You can also buy railway and air tickets through Internet banking.

Advantage of Internet Banking

As per the Internet and Mobile Association of India's report on online banking 2006, "There are many advantages of online banking. It is convenient, it isn't bound by operational timings, there are no geographical barriers and the services can be offered at a miniscule cost."

Through Internet banking, you can check your transactions at any time of the day, and as many times as you want to. Where in a traditional method, you get quarterly statements from the bank. If the fund transfer has to be made outstation, where the bank does not have a branch, the bank would demand outstation charges. Whereas with the help of online banking, it will be absolutely free for you.

Security Precautions

Customers should never share personal information like PIN numbers, passwords etc. with anyone, including employees of the bank. It is important that documents that contain confidential information are safeguarded. PIN or password mailers should not be stored, the PIN and/or passwords should be changed immediately and memorised before destroying the mailers.

Customers are advised not to provide sensitive account-related information over unsecured e-mails or over the phone. Take simple precautions like changing the ATM PIN and online login and transaction passwords on a regular basis. Also ensure that the logged in session is properly signed out.

Internet Banking Frauds

Internet Banking Fraud is a fraud or theft committed using online technology to illegally remove money from a bank account and/or transfer money to an account in a different bank. Internet Banking Fraud is a form of identity theft and is usually made possible through techniques such as phishing.

Now internet banking is widely used to check account details, make purchases, pay bills, transfer funds, print statements etc. Generally, the user identity is the customer identity number and password is provided to seure transactions. But due to some ignorance or silly mistakes you can easily fall into the trap of cyber criminals.

Here are some simple tips to prevent you from falling into the trap of cyber criminals. Remember, a simple ignorance or oversight can make a huge dent in your hard-earned savings.

Securing your account: Avoid online banking on unsecured wifi systems and operate only from PCs at home. Never reveal password to anyone. Do not even write it on a piece of paper on diary. Just memorise it. It should be alphanemeric and change it frequently.

Never reply to queries from bank online about account or personal details. The personal information should not be kept in a public computer or in emails.

Phishing: A person's personal details are obtained by fraudsters posing as bankers, who float a site similar to that of the person's bank. They are asked to provide all personal information about themselves and their account to the bank on the pretext of database upgradation. The number and password are then used to carry out transactions on their behalf without their knowledge.

Phishing involves using a form of spam to fraudulently gain access to people's online banking details. As well as targeting online banking customers, phishing emails may target online auction sites or other online payment facilities. Typically, a phishing email will ask an online banking customer to follow a link in order to update personal bank account details. If the link is followed, the victim downloads a program which captures his or her banking login details and sends them to a third party.

Spam: Spam is an electronic 'junk mail' or unwanted messages sent to your email account or mobile phone. These messages vary, but are essentially commercial and often annoying in their sheer volume. They may try to persuade you to buy a product or service, or visit a website where you can make purchases; or they may attempt to trick you into divulging your bank account or credit card details.

Nigerian Scam: Niegerian or Frauds 409 or 419 are basically the lottery scam in which some overseas persons are involved to cheat innocent persons or organizations by promising to give a good amount of money at nominal fee charges. Their intention is to steal money in the form of fee against the lottery prize.

Spyware: Spyware such as Trojan Horse is generally considered to be software that is secretly installed on a computer and takes things from it without the permission or knowledge of the user. Spyware may take personal information, business information, bandwidth; or processing capacity and secretly gives it to someone else.

"Trojan Horse" scheme unfolds when malicious software (malware) embeds to a consumer's computer without the consumer being aware of it. Trojans often come in links or as attachments from unknown email senders.

After installation the software detects when a person accesses online banking sites and records the username and password to transmit to the offender. People using public computers, in places like Internet cafes, are often susceptible to Trojans like malware or spyware.

Check sites Url: Always check the URL of your bank's web site. Fraudsters can lure you to enter your user ID and password at a fake website that resembles your bank. If you see anything other than the bank's genuine URL, it has to be fake.

Never enter your user ID or password or such sensitive information without ascertaining that you are on the right website. Always type the Web address of your bank into the browser address space. Never click on the link in the email.

Fool-proof password: Change your online banking password at regular intervals. Also, avoid easy-to-guess passwords, like first names, birthdays, kid's or spouse's name and telephone numbers. Try to have an alpha-numeric password, one that combines alphabets and numbers.

If you have several bank accounts, never use the same online banking password for all. Never select the option on browser that stores or retains user name and password. As it can easily be cracked by cyber criminals. Also, never paste your password, always type it in. This little amount of 'finger exercise' will go a long way in safety.

Always check 'last logged': Most banks have a 'last logged in' panel on their websites. If your bank has it, check the panel whenever you log in. If you notice irregularities (like you are logging in after two days, but the panel says you logged in that morning!), report the matter immediately to your bank and change your password rightaway.

Always log out when you exit the online banking portal. Close the browser to ensure that your secure session is terminated. Never exit simply by closing the browser.

Keep your system up to date: Regularly check for security updates for your computer operating system. Most security updates are aimed at reducing risks to your computer, these may be data-related or otherwise. Make sure that your operating system and browser have the latest security patches installed. And, always install these only from trusted websites.

Install a personal firewall to prevent hackers from gaining unauthorised access to your computer, especially if you connect to the Internet through a cable or a DSL modem.

Public access can be injurious: Don't leave the PC unattended after keying in information while transacting on the website. Avoid accessing your bank online at cyber cafes or on a share or public computer. Also, avoid locations that offer online connections through wireless networks (Wi-Fi), where privacy and security are minimal.

Follow Bank instructions: Banks say that appropriate upgradations are carried out from time to time by their IT departments for risk mitigation. They issue instructions to the customers to manage their accounts through virtual keyboards by way of which the characters typed by them are not identified by hackers. SMS alerts are also an important tool since any transaction carried out on account is reported to the account holder through an SMS.

Protection: Learn the ways to protect yourself from online banking fraud schemes. Detect Trojans that appear on your PC in the form of viruses, spyware or malware through Antivirus Software, anti Spyware, and Adware. Also, learn to keep your cards, documents and passwords safe, and monitor your accounts to safeguard yourself from bank fraud committed through identity theft.

Online Savings Account

An online savings account (OSA) is a savings account managed and funded primarily on the Internet.

Features

OSAs are often characterized by a higher interest rate or lower fees, compared with traditional savings accounts. Many of these high-yield accounts have no minimum balance. Account holders may link their OSAs to their existing external bank accounts for easy transfer of funds between multiple accounts. Some also offer ATM cards so customers can directly access the funds in their OSAs.

Changes in Banking and Investing

OSAs, combined with rising interest rates, have made cash an increasingly attractive investment option. They provide a relatively low risk option for investors looking for a place to park their money, especially in uncertain economic times. Inflation, stagflation, recessionary fears and stock market volatility are among the economic indicators that have encouraged more and more investors to consider cash as a way to balance their portfolios. In fact, more than 8.5 million customers signed up for OSAs with leading U.S. banks in 2005 alone and some industry experts estimate the Online Savings Account market will triple in size, from $250 billion to $400 billion by 2010.

6

The Ethics of E-banking

Introduction

In this book we aim to open up the debate on the ethics of E-banking by focusing on the activities of one case study company in the wholesale banking sector. Press and academic attention to the subject of online banking tends to focus on consumer products (B2C) and the threat they pose to traditional branch operations if concerns about privacy and security can be adequately addressed. Writers have so far largely ignored ethical issues instigated by the enormous potential of the Internet in facilitating inter-bank transactions (B2B) in the wholesale market by reducing costs.

The financial services industry has been through 'structural and operational tumult' since the mid-1990s, and innovative use of new information technology, electronic commerce and the associated cost reductions are driving ongoing changes in banking (Kalakota and Whinston, 1996). New technology brings benefits and risks and new challenges for human governance of the developments (Hamelink, 2000).

Harnessing the technology necessary for E-banking is just the first of the challenges faced by the sector. Equally important is the development of the necessary management skills to ensure the sustained success of the new processes. Intertwined in the functional perspectives of marketing, human resource management and strategic planning are the ethical perspectives. One of the new management perspectives that will contribute to long-term success in electronic commerce is the associated moral responsibility of banking organisations and their stakeholders. Because electronic commerce is still developing and is rapidly changing, there is very little experience or agreement on its related ethical issues (Turbin, et al, 2000). However, one of the few perspectives to emerge in the early stages of development is that of trust.

In any transaction trust plays a key role. Face-to-face, transactions allow for the assessment of trust on the basis of physically observed information. This is not normally part of an electronic exchange. Trust may also be based on previous experience of successful transactions with predictable outcomes. This is not yet established in electronic commerce. Where there is no personal experience, the transaction partner might rely on reputation.

Similarly, it is too early for electronic commercial activities to have built up a reputation in wholesale banking. The best the bank can hope for is to trade on its terrestrial reputation. High profile risks of electronic commerce such as security and privacy (Kelly and Rowland, 2000), the media and popular myths all act to confound the attempts of business to operate in cyberspace, not to mention the genuine imperfection of existing technology. Building high ethical standards and systems in which transaction partners can trust are imperative management requirements of the sustainable ethical enterprise.

Beyond functional issues there are ethical ideals to which the responsible businessperson should aspire. New information and communication technologies have provided the structure for the new economy (Castells, 2000) and a new economic order. Corporations often have more power and influence than public social institutions, their economic significance sometimes exceeding those of governments (Hamelink, 2000). This level of power must bring with it responsibility. We can no longer look to governments or even religion to guide our activities – we must take responsibility ourselves, whether we are individuals, companies, non-governmental organisations or cyber-networks. There is a clear need for further serious efforts to raise ethical consciousness and ethical behaviour in the 'networked economy' (Zonghao 2001).

From Medieval Trade Fairs to e-Banking

The development of money has been inextricably associated with the growth of trade and commerce. In Europe in the 1100s, rudimentary banking and foreign exchange institutions emerged as a direct product of the medieval trade fairs (Melamed, 1990). Monetary exchange and banking systems then developed rapidly as foreign and domestic trade expanded exponentially following the onset of the industrial revolution.

Although commodity-based money dates back to antiquity, money in its present primarily token form (i.e., money that does not exist in any physical form but takes the form of financial claims on banks and other financial institutions) has only assumed predominance during the past 100 years (Chown, 1994).

International trade has grown significantly in the post-war period and with it the associated monetary flows. More recently, deregulation and globalization have led to a spectacular growth in the value of non-trade-related financial transactions. Every transaction whether trade- or non-trade-related gives rise to obligations that needs to be settled through a transfer of money between the parties involved. Settlement of non-trade-related and large value trade transactions is increasingly based on the electronic large value payment systems, which have been developed since the 1960s.

Together this has led to a major expansion in payment and settlement systems which now handle payment volumes on a daily basis that collectively dwarf economic output in the main industrial countries. Electronic banking started with the use of proprietary software and private networks, but was not particularly popular until the emergence of the Web (Turbin et al 2000). The Internet and other global on-line networks have created new commercial opportunities for networked commerce. Development of an Internet electronic payment system provides opportunities for the creation of completely new sets of global and national trading relationships. The Internet offers the possibility of 'open systems' payment and settlement systems that operate in parallel to existing, more traditional bank-based networks.

Electronic banking and electronic commerce are now seen as an inevitable aspect of financial services. The new global commercial market place permits goods to be ordered and paid for electronically irrespective of location. This requires new institutional structures as well as changes to existing outdated legal, commercial and ethical systems (Kalakota and Whinston, 1996). The changes brought about by electronic commerce are similar in scope to those experienced when medieval trade fairs were established in Europe in the 11th century. The comparison is particularly apt, since that period saw the emergence of many of the banking institutional structures and payment instruments, which are now being reformed by the spread of E-banking. The case study and subsequent discussion presented here represent the findings of a pilot study into the ethical implications of electronic commerce in the business-to-business context. Semi-structured interviews were conducted with managers playing key roles in the bank's electronic commerce strategy. The study should be regarded as 'work in progress' and a number of questions for further research have been raised.

Case Study

The ABC Bank Group is active worldwide with around 1,500 branches and over 50,000 employees in more than 70 countries, including all the major financial centres. Ranked by total assets, market capitalisation and size of customer base, ABC Bank is one of Europe's leading banking groups. This case study focuses on Investment Banking, which is one of the bank's four main divisions, and in particular the business area of foreign exchange trading run by the subsidiary XYZ in the City of London. As noted earlier, press and scholarly attention to the subject of online banking has tended to focus on consumer products while the enormous potential of the Internet in facilitating inter-bank transactions by reducing costs has been largely ignored. There are increasing numbers of people in the world who are classified by banks as 'high net worth' meaning they have more than $300,000 in liquid assets. All banks are chasing this business, from which they can earn high fees for arranging and managing investments. It is estimated that XYZ earns some 40% of its profits from just 12% of capital usage in this area.

There is absolutely no incentive for the bank to offer this group of customers web-based services that will cut out the banks intermediary and advisory role and hence reduce income by cannibalising the existing lucrative business. Prospective electronic commerce projects in this business area therefore stand little chance of internal acceptance and the associated financial support. Projects which are likely to result in job losses within the bank through their automation of paper-based tasks also require support from sufficiently powerful factions if they are to go ahead, and tend to result in considerable tensions between areas of the bank reliant on traditional processing and the electronic commerce development teams. In order for an electronic commerce project to be financially supported it must demonstrate the potential to generate a positive return or be deemed necessary to keep up with competitor innovation in the area concerned, and 'not tread on too many toes internally'.

One project that met these criteria was the development of a website which offered customers access to and information about the most important Internet applications concerned with investment banking. The service provides the latest news together with selected charts and useful links. Online trading in currencies is already possible, and additional transaction applications dealing with bonds, shares and derivatives will be online very shortly. Customers have their own personalised access to the world's capital markets online, and can see and respond to changes in global currency prices in real time. The system customers are tapping into is the same as that used by XYZ for trading in the markets on its own account, in other words it is a multi-million pound investment in state of the art technology with the latest security protections.

The bank has focused upon the foreign exchange transaction as its 'flagship' online product because such activity forms a natural starting point for capturing related business from customers. Very few international banking services do not involve the purchase or sale of currency, so from handling a customer's foreign exchange transactions it is relatively easy for XYZ to cross-sell other products or services. In many cases foreign exchange trading is offered to customers as a 'loss-leader' because of this potential.

Although start-up costs are incurred in 'plumbing in' customers' systems to that of the bank, by settling transactions online the trading costs incurred by XYZ are more than halved. Fewer trading staff are required and the customer is 'locked in' through the system plumbing in process, so it is therefore more likely to use XYZ for subsequent related investment banking services. If the anticipated volume of trading is high enough, XYZ can offer to 'plumb in' a customer free of charge and still save money.

However, the real potential of such online trading for XYZ does not lie merely in automation, but in the 'white-labelling' of the foreign exchange service. This means that the online trading facility is made available to the clients of XYZ's customers, branded as if the service actually belonged to the client. For example, if XYZ's customer is an Italian regional bank, then foreign exchange transactions can be made between XYZ and all the Italian bank's clients worldwide. From the end customer's perspective, the system they use for trading appears to belong to the Italian bank, because it will be 'badged' appropriately. The advantage to XYZ is the extension the facility affords to its customer base, as money laundering regulations prevent an investment bank from accepting transactions from individuals in this area, so the Italian bank performs a useful intermediary function. For the Italian bank the attraction is the ability to 'piggyback' access to an expensive and sophisticated online system, thereby incurring prestige but none of the set up costs.

A potential problem with this system lies in the allocation of credit limits. If XYZ sets a ceiling of £20 million per transaction based on its assessment of the risk involved in dealing with the Italian bank, then the online trading system affords the same luxury to each of the Italian banks customers, who may be far less creditworthy. Consequently, XYZ developed an 'add on' system which allows the Italian bank to set appropriate sub-limits for each of its customers that are using the system. The system was developed in consultation with XYZ's Credit Managers and designed to replicate both the qualitative and quantitative judgements that were previously made manually.

The expensive Credit Manager role within investment banks is now threatened because of the success of the online system, which is now being applied to XYZ's own account trading. Ethical overview Consideration of the ethics of eBusiness has tended to focus on areas relating to the fragility of information collected and held electronically and transferred via computer-mediated communication. These include privacy of information about individuals, accuracy of information, ownership of information and intellectual property and accessibility of information held. These perspectives focus very much on the individual consumer and disregard the significant area of electronic commerce that is business to business. In the B2B case privacy based issues around information control are less critical at the personal level. By looking at a business to business case, we identify the moral precepts relevant to the case which may form a basis for further consideration of ethics in this area. These relate to: freedom of choice; transparency; facilitating fraud (ethical/illegal activities of others). It should be noted however, that this choice of moral issues is inspired by this particular case.

There are likely to be other issues which would have risen from different sets of circumstances. Hence, while we think that these issues may have wider currency, we urge continued, systematic consideration of relevant ethical issues in this context.

In this section we refer to some ethical theories to help identify rigorously observed notions of right and wrong. In particular, we identify discourse ethics as a potentially useful perspective to apply to electronic commerce. First though, on the positive side, the reduction of costs means that organisations can improve service and potentially generate more profits for shareholders and job security for employees. On the other hand, job losses are the means by which costs are cut and this has social implications for those in the firing line. The displacement of job opportunities away from face-to-face and back-office service roles to information system professionals is a common feature of the electronic commerce revolution (Turban et al 2000). Employment issues aside, however, there are also positive aspects of online trading for business customers and in turn consumers. As the case study points out, access to expensive online systems is enabled by 'piggybacking'.

From an ethical point of view, this means that high quality systems are not held by an exclusive group but made available to those other than the wealthiest, hence opening up fair access. Access to sophisticated systems comes with a catch. The need for 'plumbing in' of software and hardware, which means that business customers are locked into XYZ's facilities, is a form of restriction of free choice. When we buy one product from a certain supplier, we do not normally expect that this means our future choices of supplier are restricted in practice.

The key ethical issue here is that the business customer should be quite clear that there are significant implications for future freedom of choice of suppliers of foreign exchange and related services. In much the same way that Microsoft has been criticised for implicit locking in of customers to its software, electronic commerce through reliance on customising computer access to the specific service encourages, even forces, the user to come back to a supplier once used. As a customer –whether a business customer or consumer – once time and energy has been put into setting up the electronic access, psychological choice for alternatives are removed. This is both a clever marketing ploy, and a somewhat devious capturing of business if the customer is not entirely clear about the extent of commitment which they are making.

It is in this respect that transparency is so critical for ethical e-Banking. Cyberspace offers fantastic opportunities for disguise. This can be used for overcoming prejudices (Rogerson, 1999) but also for misleading either customer or supplier as to who you are and what you are offering. Clearly, outright fraudulent activities are to be condemned, but how far is it ethically acceptable for electronic commerce activities to convey ambiguously, by hint or absence of clarification, what it is they are offering? The white labelling aspect of our case study is illustrative here. Just like purchasing 'own label' products in a supermarket that are not actually made by the supermarket, there is an issue of misrepresentation. Branding theory demonstrates that we are drawn to products and producers that we recognise and trust (Ind, 2001). If the Italian banking consumers think that they are being supplied with the service by the Italian bank, not XYZ there is a basic problem of transparency. In the case of a packet of soap powder or cereal, there may be no real consequence other than discomfort at having been mislead. In cyberspace transactions, the consumer will be operating with significant capital as if they were dealing with the institution they know and trust when in fact it is a third party.

Given the concerns about privacy and fragility of information mentioned above this could also have worrying consequences for the party whose details are gathered by XYZ in this case. Discourse ethics states that ethical actions are those that are reached by transparent, full, open discussion including all those who are connected in any way to a decision. Here we offer some details of its basic precepts (drawn from Spence 1998). Discourse ethics theory finds its origins in contemporary philosophers Karl-Otto Apel (1976) and Jurgen Habermas' (1992) theories of real communication. It focuses on the reaching of a consensus by a process of argumentation. Kettner (1996) defines this approach as following the principle that ethically sound arrangements are those governed by unrestrained, fully participative argumentative dialogue or discourse. He goes on to outline five constraints for the use of this theory in practice:

1. Autonomous articulation of need-claims;
2. Bracketing of power differentials of the participants;
3. Transparency;
4. Participants should have empathetic ability in relation to different roles;
5. There should be comprehensive inclusion of all who will be affected.

Steinmann and Lohr (1994) define the principles of discourse ethics, explaining its categorisation as a cognitive ethical theory thus: "such a claim assumes that when there are disputes about competing moral positions, universal, reasoned solutions can be reached through sensible application". Furthering the tradition of the Erlangen school, Steinmann and Lohr have developed a particular theory of discourse ethics drawing on what Lorenzen called 'dialogical argumentation', which he suggests is the means by which the problems of communal life can be mastered. This follows earlier notions of philosophical constructivism, which suggest that a person can only really understand something as true when they have had a part in constructing it (Cooper, 1996). Steinmann and Lohr (1996) propose the transcending of personal short-term objectives as the means by which to seek social peace, which they define as a general free consensus. They take trouble to point out that their position is not one of relativism.

The normative element of their work is that peace must be held as the highest value, and social institutions must be designed to support the stability of peace. A successful exchange according to discourse ethics theory would be considered to be an argument, in the form of a thorough, constructive discussion, which enables the building of a new normative basis for a decision. Thus, through communication, an understanding of one's own and others' needs and normative groundings are reached, and then a new alternative built through consensus.

Criticisms of discourse ethics are that it assumes too optimistically that participants are genuinely seeking the best outcome, that they can be persuaded by rational argument to change their original opinion and that they do not want to force their view on others. Further, concern has been expressed that participants need to have achieved a sophisticated level of moral reasoning, and would need to be familiar with both the process of discourse ethics and the culture of participants when attempting to reach a consensus with members of different countries.

For discourse ethics theory to apply, the culture of an organisation must itself encompass values like tolerance, candour and constructive criticism, for consensus in companies to be a possibility. Adoption of a discourse ethics approach in E-Banking would mean that all transaction partners should be absolutely clear who they are dealing with and what the implications are. Where white labelling occurs, all concerned should be quite clear with whom they are doing business. The ideal circumstances of discourse theory will not of course always be possible, nevertheless the principles provide a benchmark against which action can be measured (Preuss, 1999).

We have already dismissed fraudulent activity as both illegal and unethical. What about the facilitating of fraudulent activity? How much responsibility do businesses have to prevent their products and services being used in the pursuit of illegal activity? In the US, for example, the selling and marketing of handguns emphasising the fact that the grip does not reveal fingerprints has been questioned in ethical terms (Brenkert, 2000). The Swiss banking system of confidentiality has repeatedly been challenged when criminal investigations are underway. XYZ is now enabling money laundering. While the bank itself can claim that it has not dirtied its hands, it is by implication responsible in some way. These questions require us to consider the role of business in society. Historical perspectives that the business of business is to maximise profit, are no longer acceptable in the light of limited government power to deal with the global welfare issues of which business is an inherent part. Social contract perspectives on new roles and responsibilities of business organisations encourage responsibility for actions and consequences in the B2B and B2C contexts.

In the XYZ case the issues are not limited to the B2B perspectives because of the apparent direct link to, for example, the Italian bank's customers. Here we see the features of e-Banking contributing to increasing depersonalisation, although corresponding standardisation of credit decisions. Ethically speaking, adding automatically applied rules to the allocation of credit limits can be viewed in two main ways.

First, Kantian theory is concerned with the duty of the individual to act in a way that is universalisable, reversible and demonstrates respect for persons. In practice this means that rules of action can be identified which are absolute and independent of context or consequences.

Furthermore, utilitarianism is concerned with following that course of action that maximises the greatest good for the greatest number: rule utilitarianism is where the rule applied results consistently in the maximisation of utility. Hence, according to both Kantianism and rule utilitarianism, rather than allowing favouritism, poor judgement, even corruption and bribery to determine credit limits between the banker and the customer, standard, automated procedures mean that everyone gets the same treatment. Whether this treatment is just depends on the quality of the rules applied.

Second, taking the personal relationship out of responses to credit limit applications has the effect of dehumanising transactions in the banking sector. A client's relationship with a bank or credit manager can be established over years of loyal customer commitment. Boiling this down to boxes ticked and computer-generated numbers would, according to an ethic of care, result in the loss of the development of individual relationships, human touch and use of intuition. Such aspects may be viewed as heretical to the new electronic economy, but human networks are just as important a part of business practice as electronic networks.

Interestingly, however, as with the application of standard rules, the just response to credit applications by the credit manager is reliant on the quality of decision-making that the manager applies. The difference is that we would not necessarily expect the manager to make absolutely, clinically applied standard decisions each time. The manager may include sensitive, intangible aspects in the decision-making process.

Discussion and Conclusion

We have presented some thought provoking ethical perspectives to a short case study on business-to-business foreign exchange transactions using electronic commerce facilities in one company. The example is not widely generalisable, nor does it cover the exhaustive ethical issues pertinent to B2B electronic commerce. Such computer mediated communications are developing so rapidly that it is far from clear what all the related ethical issues are, or how they can best be dealt with. The challenges of e-Banking are as great as the potential rewards if done well. By assessing this case study, we have identified some key perspectives as freedom of choice, transparency and facilitating fraud. We have also proposed discourse ethics theory as a useful mechanism for identifying ethical practice in the context of new technologies so reliant on effective communication. From this basis, we can consider the wider implications of our exploratory research into the ethics of e-Banking and develop the critical areas of consideration for a research agenda in the area.

Banks have resisted pressures for modernisation of business practices for many years. The opportunities for e-Banking may be the catalyst for change that will force the banking sector to reorganise, restructure and reconsider its institutional arrangements. No longer will the ingrained practices that suited banks but disadvantaged customers be economically sustainable (for example by applying 2 days forward value on many foreign exchange services when technology allows instant settlement). The ethics in banking cyberspace will have to be sufficiently robust to ensure public and commercial confidence and use.

The locking in of a business customer to a particular company's product lines is readily done with eCommerce. In terrestrial purchases, this might occur in relation to maintenance of a particular product (such that only the same brand replacement piece will fit), or to updates or linked products. In cyberspace software specifications and 'plumbing in' mean that the portal that a buyer uses might lead them to entirely unrelated products. This type of marketing and sales activity seriously damages the purchaser's freedom of choice.

While some may view buying all one's banking from one supplier a convenience, the crucial ethical issue is that the options available to the buyer have been significantly compromised. Where this kind of monopolising of individual choice is consciously signed up to by the purchaser, there is some defence for it. However, the rapidity of e-Banking and other electronic commerce developments would suggest that it would be unwise to limit one's choices before the sector has settled and established. Associated research topics include: How important is freedom of choice in business to business transactions? To what extent do business purchasers understand the consequences of loading software from one company? How seriously are the 'small print' warnings taken into account? Can purchasers withdraw from exchange relationships without undue cost to them?

Electronic commerce allows for the concealment of the real identity of suppliers of a product or service. This white labelling is also common practice in terrestrial exchanges, but we suggest that cyberspace, with the website as effectively a limitless 'showroom', can offer extraordinarily misleading intimation of the supplier's identity. In the case of electronic banking, this can have some enormous personal and institutional consequences. Research questions that need to be addressed include: To what extent are electronic commerce customers aware of 'white labelling'? How can websites be used to conceal identity of suppliers? How can websites be used to offer transparency in the exchange relationship?

The facilitation of fraud is another critical area of concern. The 'no questions asked' policy of banks accepting deposits in tax havens must now come under pressure for greater transparency following the attacks on the World Trade Centre and Pentagon on September 11th 2001. White labelling raises similar concerns of 'know your customer' that are surely no longer acceptable if the banking system is to be enlisted in the fight against money laundering which finances terrorism. Wire funds transfers allow legitimate customers and money launderers alike to transfer money around the world at will. An estimated 700000 wire payments are made in the US every day, moving over $2 trillionmaking it very easy for criminals to hide their transactions. Research needs to help clarify: what is the role of eBusiness in society?

How might responsibilities differ from terrestrial business? Can electronic commerce activities be held responsible for the fraudulent activities that they facilitate?

Critical in all the perspectives discussed above is that it is usually technically possible for customers to resolve problems of freedom of choice and transparency. However, it should not only be those with developed technical skills who are ensured ethical treatment in electronic commerce. Technical elitism is certainly not the solution to the divided society in which we already live. Organisations offering services and products in cyberspace have to take responsibilities for ensuring a fair and open marketplace seriously. If they do not, the essential ingredient of exchange relationships in the digital economy, trust, will not be established and business longevity will not be achieved. Trust in cyberspace must be a major area of research in the future.

The issues raised in this article and the ethical perspectives which will emerge over the next few years in relation to electronic commerce require earnest responses by the e-Banking and other sectors. We have proposed discourse ethics theory as a useful source of guidance for those seeking to act ethically in cyberspace. Legislation can only go some of the way to settling standards and guidelines, but the borderless nature of transactions is more acute still in electronic commerce than in the globalised marketplace generally. No law will reach all the electronic interfaces on which transactions will take place. More effective measures will be those that come from the pressures of professionalism and high technical and ethical standards. These take time to develop, and urgently require input from scholars to help identify and deal with ethical issues in electronic commerce.

IT in Banking –Changing Face of Banking in new Millennium

The growth of high speed networks which is part of Information Technology and communication technology is making possible applications undreamed of in the past. Now in the age of information technology voice, images data may now be transferred around the world in micro seconds. This explosion of technology is changing the banking industry from paper and branch banking to digitization and core banking. In this paper it is argued that the broad competitive forces of information and communication technology leads to irrevocable changes which allow new entrants, dis-intermediation, innovation and customer changes on a much greater scale than has occurred in the past. In the age of IT, it is fundamentally changing the delivery systems; banks use to interact with customer Evolution of Hi-Tech

Banking in India The first blueprints of adaption of IT in banks were drawn by the landmark report of Dr. Rangarajan Committee, which was constituted under the chairmanship of Dr. Rangarajan in September 1988 to draw up a perspective plan of computerization for a five yeart period commencing from 1990 to 1994 for the banking industry. This committee identified the purpose of computerization as improvement in customer service, housekeeping, decision making and profitability/productivity.

It was observed that to meet these objectives, banks have to move away from the use of dedicated and stand alone machines and move towards online real time transaction processing environment in relation to branch banking, to provide better customer service and reduce work pressure on the back office.

IT in banking has bought a new revolution in the life of a common man. Not only common man, but our nation on a whole has progressed. Computers are getting more sophisticated. They have given bank customers high expectations. Due to advances in technology, banking products and services are more conveniently delivered, thus creating new bases of competition. The bank gains a competitive advantage by having a direct marketing and accountable customer service environment and new, streamlined business processes. Growth in volume of banking business, geographical spread of operations, customers demand for quicker service, need for accuracy of data and improved control, have resulted increased use and higher dependency on technology. Information technology has been further accelerated by the advent of Internet. Corporate from office and individuals from home are able to conduct their transactions. Internet Banking is becoming a strategic necessity for banks.

Internet Banking

Internet Banking is a online Banking using Internet, The customer can access it with easy from anywhere in the world. It has made possible to conduct some banking transactions from anywhere like making payments and transfer funds to third party, open new account, details of new account, details of account, credit card and home loan balanced. The bank will be just a Click away from customer around the clock.

Core Banking Solutions

It has heralded an all new era in the banking world. It opened up new channels to transact with the customers. Now the customer can choose the channels for doing his transactions either through the

ATMs or through internet and even through phone. This is the era of anywhere and anytime banking, making the branch banking and limited banking hours a thing of the past. This is also the time of real time banking. Transactions get done instantly instead of waiting to be done in the next couple of days and weeks, especially in the case of cross border money transfers. All this is an integral part of CBS. At the same time, CBS is also helping the banks to decrease the product development and testing lead time enabling the bank to launch new products and become innovative and agile.

CBS works on open technology platforms which work on windows and other architectures, which allows for easy integration with the existing systems available in the banks and effectively deal with legacy problems. These solutions are compatible with any software and hardware systems available with the banks. The vendors customize the solutions to cater the specific needs of the bank and also integrate well with the existing systems and process in the banks. The integration is also done quickly and in a very short period of time. Some of the solutions offered by some vendors come in the form of universal banking solutions which apart from providing core banking solutions also provide solutions for wealth management, mobile banking, treasury, etc.

Most of the CBS offered by vendors provide a dynamic development interface which allows the bank to upgrade to the changing environment and grasp the opportunities accordingly. Almost all the solutions are internet based and web enabled based on open source architecture. These solutions offer 'just in time information' for different levels within the organizations and also for external people who are required and authorized to know this information. They also provide for audit trace and logging information reassuring that has done the transaction at what time and also giving the transaction details like amount location etc. these solutions also offer historical information of the transactions and provide for upgrade with every new transaction done.

IT Banking in Rural Areas

IT has revolutionized the urban sector of banking manifolds but e-banking in rural areas has not taken much care of. If e-banking is implemented in the rural sector, it would be a great boon to the rural areas. If e-banking is implemented things would be much easier. In certain areas kiosks have been put up. Where extremely easy user interfaces are used so that even very less educated people can carry out transactions. This however is not very common. If e-banking becomes common in the rural areas, the much talked about corruption would end as it would be a direct communication between bankers and the people without the need of mediators who are responsible for all the corruption.

It would lead to the commercialization of the rural sector, and would help bridge the divide between the technologically and economically rich urban sector and would help in easy transfer of funds from the urban sector to the rural sector.

The future prospects of the banks suggest that banks face a serious challenge. The basic structure of the banks is increasingly in conflict with the changing product, delivery and service needs of the customers. The future belongs to financial service providers and not traditional banks. The vast majority of large banks will create value networks.

Concluding Observations

It is true that the above changes have created a new environment and better opportunity for banks to improve their earnings so that they can be in tune with the market along with the necessary preparedness and innovative instruments to face the competition, demanding customers as well as regulators. However, these changes are wide in range and are not focused enough to fulfill the desired objective of transforming and developing the Indian Banking to global standards and thereby enabling them to cater to the diverse needs of new generation of entrepreneurs and traders due to opening up of economy and globalization. Most of the banks in India, have not yet honed their management to adapt better technology for risk management and customer relationship management. Most of them have structured some committees and departments as per regulators guidelines/directions. However they have failed to fill these with men having necessary expertise. Most of these committees operate on the advice of some middle level officers who are unable to provide the necessary vision and guidelines to these committees. In most cases these committees just fulfill the formalities under regulation rather creating the much desired expertise which is needed by bank.

Impact-of-e-Banking-in-rural-economy.html

In underdeveloped countries like India, there was a tendency for people to invest their savings in non-productive channels as real estate, gold and silver etc. socio-economic setting was responsible for this. The reason why people accumulated wealth was invested in that could be converted into cash

Whenever necessary. The savings of the owners of land or hire employees are directed to unproductive spending and conspicuous consumption. This class of people who had the power to save, but lacked the will to save. Savings of farmers have invested in bullion or in lending money to other farmers.

Some of them invested their savings in livestock. However, cattle die and dried. The savings of middle class people (employees and employees) were used for the education of their children, for the construction of residential housing and to meet unexpected circumstances. People were not previously aware of how to use their savings to socially useful purposes. To discourage hoarding and as unproductive expenditure, rural bank branches were opened to mobilize rural savings. First, they were only exercising their traditional banking and lending to accept money. Only then diversified their activities into new fields such as banking operations, leasing, housing finance, mutual funds, venture capital etc. had made a number of innovative programs for mobilizing deposits. Besides this, they were providing valuable services to rural customers through collection of checks, bills, purchase securities on behalf of clients, drafts, travellers checks, gift checks, courage to accept custody. Now customers in rural areas are encouraged to move from the current paper-based system of banknotes, checks, bank statements and cash to complete impersonal electronic banking system.

Conclusion

E-banking is a strategic weapon for success for banks to remain profitable in a volatile and competitive market today. Clearly, despite the threats posed by non-bank financial intermediaries, there is tremendous opportunity for banks large vision to reap the rewards available in electronic banking. If banks are to remain competitive, they must focus on customer retention and relationship management, updating and integration of supply and value added services, especially in the area of consumer banking. Technology has indeed transformed the Indian banking sector, but the technology itself has undergone a radical change.

It's been hard but learning journey for the Indian banking system has passed the milestones of Automated Ledger Posting Machines, mainframe, minicomputers, microcomputers and personal computers. In fact, the banking system has closely followed developments in the computer industry. The evolution of distribution channel that came later, with bank ATMs and change the rules that form the basis for development of innovative channels such as Internet banking and the last to enter the field of call centers and mobile banking.

Now, the current trend will be sustained and indeed that of centralization through the implementation of core banking solutions that integrate all banking applications, processes and distribution channels. In short, a bank has come to rely on technology like never before. In the past, the bank was influenced by technology; it now appears that the technology is influenced by banks.

Mobile Banking

Mobile banking (also known as M-Banking, mbanking, SMS Banking etc.) is a term used for performing balance checks, account transactions, payments etc. via a mobile device such as a mobile phone. Mobile banking today (2007) is most often performed via SMS or the Mobile Internet but can also use special programs called clients downloaded to the mobile device.

A Mobile Banking Conceptual Model

In one academic model, mobile banking is defined as:

"Mobile Banking refers to provision and availment of banking- and financial services with the help of mobile telecommunication devices. The scope of offered services may include facilities to conduct bank and stock market transactions, to administer accounts and to access customised information."

According to this model Mobile Banking can be said to consist of three inter-related concepts:

- Mobile Accounting
- Mobile Brokerage
- Mobile Financial Information Services.

Most services in the categories designated *Accounting* and *Brokerage* are transaction-based. The non-transaction-based services of an informational nature are however essential for conducting transactions-for instance, balance inquiries might be needed before committing a money remittance. The accounting and brokerage services are therefore offered invariably in combination with information services. Information services, on the other hand, may be offered as an independent module.

Trends in Mobile Banking

The advent of the Internet has enabled new ways to conduct banking business, resulting in the creation of new institutions, such as online banks, online brokers and wealth managers. Such institutions still account for a tiny age of the industry.

Over the last few years, the mobile and wireless market has been one of the fastest growing markets in the world and it is still growing at a rapid pace. According to the GSM Association and Ovum, the number of mobile subscribers exceeded 2 billion in September 2005, and now exceeds 2.5 billion (of which more than 2 billion are GSM).

With mobile technology, banks can offer services to their customers such as doing funds transfer while travelling, receiving online updates of stock price or even performing stock trading while being stuck in traffic. Smartphones and 3G connectivity provide some capabilities that older text message-only phones do not.

According to a study by financial consultancy Celent, 35% of online banking households will be using mobile banking by 2010, up from less than 1% today. Upwards of 70% of bank centre call volume is projected to come from mobile phones. Mobile banking will eventually allow users to make payments at the physical point of sale. "Mobile contactless payments" will make up 10% of the contactless market by 2010. Another study from 2010 by Berg Insight forecasts that the number of mobile banking users in the US will grow from 12 million in 2009 to 98 million in 2015. The same study also predicts that the European market will grow from 7 million mobile banking users in 2009 to 131 million users in 2015.

Many believe that mobile users have just started to fully utilize the data capabilities in their mobile phones. In Asian countries like India, China, Bangladesh, Indonesia and Philippines, where mobile infrastructure is comparatively better than the fixed-line infrastructure, and in European countries, where mobile phone penetration is very high (at least 80% of consumers use a mobile phone), mobile banking is likely to appeal even more.

Mobile Banking Business Models

A wide spectrum of Mobile/branchless banking models is evolving. However, no matter what business model, if mobile banking is being used to attract low-income populations in often rural locations, the business model will depend on banking agents, i.e., retail or postal outlets that process financial transactions on behalf telcos or banks.

The banking agent is an important part of the mobile banking business model since customer care, service quality, and cash management will depend on them. Many telcos will work through their local airtime resellers. However, banks in Colombia, Brazil, Peru, and other markets use pharmacies, bakeries, etc. These models differ primarily on the question that who will establish the relationship (account opening, deposit taking, lending etc.) to the end customer, the Bank or the Non-Bank/Telecommunication Company (Telco). Another difference lies in the nature of agency agreement between bank and the Non-Bank. Models of branchless banking can be classified into three broad categories-Bank Focused, Bank-Led and Nonbank-Led.

Bank-focused Model

The bank-focused model emerges when a traditional bank uses non-traditional low-cost delivery channels to provide banking services to its existing customers. Examples range from use of automatic teller machines (ATMs) to internet banking or mobile phone banking to provide certain limited banking services to banks' customers. This model is additive in nature and may be seen as a modest extension of conventional branch-based banking.

Bank-led Model

The bank-led model offers a distinct alternative to conventional branch-based banking in that customer conducts financial transactions at a whole range of retail agents (or through mobile phone) instead of at bank branches or through bank employees.

This model promises the potential to substantially increase the financial services outreach by using a different delivery channel (retailers/mobile phones), a different trade partner (telco/chain store) having experience and target market distinct from traditional banks, and may be significantly cheaper than the bank-based alternatives. The bank-led model may be implemented by either using correspondent arrangements or by creating a JV between Bank and Telco/non-bank. In this model customer account relationship rests with the bank

Non-bank-led Model

The non-bank-led model is where a bank does not come into the picture (except possibly as a safe-keeper of surplus funds) and the non-bank (e.g. telco) performs all the functions.

Mobile Banking Services

Mobile banking can offer services such as the following:

Account Information

1. Mini-statements and checking of account history
2. Alerts on account activity or passing of set thresholds
3. Monitoring of term deposits
4. Access to loan statements
5. Access to card statements
6. Mutual funds/equity statements
7. Insurance policy management
8. Pension plan management
9. Status on cheque, stop payment on cheque
10. Ordering check books
11. Balance checking in the account
12. Recent transactions
13. Due date of payment (functionality for stop, change and deleting of payments)
14. PIN provision, Change of PIN and reminder over the Internet
15. Blocking of (lost, stolen) cards.

Payments, Deposits, Withdrawals, and Transfers

1. Domestic and international fund transfers
2. Micro-payment handling
3. Mobile recharging
4. Commercial payment processing
5. Bill payment processing
6. Peer to Peer payments
7. Withdrawal at banking agent
8. Deposit at banking agent.

Especially for clients in remote locations, it will be important to help them deposit and withdraw funds at banking agents, i.e., retail and postal outlets that turn cash into electronic funds and vice versa. The feasibility of such banking agents depends on local regulation which enables retail outlets to take deposits or not. A specific sequence of SMS messages will enable the system to verify if the client has sufficient funds in his or her wallet and authorize a deposit or withdrawal transaction at the agent. When depositing money, the merchant receives cash and the system credits the client's bank account or mobile wallet. In the same way the client can also withdraw money at the merchant: through exchanging sms to provide authorization, the merchant hands the client cash and debits the merchant's account.

Investments

1. Portfolio management services
2. Real-time stock quotes
3. Personalized alerts and notifications on security prices
4. mobile banking.

Support

1. Status of requests for credit, including mortgage approval, and insurance coverage
2. Check (cheque) book and card requests
3. Exchange of data messages and email, including complaint submission and tracking
4. ATM Location.

Content Services

1. General information such as weather updates, news
2. Loyalty-related offers
3. Location-based services.

Based on a survey conducted by Forrester, mobile banking will be attractive mainly to the younger, more "tech-savvy" customer segment. A third of mobile phone users say that they may consider performing some kind of financial transaction through their mobile phone. But most of the users are interested in performing basic transactions such as querying for account balance and making bill payment.

Challenges for a Mobile Banking Solution

Key challenges in developing a sophisticated mobile banking application are :

Handset Operability

There are a large number of different mobile phone devices and it is a big challenge for banks to offer mobile banking solution on any type of device. Some of these devices support Java ME and others support SIM Application Toolkit, a WAP browser, or only SMS. Initial interoperability issues however have been localized, with countries like India using portals like R-World to enable the limitations of low end java based phones, while focus on areas such as South Africa have defaulted to the USSD as a basis of communication achievable with any phone.

The desire for interoperability is largely dependent on the banks themselves, where installed applications (Java based or native) provide better security, are easier to use and allow development of more complex capabilities similar to those of internet banking while SMS can provide the basics but becomes difficult to operate with more complex transactions.

There is a myth that there is a challenge of interoperability between mobile banking applications due to perceived lack of common technology standards for mobile banking. In practice it is too early in the service lifecycle for interoperability to be addressed within an individual country, as very few countries have more than one mobile banking service provider.

In practice, banking interfaces are well defined and money movements between banks follow the IS0-8583 standard. As mobile banking matures, money movements between service providers will naturally adopt the same standards as in the banking world.

Security

Security of financial transactions, being executed from some remote location and transmission of financial information over the air, are the most complicated challenges that need to be addressed jointly by mobile application developers, wireless network service providers and the banks' IT departments.

The following aspects need to be addressed to offer a secure infrastructure for financial transaction over wireless network :

1. Physical part of the hand-held device. If the bank is offering smart-card based security, the physical security of the device is more important.
2. Security of any thick-client application running on the device. In case the device is stolen, the hacker should require at least an ID/Password to access the application.
3. Authentication of the device with service provider before initiating a transaction. This would ensure that unauthorized devices are not connected to perform financial transactions.
4. User ID/Password authentication of bank's customer.

5. Encryption of the data being transmitted over the air.
6. Encryption of the data that will be stored in device for later/ off-line analysis by the customer.

Scalability & Reliability

Another challenge for the CIOs and CTOs of the banks is to scale-up the mobile banking infrastructure to handle exponential growth of the customer base. With mobile banking, the customer may be sitting in any part of the world (true anytime, anywhere banking) and hence banks need to ensure that the systems are up and running in a true 24 x 7 fashion.

As customers will find mobile banking more and more useful, their expectations from the solution will increase. Banks unable to meet the performance and reliability expectations may lose customer confidence. There are systems such as Mobile Transaction Platform which allow quick and secure mobile enabling of various banking services. Recently in India there has been a phenomenal growth in the use of Mobile Banking applications, with leading banks adopting Mobile Transaction Platform and the Central Bank publishing guidelines for mobile banking operations.

Application Distribution

Due to the nature of the connectivity between bank and its customers, it would be impractical to expect customers to regularly visit banks or connect to a web site for regular upgrade of their mobile banking application. It will be expected that the mobile application itself check the upgrades and updates and download necessary patches (so called "Over The Air" updates). However, there could be many issues to implement this approach such as upgrade/synchronization of other dependent components.

Personalization

It would be expected from the mobile application to support personalization such as :

1. Preferred Language
2. Date/Time format
3. Amount format
4. Default transactions
5. Standard Beneficiary list
6. Alerts.

Mobile Banking in the World

Mobile banking has come in handy in many parts of the world with little or no Infrastructure development, especially in remote and rural areas. This part of the mobile commerce is also very popular in countries where most of their population is unbanked. In most of these places banks can only be found in big cities and customers have to travel hundreds of miles to the nearest bank.

Countries like Sudan, Ghana and South Africa received this new commerce very well.

In Latin America countries like Uruguay, Paraguay, Argentina, Brazil, Venezuela, Colombia, Guatemala and recently Mexico started with a huge success.

In Colombia was released with Redeban.

In Iran banks like Parsian, Tejarat, Mellat, Saderat, Sepah, edbi and bankmelli offer this service. Guatemala have the support of Banco industrial.

Mexico released the mobile commerce with Omnilife, Bancomer and a private company (MPower Ventures). Kenya's Safaricom (Part of the Vodafone Group) has had the very popular M-Pesa Service-mainly used to transfer limited amounts of money, but has been increasingly used to pay utility bills. Zain in 2009 launched their own mobile money transfer business known as ZAP in Kenya and other African countries.

Mobile Banking in India-Guidelines

India has about 207 MM (September' 2007 TRAI Data) mobile phone subscribers, a number that is larger than the number of bank accounts or Internet users. Given the mobile tele-density of about 20% and development of secure mobile technology solutions, banks are well-positioned bridge the digital divide and introduce the unbanked sector to the financial mainstream. You may be aware that Reserve Bank of India had set up the Mobile Payments Forum Of India (MPFI), a 'Working Group on Mobile Banking' to examine different aspects of Mobile Banking (M-banking).

The Group had focused on three major areas of M-banking, i.e., (i) technology and security issues, (ii) business issues and (iii) regulatory and supervisory issues. A copy of the Group's report is enclosed. RBI has accepted the recommendations of the Group to be implemented in a phased manner. Accordingly, the following guidelines are issued for implementation by banks. Banks are also advised that they may be guided by the original report, for a detailed guidance on different issues.

However to start with, we must understand who the various stakeholders are and what there expectation are:

Stakeholders are as follows;

a. Consumers
b. Merchants
c. Mobile Network operators
d. Mobile device manufacturers
e. Financial institutions and banks
f. Software and technology providers
g. Government.

Each stakeholder group has the following expectations: To meet the following Consumer expectations:

- Personalized service
- Minimal learning curve
- Trust, privacy and security
- Ubiquitous – anywhere, anytime and any currency
- Low or zero cost of usage
- Interoperability between different network operators, banks and devices
- Anonymity of payments like cash
- Person to person transfers.

To meet the following Merchant expectations:

- Faster transaction time
- Low or zero cost in using the system
- Integration with existing payment systems
- High security
- Being able to customize the service
- Real time status of the mobile payment service
- Minimum settlement and Payment time.

To meet the following Telecom Network Providers expectations:

- Generating new income by increase in traffic

- Increased Average Revenue Per User (ARPU) and reduced churn (increased loyalty)
- Become an attractive partner to content providers.

To meet the following Mobile Device Manufacturers expectations:

- Large market adoption with embedded mobile payment application
- Low time to market
- Increase in Average Revenue Per User (ARPU).

To meet the following Banks expectations:

- Network operator independent solutions
- Payment applications designed by the bank
- Exceptional branding opportunities for banks
- Better volumes in banking – more card payments and less cash transactions
- Customer loyalty.

To meet the following Software and Technology Providers expectations:

- Large markets.

To meet the following Government expectations;

- Revenue through taxation of m-payments
- Standards.

Technology and Security Standards

The overall security framework should ensure.

- Encrypted messaging/session between consumer's phone and third party service provider/telecom company. Minimum encryption standards to be specified to make the transaction banking grade (E.g. Min 128 bit SSL)
- All subsequent routing of messages to the bank's servers must be with the highest level of security with dedicated connectivity like leased lines/VPNs.
- If any sensitive information is stored in third party systems, banks must ensure that access to this information is restricted with appropriate encryption and hardware security standards.
- All transactions that affect an account (those that result in to an account being debited or credited, including scheduling of such activity) should be allowed only after authentication of

the mobile number and the mPIN associated with it. Transactions only for information such as balance enquiry, mini statements, registered payee details, etc. may be allowed with either mobile number or PIN.

- Unless fool proof security is used in compiling and deploying the mobile banking applications, the PIN number should not be allowed to be stored in the mobile banking application on the phone. As, generally the application installed on the phone would be developed in Java, it may be possible to decompile it extract the mPIN. Alternatively, the application should be so compiled that it should not be feasible to extract the PIN on decompilation.
- All accounts, credit or debit cards allowed to be transacted through the mobile phones should have the mobile phone number linked to the account, credit or debit card. This mobile number should be used as the second factor authentication for mobile transactions.
- During the transaction, the PIN should not travel in plain text. Doing this, there is risk of the PIN being snooped out of the phone from sent items and also it being exposed at the SMSC level. Also, it may be able to snoop out the PIN during transmission, although, this is very difficult in cellular communications.
- Proper level of encryption should be implemented for communicating from the mobile handset to the mobile payments service provider's server. It has been assumed that proper security checks would be made by the banks to ascertain the security levels of the service providers. This may include PCI DSS certification in addition to bank's own audits.
- Proper system of verification of the phone number should be implemented, wherever possible. This is so as to guard against spoofing of the phone numbers as mobile phones would be used as the second factor authentication.
- It is also recommended that Internet Banking login ids and passwords may not be allowed to be used through the mobile phones. As fraudsters get more sophisticated, the chances of phishing attacks on mobile phones would become more probable. Allowing Internet banking login id and password usage on the mobile phone may compromise their usage on the Internet banking channel. This restriction may be communicated to the

customers through an industry wide effort so as to ensure that Internet banking passwords are not compromised through mobile phones.

- The payment authorisation message from the user's mobile phone should be securely encrypted and checked for tampering by the service provider or the bank. It should not be possible for any interceptor to change the contents of the message.
- Provided the above security recommendations are reviewed, the mobile payment service could use any of the preferred mode of communication viz., SMS, IVRS, WAP/GPRS, USSD and NFC. There are couple of security issues in some of these modes of communications, which are listed below:
  a. SMS is the simplest form of communication, but is vulnerable to tampering. As long as there is a second level of check on the details of the transaction so as to guard against data tampering and the mPIN does not travel in plain text, this mode of communication can be used.
  b. IVRS is also a simple mode of communication and therefore does not have any inbuilt security measures. The system should be capable of encrypting the DTMF tone entries, if required to be stored or transmitted.
  c. USSD communication uses its inbuilt encryption technology to talk between the cell phone and the operator's server. However, the decryption of the information happens at the cell phone operator's server. Vulnerability of data may exists at this point. This information should be re-encrypted and transmitted to the service provider.
- Any of the following modes of user interface may be used, provided the above listed security measures are taken into consideration:
  a. SMS
  b. Menu driven application
  c. Menu driven USSD application
  d. WAP/GPRS website.
- Formats need to be specified for exchange of information between banks. On the debit/credit card front, the exiting ISO 8583 message format may be used for communication between bank switches. However, for account number based mobile transfers, a message format may need to be frozen.

- Banks should designate a network and database administrator with clearly defined roles as indicated in the technology Group's report
- Banks should have a security policy duly approved by the Board of Directors. There should be a segregation of duty of Security Officer/Group dealing exclusively with information systems security and Information Technology Division which actually implements the computer systems. Further, Information Systems Auditor will audit the information systems.
- Banks should introduce logical access controls to data, systems, application software, utilities, telecommunication lines, libraries, system software, etc. Logical access control techniques may include user-ids, passwords, smart cards or other biometric technologies
- At the minimum, banks should use the proxy server type of firewall so that there is no direct connection between the Internet and the bank's system. It facilitates a high level of control and in-depth monitoring using logging and auditing tools. For sensitive systems, a stateful inspection firewall is recommended which thoroughly inspects all packets of information, and past and present transactions are compared. These generally include a real time security alert.
- All the systems supporting dial up services through modem on the same LAN as the application server should be isolated to prevent intrusions into the network as this may bypass the proxy server.
- The information security officer and the information system auditor should undertake periodic penetration tests of the system, which should include:
  - o Attempting to guess passwords using password-cracking tools.
  - o Search for back door traps in the programs.
  - o Attempt to overload the system using DDoS (Distributed Denial of Service) & DoS (Denial of Service) attacks.
  - o Check if commonly known holes in the software, especially the browser and the e-mail software exist.
  - o The penetration testing may also be carried out by engaging outside experts (often called 'Ethical Hackers')

- Physical access controls should be strictly enforced. Physical security should cover all the information systems and sites where they are housed, both against internal and external threats.
- Banks should have proper infrastructure and schedules for backing up data. The backed-up data should be periodically tested to ensure recovery without loss of transactions in a time frame as given out in the bank's security policy. Business continuity should be ensured by setting up disaster recovery sites. These facilities should also be tested periodically.

Business & Legal Issues

The following kinds of business applications are envisaged under the purview of this circular. Banks may permit the following transactions to its existing customers. They will encompass three key areas:

- Mobile banking (basic saving account – balance enquiry, bill payment, credit card payment, Draft issuance, Deposit booking, Stop payment request, funds transfer to another bank account including 3rd party transfers, change f personal PIN
- M Commerce (using mobile as a payment instrument either linked to a bank account or through stored value)
- Remittance: Allowing funds transfer between bank accounts, bank to cash(where the beneficiary does not have a bank account) and cash to cash
- Banks may additionally facilitate transactions for their customer's customers (E.g. Bill Payments for their corporate clients and other transactions that facilitate transactional convenience and also the inclusion of the financially excluded into the banking mainstream. Thus banks may also permit following transactions for non-customers/non-account holders.
    i. Small value person-to-person remittances (not exceeding Rs. 15,000) including the use of bank branches, ATMs and other 3rd party outlets approved by Banks or Telcos for facilitating cash in/cash out. In such cases, banks may rely on KYC processes performed by other intermediaries (such as Telcos) as detailed in section III A of this circular.
    ii. International remittances-i.e. Non resident Indians sending money back home to their families (To be read in conjunction with the MTSS guidelines)

- Considering the legal position prevalent, there is an obligation on the part of banks not only to establish the identity but also to make enquiries about integrity and reputation of the prospective customer. Therefore, even though request for opening a savings/current account can be accepted over Mobile Telecommunication, these should be opened only after proper introduction and physical verification of the identity of the customer.
- From a legal perspective, security procedure adopted by banks for authenticating users needs to be recognized by law as a substitute for signature. In India, the Information Technology Act, 2000, in Section 3(2) provides for a particular technology (viz., the asymmetric crypto system and hash function) as a means of authenticating electronic record. Any other method used by banks for authentication should be recognized as a source of legal risk. Customers must be made aware of the channel risk prior to sign up.
- Under the present regime there is an obligation on banks to maintain secrecy and confidentiality of customers' accounts. In the Mobile-banking scenario, the risk of banks not meeting the above obligation is high on account of several factors. Despite all reasonable precautions, banks may be exposed to enhanced risk of liability to customers on account of breach of secrecy, denial of service etc., because of hacking/other technological failures. The banks should, therefore, institute adequate risk control measures to manage such risks.
- In Mobile banking scenario there is very little scope for the banks to act on stop-payment instructions from the customers. Hence, banks should clearly notify to the customers the timeframe and the circumstances in which any stop-payment instructions could be accepted.
- The Consumer Protection Act, 1986 defines the rights of consumers in India and is applicable to banking services as well. Currently, the rights and liabilities of customers availing of Internet banking services are being determined by bilateral agreements between the banks and customers. Considering the banking practice and rights enjoyed by customers in traditional banking, banks' liability to the customers on account of unauthorized transfer through hacking, denial of service on account of technological failure etc. needs to be assessed and

banks providing Mobile banking should consider insuring themselves against such risks, as is the case with Internet Banking.

- Banks may determine their own pricing for the use of these services.
- Banks should get the scheme for facilitating Mobile banking approved by their respective boards/LOMC before offering it to their customers. The LOMC approval must document the extent of Operational and Fraud risk assumed by the bank and the bank's processes & policies designed to mitigate such risk.

KYC Process

Banks are permitted to rely on Financial Intermediaries as recommended by the relaxed KYC guidelines issued vide RBI circular DBOD.NO.AML.BC.28/14.01.001/2005-06 dated August 23, 2005 A Bank can sponsor the small value remittance service by entering into arrangements with intermediaries in order to manage distribution, technology and scale.

In the same spirit, Banks may partner with Telecom companies, Technology companies etc. to facilitate such small value transfers. Banks may rely on introductions from any person on whom KYC has been done and certificates of identification issued by the intermediary. Thus the intermediary can be a Telecom company, another bank or financial institution or a stand alone Trust Company dedicated to the purpose of facilitating such transactions.

It is proposed that in cases where the remitter is the owner of the mobile phone, the Bank relies on the telecom company's KYC and obtains a copy of the registration documents from the telecom company. In cases where the remitter is not the owner of the mobile phone, a letter of introduction is taken from the owner and the remitter registers with a limited KYC comprising of photograph and address proof. Wherever address proof is not available, the introducer can certify the genuineness of the remitter's address.

Regulatory & Supervisory Issues

As recommended by the Group, the existing regulatory framework over banks will be extended to Mobile banking also. In this regard, it is advised that:

1. Only such banks which are licensed and supervised in India and have a physical presence in India will be permitted to offer

Mobile banking products to residents of India. Thus, both banks and virtual banks incorporated outside the country and having no physical presence in India will not, for the present, be permitted to offer mobile banking services to Indian residents.

2. The products should be restricted to account holders only and should not be offered in other jurisdictions.
3. The services should only include local currency products.
4. The 'in-out' scenario where customers in cross border jurisdictions are offered banking services by Indian banks (or branches of foreign banks in India) and the 'out-in' scenario where Indian residents are offered banking services by banks operating in cross-border jurisdictions are generally not permitted and this approach will apply to Internet banking also. The existing exceptions for limited purposes under FEMA i.e. where resident Indians have been permitted to continue to maintain their accounts with overseas banks etc., will, however, be permitted.
5. Overseas branches of Indian banks will be permitted to offer Internet banking services to their overseas customers subject to their satisfying, in addition to the host supervisor, the home supervisor.

Given the regulatory approach as above, banks are advised to follow the following instructions:

a. All banks, who propose to offer transactional services on the Mobile services should obtain prior approval from RBI. Bank's application for such permission should indicate its business plan, analysis of cost and benefit, operational arrangements like technology adopted, business partners, third party service providers and systems and control procedures the bank proposes to adopt for managing risks. The bank should also submit security policy covering recommendations made in this circular and a certificate from an independent auditor that the minimum requirements prescribed have been met. After the initial approval the banks will be obliged to inform RBI any material changes in the services/products offered by them.
b. The guidelines issued by RBI on 'Risks and Controls in Computers and Telecommunications' vide circular DBS.CO.ITC.BC. 10/31.09.001/97-98 dated 4th February 1998 will equally apply to Mobile banking. The RBI as supervisor

will cover the entire risks associated with electronic banking as a part of its regular inspections of banks.

c. Banks should develop outsourcing guidelines to manage risks arising out of third party service providers, such as, disruption in service, defective services and personnel of service providers gaining intimate knowledge of banks' systems and misutilizing the same, etc., effectively.

d. It will become important to set up 'Inter-bank Payment Gateways' for settlement of such transactions. The protocol for transactions between the customer, the bank and the portal and the framework for setting up of payment gateways as recommended by the Group should be adopted fro Mobile Banking

e. Only institutions who are members of the cheque clearing system in the country will be permitted to participate in Inter-bank payment gateways for Internet payment. Each gateway must nominate a bank as the clearing bank to settle all transactions. Payments effected using credit cards, payments arising out of cross border e-commerce transactions and all intra-bank payments (i.e., transactions involving only one bank) should be excluded for settlement through an inter-bank payment gateway.

f. Inter-bank payment gateways must have capabilities for both net and gross settlement. All settlement should be intra-day and as far as possible, in real time.

g. Bilateral contracts between the payee and payee's bank, the participating banks and service provider and the banks themselves will form the legal basis for such transactions. The rights and obligations of each party must be clearly defined and should be valid in a court of law.

h. Banks must make mandatory disclosures of risks, responsibilities and liabilities of the customers in doing business through Mobile, through a disclosure template. The banks should also provide their latest published financial results over the net.

7

The Advantages of Electronic Banking

The difference between electronic banking and online banking is negligible. Banks have been using electronic banking longer than their customers have, and online banking is just a form of electronic banking. Banks and their customers both benefit from electronic banking.

Ease of Use

Electronic banking allows you to conveniently conduct your banking activities online. You can view you account balances and statuses from your home computer. In addition, you don't have to deal with lines at the bank or have conversations with bankers in front of other people.

Direct Deposit

Before the advent of direct deposit, Americans handled their pay differently. On payday you would receive a check (or possibly cash). You then had to take the check to your bank and deposit it, but that would require between two and ten days to clear the funds for your use.

Alternatively you could go to the bank the check was written from and cash it, then drive back to your bank and deposit the funds in order to make the funds immediately available. Direct deposit allows the banks and employers to use fewer employee hours to get the job done, saving them money. For customers and employees, direct deposit allows you to have your funds instantly available to you as soon as the transfer is initiated and completed.

Portability

If you are an online banking customer, you have the option of accessing your banking information from your home computer. Additionally you can use any computer that is connected to the Internet, and, if your bank has the ability, any smart device that can access the Internet can also give you this functionality. You can, for instance, do your banking from your local coffee shop (assuming they have a free Wi-Fi service).

Bill Pay

Bill pay is a service that banks offer to help you pay your bills on time, at the same time every month. You collect the bills that you want to be included in the bill pay service and set up your bank account to pay a certain amount each month to each biller. Online banking customers can do this from home; otherwise visit your bank to set this up.

Money Transfer

If you hold multiple accounts within the same bank and need to transfer money between them, electronic banking makes it very simple. In fact, online banking customers do not even need to leave their computer to do it. Just pick the amount you would like to transfer, and to which account it will be transferred, complete the transfer and the money is instantly transferred.

Advantages & Disadvantages of Electronic Checks

According to The Electronic Payment Association (NACHA), nearly 16 billion Automated Clearing House (ACH) payments were made in 2006. This figure represents a 14.5 increase over the previous year. Both brick-and-mortar and online merchants frequently use electronic checks to process check payments. Electronic checks can simplify and streamline the payment process for customers who use checks and for merchants that accept check payments. However, there are also cautions involved with electronic checks.

Instant Payment Acknowledgment and 24 Hour Access

With electronic checks, customers can receive instant acknowledgment of their payments. Merchants can be assured of the validity of a checking account through the verification process. With electronic checking, customers can have 24 hour access to their checking account transactions through electronic banking.

Increased Efficiency, Lower Costs, Environmental Benefits

Processing payments online with electronic checks eliminates the need for stamps and envelopes, which saves time and money for customers. Processing electronic checks also saves money for merchants in processing costs, especially in the elimination of deposit and transaction fees. Electronic checks can also be an environmentally conscious choice, since less paper is involved in printing and processing the checks.

Security Concerns, Errors and "Float"

Anytime computers are involved with sensitive transactions, there are bound to be security concerns. Fraud by unscrupulous merchants is one danger; hacking into the electronic records or interception of a transmission is another. Enhanced security must accompany any electronic payment system. There is also the danger of human error or equipment failure which can jeopardize the accuracy of transmissions or records. Customers should check their banking records carefully for unfamiliar or unauthorized transactions. Finally, consumers should be aware that electronic checks are processed much more quickly than paper checks, sometimes within hours. This process has eliminated much of the "float" that previously delayed the presenting of a check for payment for several days.

Data Protection in Consumer E-banking

Law cannot possibly be expected to keep pace with changes in technology. The recent debacle of virtual voyeurism has brought out, amongst other things, the inadequacy and vulnerability of the laws governing use of internet. Fixing liability, recording and reproducing evidence, ascertaining jurisdiction are problems which show little sign of easing. Concerns over security and misuse pertaining to e-banking activity have been mounting as more banks in India foray into electronic banking.

E-banking activities involve not just banks and their customer, but numerous third parties too. Information held by banks about their customers', their transactions etc. changes hands several times. It is impossible for banks to retaining information solely within their own computer networks, let alone a single jurisdiction is impossible. Risks pertaining leakage, tampering or blocking of data are sufficiently high to warrant adequate legal and technical protection. India has no law on data protection leave alone a law governing an area as specific as protection of data in electronic banking. Information security in e-banking presents two main areas of risk: preventing unauthorized transactions and maintaining integrity of customers transactions. Data protection falls in the latter category.

Data protection laws primarily aim to safeguard the interest of the individual whose data is handled and processed by others. 'Interests' are usually expressed in terms of privacy, autonomy and/or integrity. Data protection laws are 'framework laws' providing rather diffused general rules for such processing and making allowances for developing detailed norms as and when the need arises. Such legislation typically regulates all or most stages of the data protection cycle including registration, storage, retrieval, and dissemination of personal data. Data protection legislation of a large number of countries, such as Austria, Ireland, Japan, Luxembourg, Sweden and the UK cover only automated data processing practices.

The Indian Information Technology Act, 2000, basically a framework law, makes hacking a punishable offence under Section 66. Breach of information security is implicitly recognized as a penal offence in the form hacking. The 'appropriate government' (central/state) is empowered to declare any 'computer', 'computer system' or 'computer network' as a protected system. A ten year prison term and a hefty fine await any person who secures access to the 'secured computer system' in contravention of the provisions of the law. Despite the deterrence characterized by the penal provisions of the IT Act, 2000, a lacuna in the law is that organizations and entities can take action against those who breach data security procedure, but they are not obliged to implement data security measures to protect consumers and clients.

The IT Act does not lay down any such duty upon banks. Contrastingly, in UK, failure to undertake identification of new customers properly can create an array of risks for the bank. Under the Data Protection Act, 1998 an erring bank may face an action for damages if it fails to "maintain adequate security precautions in respect of the data". Essentially, a legal duty is thrust upon the banks, to use reasonable care and skill in disseminating information to persons who access the bank's networks either on the internet or though an ATM card.

In India, a Bank's liability would arise out of contract as there is no statute to the point. When liability is contractual it means that the bank is, by virtue of the contract, under an obligation to keep customers' data secret. If transactions are being done on an open network such as the internet then in case of a security breach, an internet service provider (ISP) may be liable, in addition to the bank. Though ambiguity persists as regards liability of an internet service provider due to dearth of decided case law on the point.

The viability of a sectoral legislation on data protection in e-banking should be gauged. India can take cue from nations which have favoured *ad hoc* enactment of sectoral laws over omnibus legislation.

Effective Method of Security Measures in Virtual Banking

In E-banking system, information is considered as an asset and so worthy of protection. Information security can support a wide variety of objectives such as compliance with laws and regulations, reducing the fraud risk and reducing the risk of unauthorized access. The protection afforded to information is usually expressed in terms of confidentiality, integrality, availability and non-repudiation. Authentication has a significant contribution to provide all these services. Now days in Indian banking system, the authentication is done through password that is not up to the level of high security measure. There is an urgent need to acclimatize the security measure in the banking system.

Virtual Banking

Any banking service delivered to the customer by means of a computer-controlled system that does not directly involve the usual bank's branch is called virtual banking. In virtual banking the traditional paradigm of a customer's integration with the bank is replaced by an electronic paradigm, which is new and innovative in banking sectors. Customer demands, commercial motivation and technological developments are the key drivers of virtual banking. In the changing environment adaptation to market realities as well as technology is causing the virtual banking revolution. Customer pull and banking push are the two engines to drive the virtualization.

Factors to be considered in Virtual Banking;

- The routine banking transaction was becoming both costly and time consuming. The banks resorted to computerization to cut cost and time overheads in handling routine transactions
- The introduction of automated teller machine (ATM) impart flexibility to bank customers and gave further boost to virtual banking

- The introduction of credit cards and debit cards helps both the consumers and retailers to be free from cash handling.

These payment systems save time and offered security in its rouse.

Technology

Biometrics is one approach to the authentication of an individuals claimed identity. Recognizing individuals through observation of particular physical characteristics is known as biometrics. A biometrics authentication is a two-stage process. During the first stage, some sort of capture device is used to take a measurement of particular physiological or behavioural characteristics and in the second stage; the measurement is compared to a stored value. Based on the comparison result the system makes an authentication decision. Biometric technologies do not actually compare the physical traits that they are designed to use as a unique identifier, rather, they create templates for comparison. This enrollment process may require the individual to provide multiple instances of the biometric trait. The initial comparison templates are created during an enrollment process.

Multifactor Authentication

One way to increase the strength of an authentication mechanism is to use multiple factors of authentication. In the case of biometrics, this could involve requiring the user to input a password or PIN (Personal Identification Number) or to produce some sort of authentication token such as smart card that contains both the PIN and any one of the biometric systems with 1:1 matching. The advantage of such is that many are designed to operate with biometric systems and have sufficient space for storage of biometric templates with them. However, assessing the extent to which an additional authentication factor can increase the overall strength of the authentication services. When passwords are used for authentication, the decision is made relatively straightforward-if correct password is supplied the result is positive authentication, otherwise the individual is rejected. A biometric authentication is conceptually different, in that the decision is based on a probability. Any organization considering the use of biometrics needs to understand the impact of this when reaching a trust decision.

Biometric Authentication

Biometrics is a measurable physical characteristics or personal behavioural trait used to recognize the identity or verify the claimed identity of an enrollee. Examples of physiological characteristics that are used in biometric device include fingerprints, the geometry of the face or hand and patterns within the iris or retina or in the layout of veins. Behavioural characteristics include voice pattern, gait and the dynamics of handwriting or keystrokes. For the authentication process the chosen characteristics must be unique to each individual. Also it is possible to measure the characteristics with the reasonable degree of accuracy. Once the measurement has been taken the data is converted into a biometric template. A template is a representation of the measurement that retains all the relevant information but takes up far less space than the original. It is this template that is compared to a template generated in the same manner during the initial enrolment procedure and based on the similarity of the two, a decision is made whether the user should be granted access.

Factors Affected

For any particular individual, it is highly unlikely that two measurements of the same characteristics will be identical. There are simply too many factors that can affect the result. The measurement may be influenced by fluctuation in the environment such as light, heat, humidity and soon. The manner in which the users interact with the capture device also has an impact on the measurement. On different occasion; an individual is likely to behave slightly differently. So the physiological and behavioural characteristics vary over time. The following variation may cause the generation of different templates.

- Fingerprint worn with hard labour and age
- Voices are affected by illness
- Signature vary depending on the emotional state of the subject
- Face change over time by addition of glasses or by injury

FAR/FRR

The permissible discrepancy between templates is determined by adjusting the False Acceptance Rate (FAR) and the False Rejection Rate (FRR). The FAR gives the measure of the probability that an individual will be falsely accepted by the system (makes an incorrect identification). The FRR is the measure of probability of the rejection of legitimate user. The balance between the FAR and FRR greatly influences both the security and usability of the system. Tuning the system to make the FAR lower will improve its security will result in a higher FRR and make the system less consumable. The FAR/FRR balance may be adjusted; neither rate provides a suitable metric for expressing the overall accuracy of the biometric system. To compare the performance of the different biometric system the Crossover Error Rate (CER) can be used. The CER is defined as the error rate of the system when the FAR and FRR are equal.

Verification and Identification

Due to the advance development of technology, the cost effective, the processing power to employ and more accurate biometric identification systems are developed. There are two ways to resolve a person's identity: verification and identification. Verification involves confirming or denying a persons claimed identity, Identity is to establish a person's identity (Who am I?). Each approach has its own complexities and could probably be solved best by a specific biometric system including the following;

Physical Biometrics

- Finger print-Analysing fingertip patterns
- Facial recognition location-Measuring facial characteristics
- Hand geometry-Measuring the shape of the hand
- Iris Scan-Analysing features of coloured ring of the eye
- Retinal scan-Analysing blood vessels in the eye
- Vascular patterns-Analysing vein patterns
- DNA-Analysing genetic makeup
- Biometric data watermarking is used to store/hide biometric information.

Behavioural Biometrics

- Speaker/Voice recognition system-Analysing vocal behaviour
- Signature/handwriting-Analysing signature dynamics
- Keystroke/patterning-Measuring the time spacing of typed words.

The following is a general user acceptance list in descending order, from the most accepted to the least accepted

1. Iris scan
2. Key stroke/patterning
3. Signature/Handwriting
4. Speaker/voice recognition
5. Facial recognition/face location
6. Finger print

7. Hand geometry
8. Retinal scan

The popularity which virtual banking services have won among customers, owning to the speed, convenience and round-the-clock access they offer, is likely to increase in the future. However, several issues of concern would need to be pro-actively attended. While most of electronic banking have built-in security features such as encryption, prescription of maximum monetary limits and authorizations, the system operators have to be extremely vigilant and provide clear-cut guidelines for operations. On the larger issue of electronically initiated funds transfer, issues like authentication of payments instructions, the responsibility of the customer for secrecy of the security procedure would also need to be addressed. So for the better security multifactor authentication is best so that Password with any one biometric system make the virtual banking with higher security in forth coming years. However, it needs to be recognized that such high cost technological initiatives need to be undertaken only after the viability and feasibility of the technology and its associated applications have been thoroughly examined.

A Suitable Research Methodology for Analysing Online Banking Behaviour

Since the inception of the Internet, the ability of websites to track the behaviour of their visitors has been considered one of the most promising facets of the new medium. The detailed records of web usage behaviour provide researchers and practitioners with the opportunity to study how users browse or navigate websites and to assess the performance of these sites in a variety of ways (Bucklin & Sismeiro, 2002). Many online retailers monitor visitor traffic as a measure of their stores' success. However, summary measures, such as the total number of visits per month, provide little insight about individual-level shopping behaviour. Behaviour may evolve over time, especially in a changing environment like the Internet (Moe & Fader, 2002). As a consequence they are unable to integrate the Internet in their direct marketing strategy. Walsh & Godfrey (2000) mentioned that the Internet offers a number of advantages. They stated that e-tailors are able to collect and analyse an extensive amount of information continuously, in a very short time and at relatively low costs. E-tailors collect three types of data: (1) basic, personal information provided on registration or via self-completion questionnaires; (2) purchasing habits; and (3) clickstream or site navigation. We are interested in the third type of data: data from clickstream navigation. Kimball & Merz (2000) see the clickstream as a new and exiting data source: "The clickstream contains a record for every page request from each visitor to our site. In many ways, we can imagine that the clickstream is a record for every gesture each visitor makes, and we are beginning to realize that these gestures add up to descriptions of behaviour we have never been able to see before". Clickstream analyses have a few important benefits in analysing online banking behaviour. Based on our experiences over the past two years these benefits are elaborated with examples from practice.

Clickstream Data

How can we analyse visitors' clicking pattern? There for we need to collect data from clickstream or site navigation. We decided to use clickstream data from an Application Server Provider (ASP). An ASP is a third party 'observer' that collects clickstream data from a website. A pixel gif is a small snippet of HTML code that is inserted into every page the bank wishes to be tracked. Each requested page sends a signal to the ASP. The ASP logs each interaction between the visitor and the website. One of the most compelling reasons to use ASP-data is that it enables the ability to identify unique users across website domains. Another reason is that additional information about screen resolution, browser plug-ins and other type of technical information can be collected. Also additional custom analytic variables (e.g., keywords) can be inserted into the pixel gif. Moreover, ASP-data generates a single data file to import for analyses. The pre-processing phase with ASP data is, comparing with the other types of data collection (e.g., web-server based or user-based) less time consuming. A file with clickstream data is like a maritime log: a detailed description of all the peregrinations on the site. There are different levels of granularity of clickstream data. What types of components are logged depends on the configuration of the server. The following types of components are most essential: Transfer log, Referral log, Agent log. For a more detailed description of different types of log components and types of collecting clickstream data see Mattison (1999); Mena (1999); Kimball & Merz (2000) and Linoff & Berry (2002).

Pre-processing Clickstream Data

To guarantee the reliability of research findings, data files have to be of high quality. Unfortunately, the quality of 'raw clickstream data' is most of the time poor. Depending on the granularity of the data in the imported file, data preparation is there for necessary and worthwhile. Pre-processing consists of converting usage information contained in the various data sources into the data abstractions necessary for pattern discovery. The extract, transformation, and load (ETL) mechanism is appropriate to get data from where it is created to the data warehouse where it will be used. Data extraction is concerned with extraction from the data sources on an ongoing basis. The data transformation programs do basic translations such as character set conversion or translating codes into human-readable equivalents. The data loading process involves that new or changed dimension data must be processed before data can be loaded into the data webhouse (Sweiger et al., 2002). In the end a few levels c.q., dimensions of the clickstream data might be loaded into the data webhouse. Analysing activity at the lowest level of granularity, the site hit, is quite useful for generating site traffic statistics and calculating many different metrics associated with site administration. But most businesses analyse user activity from a page or session perspective, requiring two new aggregate tables at the Page Activity and Session Activity levels.

The treatment of outliers, errors, and incomplete data that can easily occur due to reasons inherent to web browsing (Batista & Silva, 2001), is a relevant part of data pre-processing. We like to discuss a few difficulties with collecting and analysing clickstream data to evaluate users' navigation behaviour. The first problem is caching. Web clients save previous visited pages in the cache to reduce the traffic on the server and the costs. As a result, when a user hits the "back button", the cached page is displayed and the web server is not aware of the repeat page access. Cooley et al. (1999) use knowledge of the structure of the site to solve the problem of caching: if two pages are not connected but directly visited after each other, this means that a cache-page connected to both pages is revisited. The second problem with collecting clickstream data is proxy servers. In a web server log, all requests potentially represent more than one user. Proxy servers provide an intermediate level of caching and create even more problems with identifying site usage (Cooley, 1999). Also, due to proxy server level caching, a single request from the server could actually be viewed by multiple users throughout an extended period of time (Cooley, 1999). Another impediments to collecting reliable usage data are web spiders. Web spiders are searching the site, but do not understand the site. Web spiders are robots and they leave non-human tracks behind that are thus misleading for understanding visitors' navigation behaviour (Spiliopoulou, 2000).

Aside from counting visitors to your website, the most important information you want to obtain is the number of unique sessions, determined by the different and unique IP addresses in your access log file (Mena, 1999). However, this can be misleading due to the fact that dial-up users are usually assigned a 'dynamic' IP address by their Internet Service Provider (ISP) from a reserved lot. And, corporate users typically connect through proxy servers, which means that groups of individuals use the same address. This means that it is very difficult to identify an individual with a unique IP address.

This fact leads to two conclusions: (1) sessions are more important than individual addresses, and (2) tracking by other means is necessary whether by cookies or forms (Mena 1999). Cookies are small text files created by servers on visiting browsers' hard disk that contain an identification code. They are passed by servers to browsers so that each time a website visitor returns to a server that passed the cookie, it can recognize it and read what it wrote before, such as what pages were visited during the prior session. The absence of one unique user key is a problem in analysing visitor's behaviour on a corporate website of a bank.

The problem in the online realm is that visitors are invisible without clear definitions of a user. People come to your site, leave footprints and move on. However, those footprints are merely an indication that they were there and tell you nothing about the people who made those marks (Cutler & Sterne, 2000). Nowadays, most banks have an online banking application, where customers are able to perform transactions such as fund transfer or bill payment. A customer has a unique identification number, e.g., account number, and a password to gain access to the online applications. It is necessary to log a unique user identification key (e.g., account number or relation number) of the visitors to recognize online banking behaviour of customers.

Standard definitions of core measurements must be defined. Many e-businesses feel they have a good grasp on the basic concepts of hits, page views, and impressions. However, 'what is and what is not a page view'? Does a page merely have to requested or actually delivered? In our research different types of statistical analyses are applied on clickstream data, which contain page requests. There is more discussion about a standard definition of a session. Ideally each user session gives an extract accounting of who accessed the website, which pages were requested and in which order, and how long each page was viewed. We follow previous research and assume that a page request starts a new session if it requested after an idle period of at least 30 minutes (Catledge & Pitkow, 1995).

Analysing Clickstream Data in Order to Measure Online Banking Behaviour

Information that reflects online banking behaviour can be extracted from a file with clickstream data by applying data mining techniques. Data mining can be defined as the iterative process of detecting and extracting these patterns from large databases: it is a kind of pattern-recognition. Data mining lets us identify "signatures" hidden in large databases. (Mena, 1999).

To analyse clickstream data of a visitor's session it is possible to have a clear insight in the visitor's behaviour in detail. Not only descriptive analyses, but also explorative analyses on clickstream data are possible to get a better understanding of customers' online behaviour. Mining clickstream data is also defined as the process of applying data mining techniques to the discovery of usage patterns from web logs data, to identify web users behaviour.

The concept of applying data mining techniques to web server logs was first proposed by Mannila and Toivonen (1996); Yan, Jacobsen, Garcia-Molina and Dayal (1996); Chen, Park and Yu (1998) and Cooley et al., (1999). Since then many studies were conducted in this field, but none in the field of financial services. Down here two applications of analysing clickstream data are described: (1) website usage and (2) online banking behaviour. Regarding the latter we provide three examples to underline what types of techniques can be used to analyse online banking behaviour. These research activities show that analysing clickstream data is a suitable research methodology to measure online banking behaviour.

Website Usage

It is necessary for e-marketers to monitor the usage of the site. Monitoring means to follow and to evaluate actual number of page views, sessions and visitors. There for time series are needed to visualise the site's usage per month, per day or even per second. Analysing clickstream data during a past period provides an exact overview of the visitors' usage of the website.

Online Banking Behaviour

You cannot manage what you do not measure, and you cannot measure what you do not define (Cutler & Sterne, 2000). There are many different types of behaviour on a website. How could we define online banking behaviour? Depending on the strategy of the website, only a limited number of visitors' actions is desirable. These actions are measured by 'key performance indicators (KPIs)'. KPIs are important determinants of a successful website, and basically follow from the business process that is being supported by the site. It is possible to specify different types of desirable online banking behaviour, i.e. KPIs. E-marketers, together with researchers, must make a list with KPIs for each website. Also from explorative clickstream analyses useful and interesting KPIs can be found. KPIs should be monitored continuously. From explorative clickstream analyses also other useful and interesting KPIs can be found. Again, it is necessary for e-marketers to monitor usage of the site. There for time series of the specified KPIs are needed to visualize the site's usage in a time perspective.

Based on this type of information marketers are capable to monitor the total number of online payments on a detailed level. It is important to monitor the key performance indicators of a website. Time series are suitable to visualise the usage of a website, and the different types of online banking behaviour on a website. Time series are ideal evaluation tools. E-marketers must set themselves explicit targets for the KPIs. Alterations in the design of the website are also measured. With the proper infrastructure, time series could be reported automatically and displayed in every desired format for the end-users.

Relationship between Visitors' Surfing Behaviour and KPIs

Every company strives to reach the KPI targets. How can a bank improve and adjust the website to reach or even exceed the targets? We must analyse how the design of the website contributes to realize the KPI targets. Detailed analyses of visitors' surfing behaviour detect which parts of the website are more or less useful or absolutely important for the KPIs. With this type of analysis unknown relationships are extracted. This proves that clickstream analyses is data-driven. Perhaps unknown important factors are extracted.

Clickstream analyses offer ideas for new content. The consequences of the various alternations on the websites are evaluated. Clickstream analyses functions as a monitor for a system of KPIs as well as a tool for optimising the structure, design and content of a website.

Segmentation of Visitors' Sessions

To gain insight in visitors' online behaviour we need to analyse what groups of pages are requested within a session. If there are distinct clusters of pages, there is also a segmentation possible of surfing behaviour of visitors. We need 'correspondence analysis' to cluster pages and 'hierarchical cluster analysis' to find a segmentation of sessions based on clusters of pages. Correspondence analysis is needed to visualize the hidden structure in the datamatrix (Greenacre, 1984). Correspondence Analyse is a multivariate representation of contingency table containing information about combinations of the requested pages during one session. The 'principal inertion' of the algorithm qualifies if the representation is acceptable, and what is the importance of the axes (proportional variance) for the total solution. Pages in the figure that are requested relatively often within the same session are lying close to each other. And, pages that are not combined in the same session are lying far apart.

Groups of pages provide the right information about how to steer customers directly to the KPIs. It is also clear that this information helps content managers to decide which part of the website needs more development and what part does not. We assume that a visitor begins a session with a specific need for information. The design of the website should match visitors' needs. If a customer wants something from his or her bank, it is just one mouse-click away on the Internet. There for a segmentation of visitors' sessions-different types of information needs-is absolutely necessary for optimising the website. The segmentation is based on different typologies of sessions. Typology of sessions helps to differ in communication with different types of visitors. Clickstream analysis operates here as a tool for optimising the website as well as directing customers through the website.

Clickstream Analysis Versus OLAP

Online Analytical Processing (henceforth, OLAP) is way of presenting relational data to end-users to facilitate understanding the data and important patterns inside it. Like visualization tool in the arsenal of weapons used for extracting and presenting information (Berry & Linoff, 1997). The basic difference between OLAP and data mining is that former is about aggregates, while data mining is about ratios (Mena, 1999). Another difference between OLAP and data mining is how they operate on the data. Similar to the direction of statistics, OLAP is a top-down approach to data analysis. Manual OLAP may be based on need-to-know facts, such as regional sales reports stratified by type of business, while automatic data mining is based on the need-to-discover what factors are influencing these sales (Mena, 1999). OLAP tools are powerful and fast tools for reporting on data, in contrast to data mining tools that focus on findings patterns in data. Most areas where there is interest in data mining can also benefit from OLAP. Besides all differences mentioned above, an important benefit of clickstream analyses is that data mining provides bottom-up analysis and requires no assumptions (Mena, 1999). Besides this, when a unique user identity key, e.g. account number, is logged, clickstream data can be enriched with customer information from the back office. So, not only online customer behaviour is viewed, but customer behaviour through multi channels.

Clickstream Analysis Versus Market Research

Every year a company invests a lot of resources in market research. The outcomes of market research contribute to the development and the optimisation of products and services of the company. Market research asks customers what they think, need or wish. Unfortunately, there is a gap between what people say and what they actually do. Comparing with market research clickstream analysis has a few advantages: (i) clickstream data are collected unobtrusively and based on observed behaviour, (ii) they are free from confounds of researcher interaction, and (iii) time pattern and order of activity is recorded.

Conclusions

Banks and financial institutions still face the Internet as a 'black box' in which little insight is provided about online behaviour at the individual level. As a consequence they are unable to integrate the Internet in their direct marketing strategy. Clickstream analyses open up the black box and illuminate online banking behaviour. The detailed records of web usage behaviour provide researchers and practitioners with the opportunity to study how users browse or navigate websites and to assess the performance of these sites in a variety of ways. Pre-processing the clickstream data consists of converting usage information into the data abstractions necessary for pattern discovery. It is a hard job, but is worthy. The opportunities for clickstream analyses are far-reaching. We described the following applications of analysing clickstream data in order to measure online banking behaviour:

- Website usage: time series are accurate and easily show trends in visitors' behaviour. Clickstream analyses provide insight in customers' behaviour on a very detail level. Monitoring website usage with basic statistics foster decision-making to counteract on a possible decrease. E-marketers and content managers may decide whether or not to change the content of the website. As a result clickstream analyses integrates client focus into the daily operation.

- Online banking behaviour: depending on the strategy of the website, only a limited number of visitors' actions is profitable. These actions are defined and measured by 'key performance indicators (KPI)'. KPIs are important determinants of a successful website. KPIs should be measured continuously with time series. Based on the past figures marketers or managers can put future targets. Clickstream analyses may help to optimise the profit of a website.
- Relationship between visitor's surfing behaviour and KPIs: banks face problems in a lack of knowledge how to construct website to optimise KPIs. How can content managers improve and adjust the website to reach or even exceed the KPI targets? A logistic regression, with the KPI as a dependent variable and other types of page visits as independent variables, shows which pages are increasing the probability of reaching the KPI target. Clickstream analyses functions as a tool for optimizing the structure, design and content of a website.
- Segmentation of visitors' sessions: the design of the website should match visitors' needs. We assume that a visitor begins a session with a specific need for information. If a customer wants something from his or her bank, it is just one mouse-click away on the Internet. There for a segmentation of visitors' sessions is absolutely necessary for optimising the website.

All these applications prove that clickstream analyses functions as (1) a monitor for a system of KPIs as well as (2) a tool for optimizing the structure, design and content of a website. Based on experiences with clickstream analyses the benefits, in contrast to other tools, are:

- Different types of OLAP-tools measure site usage, but are incapable to understand online behaviour. Clickstream analyses operate as need-to-discover on the clickstream data. Perhaps unknown important factors are extracted. Hidden relationships between certain types of surfing behaviours and KPIs are found. Clickstream analyses are able to explain the mechanism of the measured behaviour at the individual level.
- Clickstream data are collected unobtrusively and based on observed behaviour, rather than self-reports, and time pattern and order of activity is recorded. Clickstream data displays

customers' online behaviour in detail; every (mili-) second customers' online banking behaviour is recorded. This type of data source can be enriched with customer information from the back office. So, not only online customer behaviour can be viewed, but also customer behaviour through multi-channels like mail or telephone.

Just the presence of a new data source is not necessarily sufficient to call for a new program of research (Bucklin et al., 2002). Future research should find out whether or not online banking behaviour is any different from off line banking behaviour. If it is not, then we already have a suitable research paradigm and a wide range of research techniques for analysing online behaviour. Studying banking behaviour is interesting because financial services are non-tangible and digitally stored, and most consumers have already bought financial service products, resulting in a high penetration of financial services among consumers. Clickstream analyses are not only applicable for online banking behaviour, but of course for any other kind of online behaviour as well. Banks or financial institutions still face the Internet as a 'black box'. Summary measures, such as the total number of visits per month, provide little insight about individual-level shopping behaviour. Clickstream analyses open up the black box and it illuminates online banking behaviour and provides opportunities to integrate the Internet in the direct marketing strategy of a bank.

Preventing Technology Based Bank Frauds

Thieves are not born, but made out of opportunities. All the major operational areas in banking represent a good opportunity for fraudsters. Majority of the fraud incidents being reported is under deposit, loan and inter-branch accounting transactions, including remittances. The advent of computerization in banks brought new technology based frauds, when committed successfully, would be difficult to track down and can multiply the financial losses of banks to unimaginable levels. A careless pressing of a button, resulted in 100 crores loss to a stockbroker in BSE, as he couldn't undo his wrong quote (Business Line). Preventive fraud management is therefore far superior to post fraud containment or recovery of losses.

Prevention is basically to limit/eliminate the opportunities so that thieves are not born and take away money by indulging into frauds. It is very difficult to look into all permutations and combinations of opportunities that thieves take advantage and prevent them so that they never surface. Only effective continuous monitoring and analysis of fraudulent activities help understand the reason behind a fraud and then take counter preventive measures.

New technology always brought some more fraudulent criminal activities developed around these technologies. Ex: Photocopiers, fax machines, credit cards, and mobile phones, ATMs, PCs and now Internet. By the time the regulatory bodies, law enforcement agencies etc. take preventive measures to cope up with the present environment and it gets stabilized, either the environment itself changes or some more new elements like new technology emerges making the criminals find a new home and commit fraud. So prevention is basically a cycle of monitor, analyse, detect, act and protect.

Technology in Banking-The Past

Most Public Sector Banks started computerization of their business, particularly branch automation based on the Ranga Rajan committee report in the eighties.

Those days the main aim was to convert the laborious manual process into simple automated process with out re-engineering any business process. The CVC (Central Vigilance Commision) strongly believed (particularly after Harshad Mehta's Scam) that frauds can take place at a higher rate due to slow and delayed manual processes and forced Banks to computerize their branches with no one actually guiding or monitoring the whole computerization in Banks. Banks went in their own way computerizing their branches, without having any holistic integrated approach not only among banks but also in their own bank with in their branches.

This led to isolated applications at branch levels, and almost every PSB (Public Sector Bank) ended up with different flavours of branch automation from different vendors mainly due to 2 reasons.

a. Software Vendor of Regional choice as maintenance charges from local vendors would be cheaper

b. No single vendor has over all presence across India.

Problems with this technology:

- Islands of applications in the branches of a bank, with dissimilar computers, operating systems and application packages. There's no integration of such application and hence forcing the manual intervention.
- Due to various flavours of hardware and software, no data integrity could be maintained even though the application was

for the same business purpose. Ex: No one could see a unified picture of overall deposits, loans customer information etc. of the whole Bank.

- Due to dissimilar application packages, Inter branch reconciliation and communication was not possible. Even if it was made possible, it was not straight through.
- Still some banks are continuing with this technology which is very out dated
- Not able to trust vendors, banks relied on half vendor based software and half in-house software. They couldn't integrate the two, without some manual intervention.

Due to the above problems, banks are still dependent on manual procedures only. More than 50% of the process of generating MIS from the branches and send to their Central Office required manual intervention. This technology helped banks, only to lessen some burden on back office. It couldn't achieve

- Better monitoring control
- Better decision making
- Faster service delivery
- Better performance
- New products or services etc.

Instead of alleviating the threats posed by manual banking, it actually increased them further, leaving lot of confusion on whom to make accountable, the computer or the computer operator.

Some of the new fraud techniques that surfaced due to computerization :

- Intentionally writing programs to siphon off the funds
- Illegal transactions between accounts
- Wrong interest calculations (Deccan Chronicle 15/12/2k2).

Today, many PSBs have computerized branches, but this computerization helped neither banks nor the customers as expected.

Technology in Banking-The Present

Introduction of foreign and private banks coupled with Information Technology and Global computer Networks, posed a big threat to Public Sector Banks. Right now, banks with no option left, but to turn to technology in order to compete (even to survive) with foreign and private sector banks.

Not satisfied with the already existing technology, banks now have decided to re-look into the whole technology adoption with fresh management goals and commitment. Many of them decided to phase out the old branch automation software in phases, with high aim of satisfying the customer and integrate the whole back office and generate MIS online. With this aim, banks are now setting up their networks so that they can have a overall bank view instead of just a branch view from all the angles of process, control, monitor, decide and act. They also chalked out plans on how to deploy their applications on this network infrastructure.

At present the foreign and private sector banks are in a position to offer the banking services through many delivery channels and integrate both front-office and back-office operations.

The delivery channels;

- Internet Banking
- Phone Banking
- ATM
- ABB.

Since it's the customer who is the king in any business, the PSBs are confused in deciding which one of the following methods suits them best

- To satisfy the customer first, just add some additional layer on the existing technology and set up proper back-office systems later
- To revamp everything – right from branch operations, to a new technology.

Many banks have taken the very first approach, i.e. some how come to forefront of the technology by offering all kinds of services on every possible delivery channel.

This requires lot of technology awareness, expertise etc. with in a bank, without which the bank can become a prey of new technology based frauds.

Frauds in Present Technology Environment

With banks deciding on setting up networks and computerize the whole banking process, to offer their services on multiple channels, they now face risks both from inside and outside. This section describes the kind of frauds that can happen in this environment.

Some more avenues for frauds in this emerging banking scenario

- Mail Spoofing – E-Mail Forgery: sending wrong information to bank customers as if its from authentic bank sources
- Web Spoofing – Web Site Forgery: Diverting the customers of a bank to an exactly duplicated forged web site and impersonating those customers on real bank site
- Attacking the User Computer: To take control of that machine
- Attacking a Bank's Server: To take control of that machine
- Media Tapping – recording the whole transactions of a bank, or customer etc. and replaying the same for their advantage
- Denying Service: Though the server is available, making it not able to render service, by poisoning the Network Infrastructure

Mail Spoofing – E-Mail Forgery

This is the first cyber crime in Andhra Pradesh. Kola Mohan, was able to convince several gullible money lenders, top banks and the state's ruling Telugu Desam party that he had won the Euro Lottery and that he was awaiting to complete a few formalities before the millions were transferred to his account in India.

He set the ball rolling in November 1998, just a few months after he actually picked up an Euro Lottery ticket in London, when a prominent Telugu daily received an e-mail (sent by Kola Mohan himself) saying that a Telugu man had won the multi-million dollar Euro lottery but no one had taken notice of this great achievement.

The newspaper promptly published a report and followed it up with an interview without making any attempt to contact any Euro Lottery representative. Other newspapers soon picked up the story and Kola Mohan became a celebrity overnight.

Now it was time to put into motion the second part of his plan. He began calling up money lenders seeking short-term loans which of course he would pay back as soon his "money arrived from London where it was deposited in a bank."

Kola Mohan's dream run continued till creditors began putting pressure on him. By October 1999, the word was out that his claims about his Euro Lottery win were fake.

But Kola Mohan was not going to give up so easily. He showed his creditors some documents issued by the Midland Bank, Sheffield, UK, where he claimed he had made some investments that were due to mature on November 17, 1999.

Around the same time, a Andhra Bank cheque of Rs. 1.73 million issued by Kola Mohan also bounced. Kola Mohan had pledged with the bank the copy of a bond certificate purportedly issued by Midland Bank Trust Company Limited, London stating that a term deposit of 12.5 million pounds was held in his name.

Cause of the above fraud:

1. *Source Address Authenticity never verified:* The e-mail system was developed trying to imitate the postal mail. Just like in postal mail, the "From Address" authenticity was never verified. Though the new mail systems have that capacity, no one can actually stop any one from setting up a mail server that has this flaw. Using this server, anyone can forge a mail posing as an authentic source.
2. *Reply can be sent to a different mail address as preferred by the sender instead of the Source Address:* Another major flaw in e-mail system is that the sender can always set on which e-mail address to get the reply to his mail i.e. the forger can send a mail with the forged source e-mail address; can set its reply address as his own e-mail address, so that the replies reach his actual e-mail address instead of the forged e-mail address.

Due to the above flaws, a forger can easily pose as any well-known personality, without the knowledge of that individual. The receiver always thinks that the mails were from the said address, and his replies go actually to the forger than to the real person.

Web Spoofing – Web Site Forgery

Hackers find new way to bilk eBay users (Source:news.com)

Someone other than Gloria Geary had access to the Washington artist's eBay account.

Using Geary's user ID, the person set up an auction for an Intel Pentium computer chip. Not only that, but the person changed Geary's password so she could no longer access her own account—or cancel the bogus auction.

Geary, who discovered the auction Friday, was able to convince eBay to pull down the auction over the weekend, but not before suffering through a stressful day of worrying about how the auction would affect her legitimate listings.

"I felt totally violated. I was shaking," Geary said. "It's appalling the ease at which they totally took over my account."

Geary is only the latest victim of an increasingly popular scam on eBay. Since January, the company has received a growing number of complaints from people such as Geary who say their accounts have been taken over and used to set up fraudulent auctions. The scam artists make a quick buck, then leave the legitimate eBay users to deal with the furor from bilked bidders.

The scam involved e-mails that asked recipients to log on to a Florida-based Web site, ebayupdates.com, and re-enter financial data for eBay, said Dean White, the Asia-Pacific "Once you've got the credit card information, you can use it for everything," White said. The fake site sported the eBay logo and colours but did not appear to have any connection with California-based eBay.

In a similar fashion, even the bank sites can be forged. The customers of the bank can be lured to log on to fake web site, which exactly looks and behaves as the original, at least till it captures the customers' username and password. These forged web site owners, pose as the real customers of the bank and log on to the real site and do transactions with the already captured username and password. The bad part of the whole issue is that the customers do not have any means of proving that it was not they who did those transactions, but some unknown persons. This kind of fraud has been increasing on Internet, to steal username, passwords and credit card info etc.

Attacking the Users' Computer

In this type, the fraudster implants a virus, Trojan horse into the victim's machine, and using that program he monitors all transactions, steals vital data like username & password and then impersonates the victim. The virus, Trojan horse can be implanted into the victim's machine by using numerous methods like e-mails, IRC – Internet Relay Chat, fake web sites.

Causes for the above crime: Though early e-mail software allowed only messages in text, due to demand from users, the software is made more intelligent in that it can now accept any kind of data, audio, video and executable files; and execute the same just by a click of button. The same is true with Web Browsers and IRC software. These are capable of downloading any kind of executable and run the same instantly.

Attacking the Banks' Servers

In all the above cases, the fraudster didn't touch the technology infrastructure of the bank and so bank is as such not responsible for its user getting impersonated.

However, in this case, the fraudster directly takes control of the bank's server; does transactions impersonating many customers (even the internal staff can be impersonated now) of the bank; and even can delete all the transaction log files of him visiting the bank's site, such that he can't be traced back.

Almost all-general purpose software like Mail Server, Web server, Operating System are plagued by Buffer-over-flow attacks that stem from bad programming practices. These buffer-over-flow flaws in software allow the fraudster execute any command of his choice on the server, by just inputting the command instead of inputting the data-like name, password etc.

Media Tapping

Media tapping involves the fraudster collect all the digital bits that travel across the physical communication wire. Only those, who have physical access to the media, can commit this kind of crime.

Denying Service from Banks' Servers

The aim of these kinds of frauds is to cause inconvenience to the bank by making it disrepute, and take away its customers. The customer just can't access the bank's services.

1. *The network protocol nature:* The TCP/IP protocol, the computer communication language, specifies how a particular task (ex: call initiation) should be performed. But it doesn't specify, how to react in case of exceptions. Different operating systems implemented these exceptions in different manners and this allowed fraudster to take advantage.
2. *Router poisoning:* Routers are like traffic junctions that lead customers to different parts of the network. Just like the signboards at traffic junctions that help motorists find their way, each router keeps routing information (called routing tables) that helps the packets reach their destination. Any one can dupe the router to change its routing table.
3. *DNS spoofing:* Computers communicate through IP numbers, which are unique numbers just like telephone numbers. Unlike telephone numbers, these numbers are difficult to remember. Since it's actually the user who instructs his computer to communicate with the other, one more addressing scheme was devised i.e. computer/host name. So, when the user types the computer name, the name is converted to IP number and using that IP, the communication starts. The service that does this

translation is called DNS – Domain Name System Service. If this DNS service, misbehaves, the user would be diverted to some other server instead of the original server.

Some of our users who automatically renew their VSNL accounts through HDFC BANK site have brought this case to our notice.

So, whenever a user was trying to renew his VSNL account, from the facility offered by HDFC, the users were being diverted to a porn site. After, verifications, the author came to know that it was because of a poisoned DNS server of VSNL.

The office's DNS server, which contacts this DNS server, also got poisoned and it too was diverting all users. Once the office's DNS server is made to point to another DNS server of VSNL, it started working properly. The VSNL authorities were informed of the same.

Technology in Banking: The Future

In the whole above discussion, the bank couldn't utilize any extra benefit from the technology apart from being able to conduct its own business on different channels; at any time and offering more convenience to customer. Instead, its now exposed to many more threats. Its old fashioned frauds in loan and deposits areas couldn't be circumvented with all these technology initiatives. Frauds that involve loan defaulters, same property given as mortgage at different banks, loans to fake companies etc. couldn't be avoided, as there's no way for the bank to check the authenticity of the information. This means, that we have to look from a different perspective altogether from every angle instead of just looking at Bank automation and how to improve Bank Service Delivery.

Many frauds are due to forged documents, forged identity, false information etc. Not only just Banks, but also almost all the organizations on which the Banks depend for authentic information should be computerized, networked and their software applications should share the information online in secure, authentic manner. Unless this happens, whichever technology the banks adopt, whatever control measures they take, frauds do take place.

Web Services/Straight Through Processing

Web Services technology allows, the servers disseminate the information in structured form using XML (extensible Mark Up Language), not only to individual operators, but also to other application servers, irrespective of which software, hardware and database they use. Using this, the other remote applications can easily avail that information to take any decision or process their own business transactions. For Ex: RBI now, allows one to verify whether an individual or a company has defaulted or has become NPA – Non Performing Asset. But to check this, one has to visit RBI web site and query their database manually. It would be difficult for a bank employee to do that, before he sanctions a loan. Similarly, Registrar of Companies database is made available on CD – Compact Disk by NIC – National Informatics Centre. But even this expects one to check individually from that CD only, for a company's information. Same is the case with Land Registration Authority. All have computerized their environments, but they are independent islands. Unless all these computerized applications talk to each other online, no one can actually use it well for better purpose.

For this to happen, RBI, Registrar of Companies, Land Registration database etc. have to set up web services and allow other applications utilize the same. In this case, whether an individual operator verifies the information or not, the loan sanction application verifies the same online and alerts him, in a platform independent way – i.e. all these organizations can set up their services on platforms of their choice but still able to communicate. At IDRBT, a prototype of how these applications interact has been developed. In our prototype these 3 applications i.e. RBI, Company Registrar and Land Registrar are hosted on different platforms and the bank loan processing application is written in Visual Basic.

Application: Online Borrower Verification

The scope of this application has been limited only to verify online the authenticity of the borrower, his company and the property he mortgages while processing a loan form. There are three checks and one direct update of the "Property Record" from the bank into the database of "Land Registration Authority".

Company Registration Check: The *Company Code* is a unique id that identifies a company that is registered with the 'Registrar of Companies'. Once the bank operator enters this code, the application contacts the "Registrar of Companies" database online and displays the entire information of the same, if that code exists. By looking at the information on screen and the information provided to him, the operator can decide on the information. Otherwise, if the code and company doesn't exist at all, the application does not allow any further actions.

Defaulters Check: In case the company is a defaulter, the complete details of where it has defaulted, amount, etc. are returned, as the application directly contacts the "RBI Defaulters Database".

The application also allows search by bank. This requires the *bank code* as the input, and all the companies that have defaulted from the bank are displayed.

Land property Check: This check is carried out only if the above 2 checks are successful. This check involves entering the *Asset ID* (which is unique), which in turn returns the current *status* of the asset (mortgaged/not-mortgaged).

The details of the asset (like the Owner, Date of Purchase, Present worth, etc.) are displayed.

The application does not allow the user to mortgage an already mortgaged asset, by displaying a message that 'the asset cannot be mortgaged'.

In case, the third check is also successful, the application asks for confirmation from the user about mortgaging the asset. If the borrower accepts to mortgaging his asset, the application updates the new status (i.e. mortgaged) in the database of "Land Registration Authority".

Though, it looked very simple in this prototype, it actually requires lot of back ground work from all the organizations. It is very difficult for all these organizations (not only the one mentioned in our prototype, but also others like Insurance, Health Department, Passport Office, Income Tax etc.) to communicate with each other and deploy these services.

Instead a National Body should decide how all these organizations could share which kind of information at what time etc.

Prevention

In this section let us discuss the prevention mechanisms. In all the sections we discussed the technology and the frauds that can occur due to that. A close observation reveals that all frauds happen due to impersonation, sniffing information on its travel and hacking into the computer. The impersonation can be for an individual, a web site, a computer, a router etc. The frauds due to impersonation, sniffing can be minimized by adopting PKI – Public Key Infrastructure. Frauds due to hacking and not able to deploy PKI, etc. can be minimized by firewalls, IDS – Intrusion Detection System.

Security Requirements

The following are the basic security requirements in a remote communication.

Authenticity: In a networked environment, asserting the source of the message has always been of importance. Particularly due to many TCP/IP and Internet applications flaws, the problems of Web Spoofing (forged web sites), IP spoofing (forged IP addresses), DNS Spoofing (forged Domain Names) are of major concern.

Non-Repudiation: The recipient of the message should be in a position to prove that he received the message only from the said sender mentioned in the message, and sender can't deny that.

Integrity: Ensures that the message hasn't been tampered in transit.

Confidentiality: Ensures that only the said recipient of the message can read, but no one else.

Authorization: Able to confirm that the sender has the right to send the message.

Public Key Infrastructure

Public Key Infrastructure assures "Confidentiality", "Authenticity" and "Integrity" of the information which 2 or more members exchange. The PKI relies on Public Key Cryptography and hashing techniques.

Public Key Cryptography: The Development of Public Key Cryptography is nothing short of a revolution in the history of Cryptography. Public Key Cryptography is asymmetric, involving the use of two separate related keys – Public Key to Encrypt; and the Private Key to decrypt with either of the two related keys being used to encrypt, and the other being used for decryption.

Its advantage is that Key Management becomes much easier. If A has to communicate with 10 persons, he need not share 10 different secret keys as in the earlier case. Instead, he just has to share his Public Key, irrespective of the number of people he communicates with. But it is computationally inefficient in terms of speed, and moreover, it also involves a trusted third party, commonly known as Certification Authority.

Hashing Techniques: PKI uses Hashing techniques to ensure the integrity of the message. A hash function generates fixed size hash code for a given message, called message digest. The main characteristics of one-way hash functions are as follows:

- No two messages can have the same message digest
- The message digest is a function of all bits in the message and any change in the data will result in a change in the message digest
- It is not feasible to compute the original message from the message digest.

Using both Public Key Cryptography and hashing techniques, the security criteria "Confidentiality", "Authenticity", "Non-Repudiation" and "Integrity" of the message can be met.

If the Public Key has been used for Encryption, only the one who has its corresponding Private Key can read the message and hence assures confidentiality. If the Private Key has been used for Encryption, only the one who has the Private Key must have sent the message, and hence assures the authenticity and non-repudiation of the message.

Sender "A" to send a confidential message to "B", he does;

- Encrypts the message with B's Public Key
- Computes the hash of the message
- Encrypts this hash (also called signing) with his own private key
- Sends all these three components to B

At the receiving end, B does;

- Decrypts the hash with the Public Key of B and gets the hash sent by A
- Decrypts the message with his own Private Key
- Computes the hash on his own of this message
- Compares the hash sent by A and the one he computed
- If they match, the message has met all security criteria including integrity, if not the message should be discarded

It's actually the software, which does all this at both the places; individuals keep only Private Keys secret.

Digital Certificates: Users of Public Key based systems must be confident that at any time they rely on a public key, the subject that they are communicating with owns the associated private key, and this applies irrespective of whether an encryption or digital signature mechanism is used.

This confidence is obtained through the use of Digital Certificates, which are data structures that bind Public Key values to subjects.

The binding is achieved by having a trusted CA verify the subject's identity and digitally sign each Public Key along with many user credentials. So instead of a Public Key, one has to distribute his digital certificate to the public.

Certification Authority: An authority trusted by many users to issue Digital Certificates and to manage the PKI.

PKI Applications: PKI can be utilized at all levels like;

- Communication among users by issuing digital certificates to users
- Communication among servers and users by issuing digital certificates to servers and users – (SSL uses this mechanism)
- Communication among network devices like routers, switches, computers etc. by issuing digital certificates to these devices (IPSec uses this mechanism).

PKI and Present Deployment: At present PKI is being used very well, for closed corporate business. However, across different networks or Internet, it still has to take a long way. On Internet, for 2 purposes PKI is being used extensively.

8

Mobile Financial Services

Across Europe as a whole, mobile phone penetration is now around 25% (ranging from the low teens in Belgium to more than half the population in Finland). Pre-paid packages were the catalyst for record sales for all four UK mobile network operators in the final quarter of 1998. Vodafone, for example, added 933K new customers in this time (of which 755K were pre-paid) and connected its 5 millionth customer on 15th January. Some 2.5 million mobile phones were sold over the Christmas period alone. The number of digital mobile handsets in circulation in the UK is now around 15 million and climbing steadily, with penetration expected to exceed 50% by 2004.

Note that penetration is likely to exceed 100% in some countries by 2002, because many people will have several mobile phones: a conventional handset in their briefcase, another built in to their car, one in their laptop computer and another in their PDA (personal digital assistant).

PCs (personal computers), despite their power and functionality, are not necessarily the best platform for the delivery of all financial services. According to ICM (a market consulting firm), 29% of the UK population were online at the start of this year. Of these, less than half (14%) access from home and there is a wide variation in household penetration, ranging from 33% of AB homes to only 2% of DE homes. For reference, UK-based market research companies use the ABCDE breakdown for demographics, so the richest households are represented by groups A and B, whereas the poorest are groups D and E. Many people access from a shared PC at home, from work, from educational establishments, libraries and so on. The mobile phone by contrast is, generally, a personal device. People carry their phones with them all of the time and don't share them with others. This makes them a good platform for such things as financial services.

Mobile phones are also digital (at least outside the US!) and GSM (Groupe Speciale Mobile) and PCN (Personal Communications Network or PCS [Personal Communications Systems] in US and Japan) services dominate. GSM has almost half of the global wireless telephony market and more than two-thirds of the digital wireless telephony market. But who cares if phones are digital or not? Well, digital mobile services are based on the use of a tamper-resistant smart card (the Subscriber Identification Module, or SIM) that provides a much higher level of security than anything available on the internet in software. The SIM was originally designed to hold a user's identification data, enabling subscribers to use their GSM handset on any network world-wide. It also allowed subscribers to receive Short Message Service (SMS) messages and store personal information such as telephone number directories. By the way, SMS is exploding. Usage in Western Europe exceeds 1 billion messages per month and is currently doubling every six months.

The GSM/SMS architecture has been wildly successful, but even back in 1993 it was clear that it would have to be extended to support the next generation of value-added services. For reasons of compatibility, it was decided to extend SIM functionality to support additional services on the existing infrastructure and exploit SMS further. The result was the SIM Application Toolkit Specification, often called the "SIM Toolkit" (STK). In this way, applications loaded into the SIM can communicate using existing network infrastructure cost-effectively and operators can add their own applications into the mobile handset using a standard platform (STK) for accessing the keyboard, menus, network and so on.

In addition to the expanding power of the SIM, the data capabilities of the mobile platform are expanding. Data rates will reach 144Kb/s with the introduction of the Universal Mobile Telephone Service (UMTS) and will then move on to 2Mb/s by 2005. UMTS is the new world-wide standard for mobile phones, and it's not that far off: NTT DoCoMo in Japan recently placed the first commercial order for UMTS equipment and expect to launch in 2001. While the higher speeds of UMTS are a year or two away, interim solutions are being found to push GSM data rates up to 14.4Kb/s and then on to 28.8Kb/s in advance of the introduction of High Speed Circuit Switched Data (HSCSD) and General Packet Radio Service (GPRS).

To summarise the situation, then, in Europe alone there are expected to be some 175m GSM users in 2001 (with 67m in Asia-Pacific and 11.5m in North America), with a couple of million new digital subscribers getting connected every month. Jupiter (5/99) forecast that Western Europe internet household penetration will triple from its current 9% by 2003: but almost half of all UK households already have a mobile phone in them. Every one of these handsets has a tamper-resistant smart card at its heart: one supplier alone (Gemplus) shipped it's 100 millionth SIM card in February 1999.

The installed base, the security and the standardisation combine to make the digital mobile handset a formidable platform for personal financial services so operators, networking companies, financial institutions and others are entering a new phase of competition to offer them. A few early examples:

- Scandanvia is, of course, way ahead in combining financial services and mobile phones. The Swedish Postal Bank (Postbanken) and Telia have a service, called Mobil Smart, that allows consumers to make Giro payments from their handsets. Merita Nordbanken's customers can check their balance and transaction logs from their mobile phones: and they do, with 50,000 customers generating 200,000 SMS messages every month. Dagens Industri, Europe's fourth largest business daily, have a pilot running allowing subscribers to receive financial data and trade on the Stockholm Exchange using Ericsson GSM PDAs.
- Citibank have a mobile banking service currently available in Singapore. Consumers can use their mobile handsets to access their account balance, pay bills and transfer funds using SMS (at a cost of Sing$0.20 per transaction). The software uses STK, in either an Alcatel or Motorola Star TAC X handset, to provide menus and functionality.
- Smart Axis, a Unisource spin-off, has been running a pilot service using both Proton and Mondex electronic purses over mobile networks.

  There are also a number of imaginative schemes around linking the power of banking and mobile networks to deliver strong customer propositions other than financial services. For example:
- Over 50% of Portuguese mobile phone customers are anonymous pre-paid subscribers. They use ATM bill payment facilities to

'reload' their mobile phones for more talk time. The advantages of this scheme, to anyone involved in the distribution of pre-paid vouchers for mobile telephony in the UK, are clear.

- Pilot schemes in Scandinavia allow consumers to use their mobile phones to pay at unattended at car parking, soft drinks in vending machines and car washes. The goods and services are charged through the telecommunications operators and show up on the consumers' bills. The benefits of such schemes, to everyone except banks, are clear.

The simplest way to exploit the mobile platform is to use the mobile phone as a personal information delivery platform in combination with banking services. A good example comes from Spain, where customers with certain banks have their account balance sent via SMS to their handset every time they make an ATM withdrawal (which is also a good way of finding out if someone else is using your card!). It would be relatively easy for my bank to send SMS messages out overnight so that when I switched on my phone in the morning I got my current account balance. Two-way SMS can extend the range of services into the transactional. Okobank, the second largest bank in Finland with 4 million accounts, was the first bank in the world to launch transactional services over GSM.

Customers can now request balance and transaction reports, access Visa card services, make domestic payments and pass on instructions over encrypted SMS links. The bank has the same SMS number (1996) with both network operators, making it very easy for customers to send messages. Operators are keen to expand these kind of services: phase 2+ SIMs with 16Kb of memory will soon be superceded by SIMs with flash memory and 32-bit processors and operators want these (at the right price) because they can only differentiate themselves on value-added services, of which finance and banking will be prime examples.

The next level of integration might be to use the mobile phone in conjunction with the internet to personalise the offering, much as Cellnet has done with the Genie service. If consumers can be persuaded to self-configure their financial services over the web, with the results (e.g. share limit minding alerts) delivered to the handset, the cost savings and increased functionality look good together. I might, for example, use my bank's internet banking service to ask for an alert when a particular debit takes place. First Direct recently launched this kind of service (for UKP2.50 per month) and other UK banks cannot be far behind. Mobile operators are implementing over-the-air (OTA) systems for their own use (such as allowing subscribers to update the phone directory in their handset by going to a web site, as Danish operator Mobiltek does), so these systems ought to available for financial services at reasonable cost.

For customers with STK handsets, these personal financial services can be surprisingly sophisticated. Swedish internet broker Teletrades is already projecting 10% of its revenue from SMS-based transactions (each transaction is accomplished using four SMS messages). Italian trading house Directa has launched a similar service. Thus the combination of STK and a handset (with no keyboard, mass storage, big screen or any other 'luxury') can deliver powerful services.

An altogether higher level of integration is to use the mobile phone as a platform for the next generation of smart card-based banking services by moving the SIM on to a multi-application platform and then providing additional functionality by adding applications. Telecom Italia Mobile (TIM) and Swisscom have placed orders for several million Java cards for deployment this year. The cards, which cost around double the $7 per card that operators pay for volume STK cards, incorporate Java SIM and Java STK applications. Operators and third party providers can then downloaded new Java "applets" over the air to phones out in the field, a good examples being TIM's equity trading application.

Secure mobile applications do not have to be based in the SIM. The synergy between, for example, a bank-issued smart card and the mobile handset looks very powerful. The bank card provides security and payment services, the handset provides to most flexible and convenient platform for using those services. Therefore, perhaps the most flexible approach comes through the addition of a second, external, smartcard interface to the mobile handset.

This would have many benefits, allowing the use of third-party smart cards without using the SIM and supporting independence between network operators and other card issuers. The use of an additional slot (in fact an additional 8 slots) is already a standard within the GSM world as it has been defined as an optional Class 3 service for STK.

This structure means that an STK application (a mobile banking application, for example) can control a second card, such as an EMV card (Europay Master Card/Visa which is the standard for chipcard credit/debit cards), for example, through the handset.

A number of manufacturers have already announced 'dual slot' handsets and work on integrating third-party cards is already underway. One of the first trials of this combination of technologies is the Visa Cash pilot, enabling a thousand customers in the Leeds area to download e-cash over Cellnet's GSM network on to a smart Barclaycard by inserting it into a specially designed Motorola Star TAC mobile phone. Merita Nordbanken is to pilot a WAP-based service using smart Visa cards for online payments.

France Telecom is planning to launch a service with Carte Bancaire later this year so that consumers can pay for goods and services by inserting their CB card into the second slot. Further afield, Mobile One in Singapore will soon launch second slot phones to take the NETS e-purse and for remote loading and payments.

It is important to note that all of the technological aspects of these services are in place already: it's really not difficult to get personal financial services on the move. For many organisation, the imperative for doing so is more about positioning for the arrival of 3rd generation (UMTS) services in the near future. The thinking is straightforward: service providers can learn about business models and relationships by deploying basic services using STK, SMS and two-slot handsets. This means that they have all of the non-technical factors in place for the arrival of the powerful next generation handsets, WAP (Wireless Application Protocol, the emerging standard for mobile handsets) and high-speed data connections that will become consumers' indispensable companions.

It is the non-technical factors that pose all of the really hard questions about the branding of services (and the smart cards that drive them), applications, loyalty schemes and even the money used in transactions. It is a reasonable technological prediction that multi-application smart cards and financial services will be central to the next phase of the evolution of mobile services, but it is virtually impossible to predict what this will mean in business terms.

The Internet Banking Horizon: Bleak or Bright for Community Banks?

As the sun goes down in a small Texas town, a customer of a small community bank logs onto the bank's Internet banking system to pay bills. According to industry experts, this remote online banking customer is certainly not alone. More and more consumers are banking on the Internet, and so are an overwhelming number of businesses of all sizes.

Why, then, do industry opinions and predictions about the future of Internet Banking vary so dramatically? On which statistics should bankers base their Internet purchasing decisions? What's smoke and what's fire in this new, blazing industry? This is a looming concern in the minds of today's bankers, especially community bankers, striving to remain competitive in a rapidly changing banking landscape. The mega-banks in the industry have been online for some time now, and many community banks have followed suit with transactional websites.

According to American Banker, more than two-thirds of the 227 transactional Websites counted in June of 1998 by the FDIC are offered by banks and thrifts with assets of less than $500 million. While this remains a small age of community banks (there are over 10,000 in the U.S.), the rate of adoption of Internet Banking does not seem to be subsiding at this point.

Growth of E-commerce

The growth of electronic commerce as a whole speaks volumes about the potential growth for Internet banking in particular. By the end of 1997, 10 million people across the United States & Canada made purchases—from airline tickets to books and automobiles—on the World Wide Web, up from 7.4 million people just six months earlier. According to Forrester Research, 43% of United States households have PC's, and demand is growing among low-income consumers.

In addition, 25% of United States households now have Internet access. The U.S. Department of Commerce also reports that Internet traffic is doubling every 100 days, and business use is growing fastest. As consumers and companies become more familiar and comfortable with making purchases online, this increase in knowledge and comfort level will benefit banks by bringing more retail and commercial consumers to their virtual branches. Even smaller banks and rural institutions will see more consumers moving online to take advantage of Internet convenience.

Industry Predictions

Business-to-business commerce on the Internet is expected to grow forty-fold, from $8 billion in 1997 to $327 billion in goods and services traded between companies, by the year 2002, says Forrester Research. Mentis Corporation predicts that by the year 2000, an estimated 50% of all banks and 40% of banks with less than $1 billion in deposits will offer online services to their customers. The FDIC estimates that the number of financial institutions with transactional websites will increase by more than 50% by the year 2000. According to some industry sources, however, the future is not so bright. Only an estimated 4-5% of online surfers currently bank on the Internet. In addition, a recent poll by PSI Global found that out of 1,000 online users who do not bank online, only 29 believe that online banking is safe.

This perception from consumers merely tells banks that educating consumers on the safety and risks involved in Internet transactions is key to attracting and retaining more online clientele. Despite the message from industry soothsayers who predict that industry growth and consumer acceptance of Internet banking is still decades away, Internet banking continues to spread like wildfire.

9

The Evolution of Online Investment Banking

Introduction

In the past few years there has been a growth in Internet markets where companies and investors can buy and sell initial public offerings (IPOs) of corporate stock. In fact, by early 1999, the mechanics of Internet IPOs had quickly progressed from the first phase, a partial distribution of IPO shares directly to investors via the Internet, to the actual determination of the offer price and the allocation of shares through an online auction process.

Internet-based investment banks provide companies with a choice of whether to use a traditional investment bank, or one that provides the new online services to distribute some portion of their IPO.

When companies are considering an IPO they must first evaluate the financial issues to decide whether it is a viable financing option, and second they must identify which channel(s) they wish to use to distribute the IPO. In this article we focus on the second decision. This is an important topic because it potentially affects all public companies, or companies considering going public, the investment banking industry, and all stock investors. The importance is also indicated by the fact that in 1999 a record $74 billion was raised through 511 initial public stock offerings with new issues posting an average first-day gain of 68.3 [Kapadia 2000].

Traditional IPO Process

The traditional IPO process involves the issuing firm, an investment bank that acts as an intermediary between the seller and buyers, and a select group of typically larger investors. The investment bank provides services such as pricing the stock, forming syndicates of investment banks and their brokerage arms to distribute shares, providing access to a select group of large investors to facilitate distribution and, if need be, supporting prices in the IPO after-market by placing its own buy orders for the stock. Prior to the offer, the investment bank contacts its buying clientele and explains the details of the offer and the selling company.

During this time the investment bank assesses interest in the IPO and takes preliminary subscriptions for shares. The bank then uses this information to determine the price and the number of shares to sell. Because many IPOs are over-subscribed, the bank pro-rates the shares during the final distribution based on the original subscriptions. This service comes at a price, however, as the investment bank receives a commission — typically based on the amount of money raised in the IPO.

This process has been used for IPOs for well over a century, but some questionable activities have evolved during that time. There is the practice of spinning, where the investment bank allocates shares to favoured or potential customers in hopes of winning future business. One could argue that by spinning, investment banks preclude the average investor from some potentially attractive IPOs. There is also underpricing. The stock price run-up of the average IPO on the first day of trading is so great, that it appears that investment banks are often setting the offer price too low. Theories have emerged to explain the existence and magnitude of underpricing and defend it as an efficient way to clear the IPO market. However, there is still a real possibility that many companies are being sold too cheap.

Consider the case of Theglobe.com, a Website builder that debuted in February 1999. Theglobe's bankers, Bear Stearns and Volpe Brown Whelan, underwrote its shares for $9, raising $27.9 million in capital. On the first day of trading, the price rose to $63.50. Had Theglobe sold the IPO for $63.50, rather than $9, the company would have collected not $27.9 million but $197 million-seven times the money to build the brand and develop new products [Tully 1999]. Given these transaction costs and a less than open IPO market, a new information technology enabled IPO may offer a solution.

Online Investment Banks and the Changing Role of Intermediaries

The primary difference between the traditional and online IPO process is the role of the intermediary. Bakos (1998) identified eight functions of a market that are facilitated through intermediaries. They include determination of product offerings, search, price discovery, logistics, settlement, trust, legal, and regulatory. The differences in the anticipated phases in the diffusion of online IPO processes can be described using these intermediary roles. The phases occur as the participants in the process search for greater market efficiency (reduced transaction costs).

The roles of intermediaries in Phase I, partial share distribution via the Internet, include providing market access and IPO information (search), IPO share offer price information (price discovery), as well as informing the investor that the intermediary feels that the selling company is reputable (trust). For Phase II, price determination via the Internet, the search and trust roles are similar, but the share price is determined not by an offer price but through an auction or negotiation mechanism. The future may bring a Phase III, dis-intermediation, where the IPO process intermediary is no longer necessary. This phase will only take place when the trust between the share buyer and seller can be facilitated without an intermediary firm.

Each form of online IPO involves the same seller, but a different form of intermediary. The online investment bank provides an Internet-based IPO offering a more open IPO market with access to a larger number of smaller investors. Bob Lessin, CEO of Wit Capital, identified this as a primary goal: to level the Wall Street playing field by giving the little guy, individual investors, a chance to invest in a company when it first offers shares to the public and before the stock actually begins trading in the markets [Dorsey 1998]. An example of a phase I online IPO process is Wit Capital. It allows the investor to subscribe to shares at the offer price via the Internet, using Wit Capital's homepage to peruse pertinent documents concerning the issuing firm. While only a small portion of shares is now allocated to those online investment banks in the distributing syndicate, it appears to be expanding.

The next phase of the online IPO process has been developed by William Hambrecht, owner of W. R. Hambrecht & Co. Using Mr. Hambrecht's plan, dubbed OpenIPO, investors submit bids for the number of shares they would take and at what price. After a few weeks of taking bids, the offering price is set at the lowest price at which all shares can be sold. Those bidding above the offering price will get all the shares they asked for at the offering price; those bidding at the offering price will get a portion of their bid; and those bidding less than the offer price will not get any shares. No more than ten per cent of the shares sold can go to a single bidder, and Hambrecht reserves the right to limit the purchase of anyone seeking to buy more than one per cent [Bransten and Wingfield 1999].

As of the end of 1999 there has not been a significant amount of IPO share sales directly from companies to investors without any intermediary. But, the potential savings in fees and commissions for both the offering company and the investors may be large enough to move toward a disintermeidated process.

Summary and Conclusions

Raising equity in public markets involves many choices for the issuing firms. Among these choices is how much stock to offer and at what price. They must also decide whether to use an investment bank to underwrite the issue and, if so, which investment bank.

Traditionally, the underwriter pre-sells the entire offer to its clients-thus determining an optimal offer price and the demand for the issue. However, this traditional method has led to some questions as to some of the practices of the underwriter.

For example, is the offer price discounted in an effort to satisfy the underwriter's preferred customers? While there are theories describing deep discounting as an equilibrium market clearing process, the practice suggests that the firm may not have received an optimal price for its stock. Recently, the IPO process has experienced some significant changes involving the Internet In the first phase, a portion of the issue was distributed via the Internet.

A preliminary analysis suggests there has been no fundamental changes in the underlying mechanics of the IPO. In the second phase, both the offer price and the investors are determined through an online auction mechanism.

This may result in a more efficient offer price for a company's IPO and certainly implies a gradual dis-intermediation process as the need for brokerage and other solicitation activities of investment banks is mitigated. However, if deep discounting is required to clear IPO markets, an analysis may uncover the same phenomenon regardless of the price discovery and distribution mechanism.

In the future, when firms are deciding how to distribute their shares, they must compare the risks associated with using a new, relatively untested, online investment bank to distribute a portion of an IPO versus the potential increase in capital received resulting from this new process.

Internet Payments: Momentum or Muddle?

As movements in the Internet payments market indicate, the state of payment transaction processing in the Internet space remains nearly as liquid as ever. SET is late coming to market and now battles firmly entrenched SSL-based offerings. Payment companies, both public and private, are having a slippery time of it trying to establish strong market share and turn a profit-or in some cases even recoup money sunk in R&D holes.

Following the jagged path of one company, Cyber Cash, gives an indication of the difficulty even the earliest mover has had in making a living selling payment systems geared toward the Internet. Looking to crack the consumer and merchant behaviour problems it has faced since the public introduction of its wallet in late 1994, Cyber Cash has now released its thin wallet-aimed at reducing the high transaction drop-off rate. Earlier this year, the company made a series of announcements: acquisition of competitor ICVerify to move it beyond the Internet payments space; a technology swap with IBM to gain a SET solution while giving IBM an SSL-based product; and the acquisition of customers from the payments business of First Virtual Holdings, another early mover.

The list of fluid business models continues. Veri Fone, the market share leader in physical POS solutions has struggled with its SET product and has recently undergone a restructuring into hardware and software business lines. IBM, as mentioned, has had to look to Cyber Cash for a near-term solution. On the SET side, Irish firm Trintech has not met great success with its products and has gotten more funding tweak its products, and even ambitious must wait in part for other powers (such as the credit card associations) to make SET happen. SET in itself is a story-and bodies are falling to the wayside with frequency over the slow-moving standard, including heads of SET teams at Veri Fone and Master Card.

SSL, Anyone?

Looking over the remaining landscape reveals a patchwork of out-of-the-box and homegrown solutions for getting payments from the consumer to the bank and the money in the merchant's till. Clearinghouse solutions such as Cyber Source and Order Trust co-exist with POS product/service combos such as Clear Commerce, and Open Market's Transact. All of these are SSL-based systems, but none take into account the unique business model of the Internet and all use the time-tested physical electronic payment infrastructure. Lowest on the food chain are the likely thousands of merchants who take a credit card number unsecured, secure over SSL but hand-entered into a POS box, or just have the buyer call or fax the number.

This diversity of methods and solutions (though some would call it chaos rather than diversity) maps somewhat to the development of the non-Internet electronic payments world some 20 years ago. However, in today's market, several market leaders have emerged-such as Veri Fone on the POS terminal side and First Data on the processor side.

In this market, the processors have remained the same, but the POS market that has changed and middlemen such as Payment Net and Cyber Cash have emerged. The fundamental difference between old-school electronic payments and the Internet is that the POS environment is more distributed, with more pieces scattered to the client, merchant, acquirer, and sometimes the processor. The penetration is contingent upon both the brand of "cash register" chosen as merchant server and the flavour of Internet payment available from the merchant's bank-if the merchant can even get an account at all.

Controlling the Chain

While this distribution schema is also somewhat existent in the physical payment schemes of today, in the Internet space vendors fight to control the whole payment chain from end to end-which makes breaking into the market harder. At the same time, payment technology vendors struggle with the paradox of asking the consumer to form loyalties to a client component for which the vendor's brand is secondary, while asking the financial institution to stake its brand on untested and untrusted new software.

This is the fundamental reason why some vendors, such as Cyber Cash and the SET vendors, have lowered their profiles even more and receded into the background as a processor.

Transparency has become one of the top priorities in the industry, with efforts made to lift the download, installation, and maintenance burdens off of the merchant and customer. Cyber Cash lightened the load on merchants with Cash Register and will do so again with the thin wallet Product, Insta Buy and the Agile Wallet. Globe Set has gone server-side with some of its components, and we expect similar announcements to follow. It seems thin is now "in" for Internet payments.

Banks Must Take Over

It hardly seems to need mentioning, considering that banks are in the payment business, but banks now have a golden opportunity for additional service revenue laid at their feet. Banks, of all parties involved, have the most arrows in their quiver when it comes to being successful payment merchants.

They have large operation centre environments and big iron in the back office, which can handle not only large volumes but hosting of server-side wallets and public key infrastructure as well. They also need new sources of service revenues as lucrative assets bleed off to mutual funds, insurers, etc. Lastly, but most importantly, they remain the most trusted link in the chain.

Opportunities for banks to increase their presence in this space are multiplying quickly. Internet user numbers are reaching the critical mass needed to justify the medium as a stable channel. Likewise, the big merchants that banks love to serve are now moving online and high-traffic points are becoming clear.

Citibank's deal with Netscape's Netcenter and buy-in to Trans Point demonstrates that some banks are recognizing the value of the medium for branding, and with the competitive nature of the portal business alone, we expect copycat deals will follow quickly. This will create, among other things, a co-branding opportunity for payment client distribution and joint marketing opportunities for merchant customers.

Conclusion: Time to Strike is Now

We believe some banks will soon take up this challenge and see the obvious (and now stable) connections between marketing, payments, and the Internet-as is occurring in the smart card and bill payment markets. We believe some large partnerships will soon emerge, spurring activity among banks to grab the branding opportunities that have been present for several years. We expect this to be a marketing land-grab at first, as smart cards, SET, and bill payment are backed up behind Y2K and Internet banking in the technology queue. Nonetheless, we believe opportunities inherent in the integration of the Internet and its related opportunities will be a key differentiator between banks that will fully realize the value of their technology investments in the next decade and those that won't. Internet payments remain a muddle at present, but in our opinion the chance to turn that muddle into momentum for a group of key players is at hand.

Internet Banking Services vs. Proprietary Solutions: Why the Internet is Deemed to Succeed

Will Internet banking ever take off? Should Banks consider deploying the infrastructure and acquiring the necessary know-how to run an Internet based service?

After all, there are several other ways to make payments electronically, such as home and corporate banking dial-up services, value added networks (VANs), POS, etc. These systems have been designed specifically to deal with payments, whereas the Internet, an insecure network, has been developed for completely different purposes. Moreover, existing electronic payment procedures integrate well with the current world banking system, which is based on political and economical boundaries which separate the economies, isolating the banking systems from systemic risk. The Internet, on the other side, is intrinsically international.

Why should Internet services eventually take off? To this question, there can be several answers. First of all, the cost of a communication network is largely fixed. Therefore, the production of network services is subject to economies of scale. For instance, it has been calculated that the break-even point for the U.S. ATM network is achieved with at least 1,000 interconnected ATMs and with at least 2,000-2,500 operations per month on each machine. The more a network is wide, and the more are its users, the less will be the average cost. Proprietary networks, designed for one or a few banks are, therefore, economically less efficient. Economic forces push towards the integration of networks. As the Bank of Italy recognises, "the advantages of new technology can only be achieved with systems accessible by a large number of users and able to interconnect". According to a research by the Hitachi Research Institute, today VANs are frequently designed to be able to interconnect with VANs of other companies and of banks, in order to maximise the amount of data that can circulate in electronic form.

This need puts the Internet at an advantage: it is already, today, the point of connection between many company networks. It offers a common protocol, TCP/IP, that allows each machine to connect to any other. While negotiations to achieve a common world-wide EDI standard never seem to reach an end, the Internet is already a de facto communication standard. With the potential to become a generic network, where all sorts of information travel, from usenet to images, from payments to advertising. Such a network would avoid duplications of functions, and be economically very efficient.

Furthermore, since the value of a payment instrument is directly proportional to the number of its users, it is normally difficult to find a balance between competition and co-operation. If banks start building competing payment networks, none of them will reach the critical mass of users to achieve profitability. On the other hand, if they co-operate and design only one payment system, the industry risks turning into a cartel. The solution could be to make the payment system independent of the physical infrastructure, the network. This can only be achieved if the network is a simple, "neutral", communication medium, such as the Internet. This would allow anyone to deploy his own software-based payment system, without having to undergo the huge investments necessary to build the communication network, which would give an advantage to large firms over small ones.

Internet payment systems are, mostly, software-only solutions, relying on the existing hardware and network infrastructure. This means that even small companies can afford to design and deploy their own payment system. Most of the companies which are developing payment systems are, in fact, quite small. At the same time, all Internet payment systems use the same protocol, TCP/IP, and can therefore be interconnected more easily. Competition is thus enhanced, without undermining profitability and interoperability.

But what about the most important feature of a payment system, security? Any successful payment system will be subject to intense attacks. The difference between Internet payment systems and specific EDI networks is that, on the Internet, it is much easier to intercept and monitor messages. However, any electronic payment system needs to reach households and firms. Whereas the network backbone can be designed in a safe way, data can only reach the customers through the telephone lines or TV cables. Telephone lines are not much more secure than the Internet itself: anyone with a superficial knowledge of electronics can tap communications by connecting on the cable somewhere on its way to the customer. Security will have to be provided by protecting the message itself, not the communications line. This can only be achieved through encryption. And, under this respect, the Internet is not at a disadvantage.

On the demand side, the most important trend for what concerns payments is, today, the globalization of markets. Whereas in the past this tendency involved only large multinationals, the integration of European markets and the lowering of trade barriers imply that even medium and small companies have to compete in the international arena. This, in turn, gives rise to one unsatisfied need: that of fast, homogeneous, international payment procedures. Today's banking system is not designed to satisfy the payment needs of many small and medium customers. Whereas large corporations and institutions can move capital from one country to the other and change it from one currency to the other in real time, the typical retail international payment takes from days to weeks, and can be very expensive. The banking sector does not have the incentives, per se, to improve the situation, since the slowness of payments imply a revenue from the so-called "float" for the bank: between the time when the payor makes the payment and the time the payee receives it, the bank can earn an interest on the money.

On the other hand, Internet payment systems are designed as international, and compete on a global market. Being almost fully automated, they remove any "alibi" for slowness, and are a spur for the improvement of conventional banking services.

Finally, the Internet is a potential market. There is a multimedia communication protocol, the WWW, companies, and about 30 million customers world-wide. The only element which is missing is safe payment systems. If banks miss the chance to enter the market, they could lose their monopoly over payment services. Once people get used to Internet payment systems for on-line shopping, which promise to be very efficient, why should they walk to their bank to make a wire transfer?

The Use of "Internet Money"

The debate around electronic commerce and payments on the Internet is being carried out with little reference to the way the residential user will use the new form of Internet money, that is money which uses the Internet as the main transaction mode. Instead of the user being at the centre of the discussion, the focus has been on the new payments instruments such as e-cash, stored value cards and electronic checks and the growing use of e-mail and the Internet as transaction media.

This is resulting in public policy and corporate decisions being taken without understanding how this new form of money will shape and be shaped by social relations and cultural values. It has prevented the realization that a new form of money is emerging, which is different from previous electronic and non-electronic monies. It has also blocked questions of how and why people mix and match different forms of money. This is why we are again hearing the prophecies of the 1970s and 1980s, that we are at the threshold of a cashless, checkless, branchless society.

In this paper, I place the user at the centre of the discussion. This shifts attention away from payments instruments and transaction modes within the banking framework and focuses it on forms of money. The new form of Internet money is discussed in the first section. In the second section, I show how people continue to use a mix of new and traditional forms of money, though the balance in the mix is changing. In the third section, I submit that the reason for the mix is that people use different forms of money as one of the ways of separating the multiple kinds of money that exist in the market and non-market spheres of life. Information is the key to the congruence between the form and kind of money.

This analysis is primarily based on open-ended interviews of 50 persons from 24 predominantly middle-income Anglo-Celtic households in Melbourne and the surrounding rural areas, between March 1995 and February 1996. Their use of electronic money was investigated within a wider framework of the use of information and communication technologies in the home. The analysis also builds on my doctoral thesis entitled Marriage, money and information: Australian consumers' use of banks (1994).

Internet Money: A New form of Electronic Money

Forms of money combine transaction modes and payments instruments. They can be broadly grouped as physical and electronic, depending primarily on the transaction medium used. Physical forms of money include physical payments instrument and physical transaction media. They comprise cash and checks transacted person-to-person and across the bank branch or post office counter. It would also include checks sent by mail. Along the continuum between the physical and the electronic are plastic cards transacted physically across the counter. Electronic forms of money include those that involve payments instruments with no physical representation such as direct debit and credit and the electronic versions of cash and checks. Plastic cards used with electronic media such as automated teller machines (ATMs); electronic funds transfer at point of sale (EFTPOS); the telephone and fax; email and Internet form the most common instance of the electronic form of money. It has to be noted that an electronic transaction such as getting cash from an ATM or cash-out from EFTPOS yields a physical payments instrument.

Moreover, an electronic money transaction often results in an immediate physical record as with credit card payments over the counter, ATM and EFTPOS payments and withdrawals.

The new Internet money, that is the form of money using Internet as the main transaction mode, builds on payments instruments such as credit cards and direct debit and credit and electronic versions of cash and checks. It differs from earlier forms of money in that it is both impersonal and virtual. There is no identifiable person at the other end of the transaction as when paying via EFTPOS or with a plastic card across the counter. It does not result in physical cash unlike the ATM or EFTPOS withdrawals. Internet money also does not automatically generate a physical record which is evidential in nature. The closest approximation to Internet money is using the plastic card over the phone, fax or mail. But the phone, fax and mail are less virtual than the Internet, in that the potential for personal interaction and a physical record of transaction, is greater.

A Mix of New and Old Forms of Money

For most Australians, cash, the check and the branch remain the dominant payments and transactions mechanisms. Despite a fast rate of growth in electronic payments and transactions, these traditional forms of money continue to remain important for Australian consumers.

- Cash remains the most popular and convenient way of paying for everyday transactions of small value in Australia. Though there is no hard evidence, it is estimated that some 90 per cent of the number of transactions are in cash.
- The check is the most popular form of non-cash payment in Australia. In 1995, its volume (38%) exceeds that of credit cards (10%) EFTPOS (13%), ATM (17%); direct entry credit (18%) and direct entry debit (4%).
- Though high-value electronic funds transfer is now for the first time higher in value (63%) than checks (35%), checks continue to dominate over retail low value electronic funds transfer which remain unchanged between 1991 and 1995 at 2%.
- Though payment by cards is increasing, it still comprised only 0.1 per cent of cashless transactions in value.
- The number of ATMs and EFTPOS outlets is increasing in Australia. However Australians continue to conduct about 50 per cent of all transactions through the branch (Ayling, 1996). Empirical research suggests that the branch remains an

important access point for banking, even when persons have electronic access.

It is difficult to go beyond this picture to detail the use of different payment and transaction mechanisms. As the Australian Payments System Council notes in its 1994-1995 annual report, "Limited data are available on the number of payments, and there is limited detail on the relative usage by consumers of different payment instruments". Hence there is no data on the public record about the use of different forms of money. However, the macro picture shows that even 22 years after Bankcard was introduced in Australia and 15 years after the first bank ATM, physical forms of money continue to dominate.

Socio-economic factors like income and literacy are important for drawing the outer limits of access to bank accounts, plastic cards, personal computers and modems. Access to bank branches and ATMs is also a limiting factor in some rural areas pushing people more to the use of EFTPOS on the one hand and checks paid personally or across the post office counter on the other. These factors are less useful, however, for predicting the way people use different forms of money.

The micro picture shows that even among the early adopters who use Internet money, there continues to be a mix of different forms of money. The quality of this mix varies even for different members of a household, where the wife may use more cash from the bank branch, ATM or EFTPOS than the husband who may use more checks and the credit card. Some of the differences of the mix can be explained by life stage and gender roles. However one needs to go further than this to explain why a person in Melbourne who uses Internet money to buy books from Boston and information services from Colorado also pays his utility bills by checks at the bank branch or the post office.

Matching Forms of Money to Kinds of Money

In this section, I argue that people continue using various forms of money, because this is one of the ways they separate grocery money from mortgage money; tax-deductible expenditure from non-tax deductible expenditure; utility bills from discretionary spending on the weekly Tattslotto or scratch tickets. These different kinds of monies require different levels of information for accountability. For instance, it is important to have a physical record for tax-deductible expenses for the Tax Department. Similarly it helps to be able to prove that utility bills have been paid. Hence the popularity of checks for these kinds of monies. The need for certainty that the mortgage has been repaid makes direct debit the most frequent option. Credit cards used across the counter are the most frequent choice for paying for incidental business expenses. Often a separate credit card is devoted solely to business expenses so that the statement of accounts is separated from personal expenditure on the pesonal credit card.

It is usually not critical to have an evidential record of grocery expenditure. It is important though, if one is on a tight budget, to know on a continuing basis how much money has been spent and how much money remains. This explains the popularity of physical cash, for that alone gives immediate information on money spent and money still in hand. This association of cash and grocery shopping is further strengthened by a general aversion to the use of credit for food.

The information dimensions that are important for forms of money and kinds of money are those tat relate to time; range and record. Does it yield or require immediate information or will retrospective information suffice? Does it give information on money spent or also money still in hand or in the account? Is the record evidential, discretionary, or is there no record at all? On these information dimensions is also overlaid a person's sense that some information is more reliable than others. Preliminary analysis of the qualitative data shows that reliability of information is related to whether the information is obtained personally or impersonally; whether it is physical or virtual. These aspects relate to the payments instrument and to the mode and context of the transaction.

An investigation of psychological factors is important to discovering why some persons are more comfortable only with personal and physical information while others can handle different degrees of impersonal and virtual information. However, it is a more complicated issue than putting one measure of reliability against one personality type, for as noted earlier, the same person can use both forms with equal ease for different kinds of money.

The preliminary conclusions from the qualitative research are that where possible, a person tries to personalize electronic money, either through familiarity with the merchant, the intermediary, or the individual recipient. This is an important point to verify, for the use of Internet money will depend on users' comfort with the impersonal and virtual nature of this form of money. Or conversely Internet money will be shaped by users' desire to personalize the money and/ or ensure that some part of the transaction generates a physical record.

The Role of the Central Bank in the Growing Industry of Internet Payments

What role could, or should, Central Banks play in the Internet payments industry ? It is a difficult question, as it is not yet clear how, and to what extent, such industry will develop, and whether governments will allow such developments. According to some, Internet payments are a matter of private initiative, and the Central Bank should play no role at all. They dream of an unregulated world, where multiple currencies, as well as baskets of currencies and other assets, are equally accepted as means of payment. Others point out at the risks of such a scenario, and at the increased volatility and unpredictability of financial prices that it could cause.

Economic theory is not helpful either. Even though the payment system as a whole is crucial to economic stability, and is, indeed, one of the main concerns of Central Banks, it is seldom taken into account in economic models. It is normally considered as part of the institutional context or analysed through its effects, mainly on the banking system, the monetary and financial markets, the instruments of monetary policy. The problem with this approach is that it is static, as it considers the payment system and the institutional context as given. Furthermore, if the traditional Central Banking institutional model is clearly becoming rapidly outdated, elaborating a new one poses several problems.

Globalization and the growing integration of national payment systems, as well as the increasing amounts of payments handled through private clearing houses requires an international approach, at least on a G10 level. However, as Mr. Padoa Schioppa, of the Bank of Italy, says, "*the road to define a new institutional model must be different from the ones adapted in the past. At the beginning of this century, an agreement on how to manage a monetary system based on currency and deposits was only reached after a financial and monetary crisis. It would be extremely dangerous to pass through a similar learning process today, not least because payment systems in the industrialised world would amplify the problems of any single market operator, diffusing its effects to the whole economy*".

Traditionally, Central Banks have four duties: they manage monetary policy, they supervise the payment system, they promulgate regulations, and, in many countries, they supervise the banking system as a whole. Each of there roles is going to be affected, in a way or another.

As a monetary authority, the Central Bank will have to adapt its procedures to the new context. I believe that its ability to control monetary aggregates will not be seriously thwarted, at least in the short and medium run. Internet payment instruments are indeed a new financial instrument, significantly different from traditional ones, but many innovations have changed and are changing the banking and financial industry. Furthermore, current and projected volumes for the next few years are not large enough to have significant macroeconomic effects. Probably changes and adaptations will be required in the econometric models used to predict the trends of economic variables, as variables such as the velocity of money, capital mobility, etc. could be affected.

Other effects could derive as a result of the current trend of institutional de-specialisation. Today the monopoly held by banks over the payment industry is increasingly being threatened by non banks. Department store credit cards are an example of such new competitors. Internet payment instruments, if provided by non banking institutions, could increase this tendency. As Central Banks enforce monetary policy through their "special" relationship with banks, a decreased importance of such institutions could decrease its effectiveness.

The role of the Central Bank as supervisor of the payment system will be affected too. Central banks can take part in the payment system in three ways:

- through consulting and moral suasion it can spur market operators to adopt certain behaviours, which it believes to be positive for efficiency and stability
- it can promulgate rules which bind market operators to certain behaviours (ex. legal reserve requirements)
- it can choose to offer directly certain services, if the other two options are impossible or too costly (ex. the supply of currency).

It is yet unclear what approach the Central Banks will adapt towards Internet payment instruments. It is likely that, as long as Internet payment instruments are growing, Central Banks will refrain from imposing limits and regulations, to avoid impairing growth. And it is quite unlikely that Central Banks will ever offer Internet payment services. Before deciding to what extent Central Banks should be involved, a serious analysis of the effects of such instruments on the international settlement system should be done. Even if Internet payment instruments target the retail sector of the payment market, and therefore do not imply the same systemic risk of large value payments, at an aggregate level they could still become relevant. Furthermore, current international settlement systems are not made to handle vast amounts of small payments. In the medium term, new ways of settling such payments should be devised.

As a regulator, and as an advisor to the government, the Central Bank is faced with several significant questions:

- how to preserve the integrity of the payment system ? Who is responsible for settlement ? What settlement system should be provided ?
- How to protect customers from bankruptcy of a supplier of payment instruments ? How to treat, from a legal point of view, the new digital instruments ?
- How to deal with the international implications of the Internet ?
- How to ensure competition and transparency ?
- What, if any, standards should payment instruments meet ?
- How to avoid that the new instruments be used for tax evasion or money laundering ?

As a supervisor of the banking system, the Central Bank has to rethink its special relationship with banks. As already said, institutional de-specialisation currently implies that banking institutions face more and more competition from non-banks. The industry of Internet payments is a typical example, as most of the companies who are offering payment services are non-banks. Whereas, in the past, it was sufficient to monitor banking institutions to guarantee the stability of the payment system, today too many payments are not being intermediated by banks any more. Therefore, the scope for offering settlement services and credit of last resort only to banks is becoming less and less relevant. In the future, if Internet payment instruments, as well as several other payment instruments managed by non-banks, are going to take off, it is foreseeable that the regulations applied to banks will be extended to all the companies who wish to operate in the payment industry. This would avoid unfair competition (if non-banks are not subject to the same rules as banks, they have an unfair advantage) and instability. This is the opinion expressed by the Payment System Task Force of the EU.

Furthermore, traditionally Central Banks only monitor national banks. The development of Euromarkets has pushed the Central

Banks of G10 Countries to extend their supervision to foreign subsidiaries of national banks. Internet payment instruments are a further step forward, being completely independent of physical location. It is possible for national companies to sell their products abroad, and for foreign ones to compete in the national market just like national operators. Suppose a European Bank located in Cayman Island starts selling US$ denominated payment instruments to customers in Japan. Which Central Bank, if any, should be responsable?

The problem is even more serious than for other international assets and financial instruments, as Internet payment instruments target families and consumers, and not just financial operators. This means that there is a stronger "*need for protection*" from risks.

It is, however, difficult for a Central Bank to extend its powers to foreign companies, as this would infringe the sovereignty of other States. There are, however, ways to exert some kind of control. For instance, Central Banks can use their powers of moral suasion. In the case of Internet payment instruments, Central Banks could decide to provide those operators who accept to submit themselves to Central Bank controls with a digital certificate proving the stability of the operator. Such certificates would tell customers anywhere in the world that they are accepting a payment instrument which has been declared secure by an independent, non-profit driven institution such as the Central Bank.

Users would quickly learn how to distinguish between certified suppliers and uncertified ones. Such certification would prove to be extremely useful in the process of reputation building, essential to any payment instrument supplier, and could contribute in avoiding crisis of confidence. To conclude, Internet payment instruments will significantly affect Central Bank operating procedures. For the moment, there are no risks of systemic instability, but as these new instruments take off Central Banks will have to adapt their behaviour to take them into account, to avoid that certain behaviours become customs. Such changes will have to take place early enough to avoid that some crisis of one operator gives rise to an overall crisis of confidence in Internet payments.

The Role of Check Images in Internet Banking: An Introduction

Given that we will have to continue to deal with paper checks, at least in the near future, how might we integrate them into the non-traditional forms of banking? One option is not to integrate them. Simply stated, paper forms of payment remain paper and are accessed through traditional methods, (paper checks returned or via microfilm). Another option is to transform the paper checks into electronic information, or digitize them. Digital technology will not only offer integration of this traditional payment form with alternative delivery systems, but it will also enable more efficient processing of checks.

By definition, imaging is digitizing information, (transforming information into a series of ones and zero's) for storage and retrieval. Digital check images can be stored in the same way as digital data, (i.e.: written to magnetic disk, optical platters, or to tape). Check imaging is not new, but technological advances in microprocessor speed, storage, telecommunications, data compression algorithms, and artificial intelligence pattern recognition have assisted in making check imaging more practical and possibly profitable.

Operational Benefits to Digitized Check Information

Banks process millions of checks per day. Conventional processing of checks involves reading MICR (Magnetic Character Information Recognition) line information on items to determine issuing bank. If the issuing bank is one other than the bank of {first deposit}, that check must be physically delivered to the issuing institution to collect the associated funds. Banks in turn withdraw the appropriate funds from customers accounts.

Banks spend a considerable amount of money delivering checks to the issuing financial institutions so that the institution that accepted them can collect the funds. The money that is in limbo while this is happening is money that the check issuing institution can invest. This is currently worth millions per day. If the check images were electronically presented in lieu of the physical paper, checks could be cleared instantly. Checks could be truncated at bank of first deposit and instead of flying checks, images could be electronically transmitted among financial institutions, the Federal Reserve Banks included.

Banks also spend a considerable amount of money storing paper checks and copies, (microfilm). By law, banks must retain this microfilm for a minimum of 5-8 years, (varies state by state). The cost is magnified considering the expense to perform research and inquiries based on this microfilm. Truncating checks and utilizing images can drastically reduce the research functions related to checks. Image technology alone does not bring about all of these benefits. Workflow plays a significant role. Check imaging offers the vehicle by which workflow can be implemented to achieve notable processing benefits.

Potential of Digitized Checks in Internet Banking

Finally, there are options to interface with alternative delivery mechanisms for banking. Because check images can be stored on a variety of media, this creates the potential for check archive systems where check images are stored in a repository. Any authorized user, internal or external to the bank could access a picture of a check in this archive. The Internet provides an extremely viable delivery mechanism for customers external to the bank. For those who still have a requirement to see all their checks with a bank statement, actual checks can be eliminated by digitized pictures enclosed with statements.

The future of alternative forms of banking looks promising and checks appear to be in the equation for some time to come. Image technology provides the opportunity to integrate these two in a harmonious relationship for the banking customer.

10

Public Finance: Practice and Theory

Public finance has both normative and positive elements, and moving between theory and practice requires attention to help us understand both what policies government should adopt and whether it is likely to do so. We should not be surprised when bad policies are adopted in spite of better policies being available if our political system is structured to deliver bad outcomes, for example, if our political environment gives politicians strong incentives to serve narrow interests at the expense of the common good.

But I will focus here on examples where the contrast between normative and positive outcomes is not so clearly explained, and thus where understanding the reasons for observed policy practices might help us develop better positive theories. It is very tempting for an economist frustrated by the state of public policy simply to conclude that politicians do some of the things they do because they do not understand the economic consequences of their actions.

Undoubtedly many public policy actions can be attributed to mistakes and misunderstandings. But when the behaviour in question is widespread and persists over time in the face of information and discussion of its economic consequences, we should consider alternative explanations. There is no shortage of puzzling economic policies practiced by national governments around the world, so my list will be selective. I will focus on cases where standard arguments (misalignment of incentives, corruption, rent-seeking, concentration of benefits, imperfect information, etc.) seem insufficient to explain the divergence between positive outcomes and normative prescriptions, and I will draw most heavily on examples from the United States, with which I am naturally most familiar. For each of the examples on my list, I will discuss the current public policy practice. After presenting my examples I will consider how our positive and normative theories may need to be expanded to understand why things are the way they are, and the lessons we might take for the practice and theory of public finance.

Piecemeal Progressivity

Who should bear a society's fiscal burdens? Most advanced economies have determined that the most equitable approach is a progressive distribution, by which we mean that those with a higher ability to pay, as measured, for example, by income (or consumption, or wealth) should pay a greater share of their before-tax income than those with a lower ability to pay.

How progressive the burden should be, and whether the focus of progressivity should be throughout the income distribution or primarily among the poorest, are reasonable questions for which there is no simple "right" answer. But what is clearer (or at least seems clearer before we confront actual practice) is that what matters is the overall progressivity of the fiscal system.

With many instruments of tax, transfer and spending policy at its disposal, the government can achieve a given degree of progressivity in many ways. As some instruments will be better suited to achieving progressivity than others, it makes sense that the government would utilize those instruments for equity.

As a rule, it is easiest to achieve progressivity using instruments that rely on individual characteristics related to the objective. Most simply, we can use a progressive income tax to achieve a progressive outcome if we wish to place a higher relative burden on higher-income individuals. We may do better still by augmenting our system with instruments based on other characteristics that relate to ability to pay, such as having a disability, being elderly, or having children.

By contrast to these direct taxes and transfers, based on individual characteristics, systems of indirect taxation that are transaction-based are much more difficult to make progressive, because, as the category name suggests, they relate only indirectly to individuals: our objective is progressivity with respect to individuals, not the transactions in which they engage. For example, to achieve progressivity under a value-added tax (VAT), we must determine which goods and services are relatively concentrated among the poor, such as food, and tax these commodities less heavily than others, while at the same time imposing an unusually heavy tax on items preferred by the rich, such as yachts, jewelry, furs and luxury automobiles.

The problem with varying VAT rates in this way, though, is that because we are subsidizing food rather than food purchased by the poor, most of the food subsidy goes to the non-poor. Thus, we would need huge variations in tax rates among commodities to effect much redistribution, which even so would be limited, and in so doing we would produce massive distortions in the purchasing decisions of households, rich and poor alike. In short, if we have a progressive direct tax at our disposal, there is a very convincing argument for using that tax, perhaps in conjunction with other programs based on observable individual characteristics, as our main vehicle for achieving progressivity. And yet, it is standard practice for indirect taxes to reflect the desire to achieve progressivity in their design.

Value-added taxes around the world commonly exempt or tax at a reduced rate food and other necessities. The same practice is observed for the sales taxes imposed by individual states in the United States. Even though there is no sales tax or VAT at the U.S. national level as yet, we have had an important national episode of attempting to use indirect taxes explicitly for distributional purposes.

In 1990, President George H. W. Bush and Congress agreed to introduce a new set of excise taxes on specific luxury goods, indeed on those same goods mentioned above (yachts, jewelry, furs and luxury automobiles) as well as personal-use private aircraft.

This observed practice of what one might call "piecemeal progressivity" is also observed in the administration of some government spending programs, as discussed further below. Its influence is seen even in the law, where a widely-held view suggests that there is a role for the setting of legal rules in part on the basis of distributive objectives.

For example, if those likely to cause damage in a particular context are wealthier than those suffering the damage, then one might assess higher transfers from the violator to the victim, or to the state, than the actual damage caused, in order to further distributive objectives. As in the case of indirect taxation, one can argue for using other, more effective instruments to achieve distributional objectives, leaving legal rules to be designed to promote efficient outcomes that relate penalties to the damage caused. Yet, even in societies with progressive taxation, the shaping of legal rules for redistribution retains its appeal. Perhaps the most remarkable illustration of this practice is the system of speeding fines in Finland, which are based not only on the severity of the offence but also on the violator's income.

This system has resulted in fines as high as €170,000 for a single speeding violation, an amount clearly in excess of the social damage imposed by speeding. What drives the design of the VAT, U.S. luxury taxes, and other policies such as legal rules to incorporate the objective of progressivity when other methods exist and are already in use that are evidently better structured for achieving progressivity? We can start by discarding a common wrong answer, that to make the income tax more progressive would require such high marginal tax rates that the economic distortions would be unacceptable, so that using other instruments is preferred.

This answer is wrong because the other instruments impose the same economic distortions as the income tax, plus others in addition. It does not matter if taxes lower my income or raise the price of the things I buy, and raising the prices of some things I buy and lowering the prices of others introduces another set of economic distortions, to my choices among the things I purchase.

A related argument is that overall tax enforcement might be enhanced by relying on several taxes rather than just one. But this argument, even if it is correct, applies to the revenue we collect from taxes, not their contribution to overall progressivity, and the two do not have to change together. For example, we might lower income taxes and raise indirect taxes while still relying entirely on the income tax to provide a given degree of progressivity, by making the remaining income tax even more progressive.

Perhaps the most common justification for piecemeal progressivity is that while using the income tax might be preferred, this is not politically possible and so other means, even if inferior in nature, must be used. But this argument essentially assumes the conclusion, for it fails to explain why a society would force itself to use one method to achieve an objective when another, superior method is available. This is not an issue of some groups gaining at the expense of others as a result of using the inferior method, since we are, roughly, collecting taxes from the same individuals, but in a less efficient manner.

Some insight into this puzzle might be gained from the 1990 U.S. luxury tax experience. When President Bush and Congress introduced luxury taxes, they did so while also increasing the marginal income tax rate on the highest income individuals from 28 percent to 31 percent. Already under pressure for reneging on his famous 1988 campaign pledge, "read my lips: no new taxes," President Bush would have had to accept even higher increases in the top marginal income tax rate to produce the same revenue and the same estimated tax burden distribution without relying on the luxury taxes.

Introducing the tax increase in pieces, therefore, may have been viewed as a way of hiding the total increase in effective marginal tax rates at the top. Note that a generally different approach was taken by the Tax Reform Act of 1986, which was designed to maintain the existing degree of progressivity by balancing reduced marginal income tax rates with other changes in tax provisions that increased tax burdens.

In 1986, the effects of provisions taken together were emphasized, rather than hidden. Even in 1986, however, the effects of some provisions were presented separately. In particular, the corporate tax increases used to finance individual income tax cuts were commonly left out of presentations of the legislation's distributional effects, perhaps hiding a progressive shift in the tax burden.

The lesson from the U.S. experiences of 1986 and 1990, then, may be that politicians seek to obfuscate distributional effects of tax changes when these changes lead to increased progressivity. Or perhaps the lesson is that politicians do this when they wish to hide the results from their supporters, as might have been the case for the Republican presidents in 1986 and 1990. But how well hidden can the results have been when they were contained in the same piece of legislation and highly publicized? Much has been written recently about the salience of taxation potentially having an impact on individual decisions, although we have little evidence regarding the effects of provisions on such a grand scale, or about whether the salience of tax provisions changes over time. Can individuals who have been subject to the VAT for their entire lives still fail to comprehend that progressivity achieved through the VAT is a substitute for progressivity achieved through the income tax?

And why would the attempted obfuscation take the form of understating progressivity, rather than overstating it? One could argue, I suppose, that politicians are seeking to produce a just society without alienating those who can exert a powerful role in election outcomes, but one could just as easily imagine a world in which politicians make hidden transfers to the powerful to ensure their continued support, producing a tax system that is less progressive than might be apparent. Finally, it might simply be the case that individuals are naturally disposed to thinking about government policies individually, so that an apparently regressive tax seems unfair, even if it is part of an overall fiscal system with a suitable degree of progressivity, and income-based speeding fines seem fair, even if they provide much distorted incentives to those who drive.

In summary, though the economic arguments against doing so are compelling, piecemeal achievement of a progressive distribution of the fiscal burden is a standard feature of national fiscal systems. Why this occurs is still something of a mystery if we use our standard theoretical tools for analysis.

Minimum Taxes and other Individual Limits

The theory of public finance suggests that we should decide on a desired tax base and rate structure and then impose taxes accordingly. But tax codes are filled with additional provisions that seem to reflect ambivalence on the part of tax authorities. While the main provisions of a tax code may specify that a particular type of income is taxable, or that a particular expense is deductible, other provisions override these general principles in particular circumstances in a manner that typically makes tax systems much more complicated.

Among the restrictions of this type that are very common around the world are those that limit deductions for tax losses and interest. Both deductions would be appropriate under the principles of standard income tax design, but one is unlikely to find any tax system that offers unlimited deductions for losses and interest.

In many or perhaps most instances, however, limits on deductions for losses and interest can be rationalized as a tool for overcoming some other defect in the tax system that may be difficult to address directly. In the case of losses, for example, tax authorities may be concerned that a business showing a large loss is more likely to be engaged in fraud than a business reporting income. If fraud is hard to detect, then limiting deduction for losses represents an alternative, even if a very imperfect one that also discourages risk-taking, as we have understood since the work of Domar and Musgrave (1944). Indeed, tax systems commonly allow losses to be offset against previous or future income, attempting to cushion the impact on legitimate firms.

For individual taxpayers, limits on the deduction of capital losses is necessitated by taxation of capital gains only on realization, which gives taxpayers the opportunity to realize losses and hold gains.

Likewise, some limits on interest deductions are aimed at restricting other undesired behaviour. Under so-called "thin capitalization" rules, for example, which limit interest deductions based on the share of debt in a local subsidiary's capital structure, countries seek to prevent multinational companies from using unlimited interest deductions to shift profits generated locally to tax haven countries with low tax rates.

But there are other limits imposed on the basic income tax structure that are more difficult to rationalize. Perhaps the most significant of these is the "minimum tax," so named because it is designed to establish some minimum tax liability for taxpayers who otherwise would owe little or no tax.

The United States imposes minimum taxes in conjunction with both the individual and corporate income taxes. The basic approach of the minimum tax is to apply a lower tax rate schedule than the regular income tax to a broader tax base that includes more income and permits fewer deductions, so that taxpayers who have relatively high levels of such included income and excluded deductions will face a higher tax liability under the minimum tax, even with its lower tax rates, than under the regular income tax.

Under the U.S. individual minimum tax, for example, taxes paid to state and local governments are not deductible, whereas they are deductible to a considerable extent under the regular income tax, so that taxpayers with high state and local tax liabilities are more likely to be subject to the minimum tax.

The origins of the minimum tax tell us something about the motivation behind it. The U.S. minimum tax was introduced by the Tax Reform Act of 1969, following the disclosure by the government that many very high-income individuals had paid no income tax at all through combination of non-taxable income and substantial tax deductions. At first, the minimum tax affected only around 20,000 taxpayers per year and accounted for little revenue. But in recent years, the individual minimum tax has affected around 4 million taxpayers, and its added tax liabilities have accounted for 4 percent of all income tax revenues.

Thus, the minimum tax was introduced as a small measure to deal with outrage about the apparent unfairness of the tax system, but it has become much more important over the years. Unlike in the examples given above relating to limits on losses and interest deductions, however, there is no issue here of the government being unable to address the perceived problem more directly. For example, if the deduction of state and local taxes is seen as inappropriate, the government is fully able to curtail such deductions under the regular income tax.

The original minimum tax may have been justified as a cosmetic measure, the government believing that the tax system as structured was appropriate but needing to deal with public perceptions that it was not. But the current minimum tax is much more than a cosmetic measure, so why does it still exist?

Common explanations offered in the United States provide little real insight on this question. Some suggest that it would be difficult to find additional revenue to replace what would be lost by repeal of the minimum tax, but this argument could be used to explain why any tax remains in place and fails to explain why any tax would ever be reduced or repealed.

In recent years, others have argued that the minimum tax promoted the objectives of Republicans, because the states with the highest state and local tax burdens (and hence having taxpayers more likely to be subject to the minimum tax) all leaned toward Democrats. But this reasoning fails to explain the durability of the minimum tax through periods of national control by Democrats as well as Republicans. In short, the philosophy behind the minimum tax, as currently structured, seems to be that it is acceptable to reduce one's taxes to a certain extent through straightforward arrangements laid out in the tax code, but that limits should be placed on the ability of any single individual to engage in such tax-favoured behaviour.

These limits have their economic costs, because they distort the allocation of activities among individuals. For example, some of the deductions disallowed under the minimum tax are for costs associated with natural resource extraction, so taxpayers are discouraged from concentrating too much individually in such sectors. Placing limits on each individual can also lead to a reduction in the overall amount of the activity that takes place.

But if such an overall reduction is the policy's underlying objective, it could be accomplished more efficiently by reducing the tax benefits uniformly, for example by reducing the fraction of expenses that are deductible. Lest one think that the minimum tax is just an inexplicable historical accident, one can find instances of similar provisions elsewhere in U.S. policy. Perhaps the most important is the U.S. system of agricultural support payments to farmers of various crops.

Under this system, there have been limitations in place since the Agricultural Act of 1970.

These limits, as most recently amended by the 2008 Farm Bill, take the form of ceilings on the size of payments that any individual farmer can receive. It is noteworthy that the payments are also subject to an income limit, with farmers having income above the specified limit (now $750,000 per year) not eligible to receive any payments.

Thus, the system of agricultural support payments reflects both of the anomalies discussed so far, individual limits on the receipt of government tax or spending benefits, and the use of government programs other than the system of direct taxation to achieve distributional objectives.

Thus, one might justify some of the limits placed on individuals and firms in their use of tax benefits as accomplishing objectives that are administratively difficult to approach more directly. But this is not so of the minimum tax, nor is it the case for agricultural support payments. It may be that these tax and spending benefits exceed those that are socially desirable, and that the limits placed on individuals in their use serves the purpose of limiting overall take-up as well. But the logic of this approach presumes that directly attacking the overall level of activity is more difficult to achieve, politically if not for other reasons.

Perhaps only through the guise of placing limits on individuals can the government achieve such overall limits.

And why would placing limits on individuals seem attractive? If citizens think of the progressivity of programs individually rather than on an integrated basis, as suggested above as a possible explanation for the practice of piecemeal progressivity, then placing limits on individual access to tax deductions or spending benefits may also be viewed as furthering the objective of progressivity. Thus, the two types of anomalies we have explored thus far – piecemeal progressivity and individual limits – may be closely linked, and not simply because in both cases the government may be trading economic efficiency for reduced perception of its ultimate objectives.

Quantity-Based Restrictions

Countries around the world struggling to develop policies to counteract global warming have devoted renewed attention to alternative tax-based and quantity-based mechanisms for limiting particular activities, in this instance the emissions of greenhouse gases. Quantity-based approaches are typically based on the use of tradable permits, while tax-based approaches rely on taxes placed on emissions.

As is well understood, these two approaches are closely related, in that one can determine market equilibrium by setting either the price or the quantity and letting the other respond. Indeed, if tradable permits are auctioned off, then the government will receive the same revenue, emissions will be the same, and producers and consumers will face the same prices, as in the case where the government levies a tax on emissions sufficiently high to produce the same level of emissions.

There are, of course, subtle differences between controlling quantities and controlling prices when there is uncertainty regarding market responses or imperfect competition among producers. But a major potential difference between these two approaches is revenue, should the tradable permits be given away rather than sold by the government. The advantage of raising revenue through corrective taxes or permit auctions has been central to discussions of the so-called "double-dividend" hypothesis, which notes that funds so raised can be used to reduce other taxes.

Given that tradable permits and emissions taxes can be used to implement the same underlying policies, one might ask why the permit approach has gained such prominence given the long-standing existence of taxes on certain pollutants, such as motor fuels.

An answer sometimes offered is that the tax effectuated when tradable permits must be purchased is an implicit one. This answer is not very convincing if all of the permits are first auctioned off by the government, for then the payments for permits and payment of taxes involve essentially identical transactions. On the other hand, if the government wishes to give away at least some of the permits, then this approach may be easier politically, especially if the recipients are industrial polluters, than making transfer payments of the same value to the same recipients, as would be required to produce the same outcome under an emissions tax.

This leaves aside the question of whether and to whom compensation should be paid when the revenue could instead be used to reduce other taxes. But beyond the issue of compensation, there are other policy choices that are more difficult to justify, such as restrictions on the trading of rights to pollute.

For example, the United States has since 1975 imposed Corporate Average Fuel Economy (CAFE) regulations on automobile manufacturers to increase the average miles per gallon of gasoline for the average automobile sold by each manufacturer. (Other countries impose similar rules that are even more restrictive.) Leaving aside the fact that regulating fuel economy is a very imperfect way to regulate emissions (which depend not only on fuel efficiency but also on the intensity of driving) another problem with CAFE standards is that they are not tradable.

Thus, it is not permissible for one manufacturer that makes small cars or is very adept at making cars fuel efficient to sell unused "CAFE credits" to another manufacturer facing higher costs of meeting the uniform standard. The consequence is an increase in the total cost incurred by manufacturers as a group to meet the CAFE standard. Unlike on the issue of whether to pay compensation, where lobbying by one group might explain the outcome, there are no obvious winners from the policy of not allowing trade. Why, then, are the quotas assessed on individual firms not tradable?

Here, we again confront a case where practice goes beyond our theory. One possible explanation is that there is, among many observers, revulsion to the idea of allowing the purchase of a right to engage in an activity that is viewed as socially undesirable. Allowing purchase of the right to pollute, so the argument goes, implies that pollution is acceptable and that those individuals or countries with greater resources can shift their moral responsibilities for reducing pollution onto others.

Of course, any standard that does not eliminate pollution entirely implies the judgment that pollution is acceptable, but the perception of fairness and justice here goes beyond such logic. It is also not clear that the same objections would be raised to the imposition of a tax on emissions, even though as already discussed such a tax would result in essentially the same outcome as the auction of tradable permits. Paying for the right to pollute and paying the same amount in the form of a tax on pollution may be equivalent economically but not necessarily in the eyes of some observers.

This perspective regarding the morality of purchasing the right to engage in socially undesirable activities may also help us understand Finland's approach to speeding fines. Such fines may not simply be viewed as another tool for redistribution, as suggested above, but may also be perceived as a fair way of preventing wealthy individuals from "purchasing" a disproportionate share of the "speeding rights" from those with lower income for whom a uniform fine would be more difficult to pay. That is, even if it is efficient for wealthy individuals to speed more frequently, some may perceive this as intrinsically unfair. Another striking anomaly regarding the choice between tax-based and quantity-based restrictions comes from the area of international trade policy, where import tariffs and import quotas are the relevant policy instruments.

As in the pollution-control context, the two instruments are basically equivalent if the quotas are auctioned off and then tradable, but in the trade context it is rare to observe the sale of quotas, at least explicitly (i.e., leaving aside bribes and other payments made to obtain them). This is the case even though the transfer via the free grant of a quota goes to a foreign producer, presumably with less political influence than a domestic one. Of course, imposition of either tariffs or quotas imposes social costs from forgoing gains from trade, but a country might be enticed to adopt these trade restrictions nonetheless, either to improve terms of trade, thereby making its residents better off at the expense of the rest of the world, or simply to help some of its residents at the expense of others by protecting certain domestic industries.

Thus, it is not hard to understand why countries might and do erect trade barriers. But why they would use quotas, thus granting rather than selling "quota rents" to foreign producers, requires further consideration, particularly given that these rents are not small. For example, one compilation of estimates put the quota rents from major U.S. trade restrictions (on automobiles, dairy products, steel, sugar and textiles) at between \$7 billion and \$17 billion around 1985, around 1 to 2 percent of federal revenues or 12 to 28 percent of corporate tax revenues, and of a magnitude similar to actual tariff revenues (\$12.2 billion in 1985, according to the Bureau of Economic Analysis.)

It is hard to think of an explanation for this gift to foreigners that does not involve differences in perceptions about the two policies on the part of domestic residents. Whereas tariffs, as taxes, might be seen as contributing to an increase in prices, at least of imported goods, the impact of quotas might be harder for some to comprehend, particularly when such quotas are "voluntary," as was the case for the U.S. automobile quotas imposed on Japanese producers in 1981. Making quotas marketable could clarify the close relationship of quotas and tariffs and, in doing so, make domestic consumers more aware of the losses they suffer as a result of the policy.

Thus, once again, government might be willing to accept additional social losses in furtherance of a policy objective, in this case the protection of certain industries or a terms-of-trade improvement rather than the achievement of a more progressive fiscal system. As this case suggests, however, the government's ability to confuse voters may contribute to greater policy flexibility without contributing to better fiscal policy.

In summary, tax-based and quantity-based methods for controlling activities are very similar in nature but are applied differently in practice. Two particular elements of common practice that are difficult to square with the basic theory of public finance are limits on the ability to trade quotas and the granting of import quotas without compensation, both practices that harm domestic residents as a whole without providing appreciable benefits to any particular group. It is conceivable that an expanded view of fairness might help explain the former and that the latter might derive from a desire on the part of policy makers to mask the effects of restrictive trade policies on prices.

Dedicated Taxes

In general, the sources and uses of government funds need not be related. If a public spending project, a transfer program, or a tax incentive needs to be financed, then we might wish to take the distributional effects of the program into account when deciding who should bear the burden of taxation, but there is no need to specify where the revenue comes from, given that money is fungible.

There are, of course, particular cases in which it makes sense to tie taxes and spending together, as in a public pension or unemployment compensation program, where the benefits received are related to the taxes paid, or at least to the earnings on which the taxes are based.

Then, tying taxes to spending can establish a link between benefits received and taxes paid, and so may lessen the perceived burden of the taxes. In many cases of such apparent linkage, however, the actual relationship between taxes and benefits at the individual level is weak or nonexistent.

For example, the U.S. old-age pension system – Social Security – is financed primarily by payroll taxes on workers, and the benefits that accrue are based on the earnings that are subject to the payroll tax. But the formula used to calculate benefits incorporates so many transfers, from single individuals to married couples, from high-income workers to low-income workers, from young workers to older workers, and from future retirees to current retires, that the actual linkage between taxes and benefits at the individual level is weak.

In other cases where there are dedicated taxes, the linkage between spending and taxes is essentially nonexistent at the individual level even if the spending and taxes bear some intuitive connection. One example is U.S. federal gasoline taxes, which are earmarked for a highway trust fund used to finance road construction.

Though the relationship of gasoline taxes and highway spending may have some logic, the number and quality of roads on which any individual can drive are unrelated to the gasoline taxes that individual pays. Furthermore, there is no requirement that highway trust fund accumulations actually be spent on highway construction over any specified period.

Another example comes from the U.S. Medicare system, which provides medical care for the elderly. One component of that system, hospital insurance, is financed through a 2.9 percent payroll tax. One does need to have been a worker to qualify for Medicare, so there is some connection between taxes and benefits. But once qualified, the health care one receives is in no way related to the payroll taxes one has paid. A third example comes from President Obama's recent budget, which would institute a new cap and trade system for greenhouse gas emissions and explicitly dedicate a portion of the revenues – $15 billion per year – to the development of clean energy technologies. While both sources and uses of funds go toward reducing pollution, there is no reason to think that the appropriate level of spending on new technology is related to the level of payments by polluters.

Finally, there are some cases where dedicated taxes bear no relationship at all to the expenditures to which they are committed. A nice illustration comes from the practice of direct democracy under the California proposition system.

In November 2004, California voters approved Proposition 63, also known as the "Mental Health Services Act." Proposition 63 provides state funding for certain new or expanded mental health programs through a personal income tax surcharge of 1 percent on a taxpayer's income in excess of $1 million. (There has, of course, been a long-running dispute since the days of Fitzgerald and Hemingway as to whether the rich are really different, but the dispute has not centred on whether they suffer a higher incidence of mental illness.) And, at the U.S. national level, there have been frequent discussions of introducing a value-added tax and dedicating it to the provision of universal health care.

Thus, although dedicated taxes can sometimes act as user fees, we see them in many more instances where such a mechanism is either imperfect or nonexistent. And where there is no natural linkage of taxes and benefits, there can be real economic costs to reliance on dedicated taxes. We may end up relying too heavily on some taxes than others, thereby reducing the tax system's efficiency, and our mix and level of public spending may be distorted by the connections of particular types of spending to specific sources of funding.

Why, for example, should California's spending on mental health services rise and fall with the incomes of millionaires? Further, if the practice of tax dedication becomes widespread, the ability of government to shift funds among different categories of spending as circumstances change is limited.

What might explain this common phenomenon of tax dedication? One possibility is that tying taxes to spending helps to overcome taxpayer skepticism. For example, taxpayers might be more willing to pay taxes if they perceive that these taxes are spent on something that they value, even if there is no tax-benefit linkage at the individual level. Tying taxes to spending programs that can be seen as related increases the chance that taxpayers will perceive such value, as in the case of gasoline taxes being used to finance highway construction. This might mean, of course, that spending programs for which related taxes are more difficult to identify may suffer.

A second objective of tax dedication might be either to protect or to limit the amount of a particular type of spending. Those who introduced California's Proposition 63 succeeded in placing a claim on a specific source of revenue, thereby helping to insulate mental health spending from the normal budget process in which this spending would have to compete with other potential uses of funds.

On the other hand, one of the reasons advanced for providing a dedicated source of revenue such as the VAT for health care has been to try to force health spending growth to conform to the growth of VAT revenues. In either case, though, the influence of tax dedication on funding need not go in the right direction from a social perspective.

Third, tax dedication, particularly where there is some tax-benefit linkage, may be used to accomplish social objectives. Wilbur Cohen, Secretary of Health, Education and Welfare under President Lyndon Johnson and one of the important architects of U.S. social insurance programs, was said to have argued that programs for the poor are poor programs.

That is, it might be more difficult to maintain a healthy transfer program for the elderly poor than to embed such a program in a universal public pension system with a dedicated tax by making pension payments higher for low-income retires and lower for high-income retires than actuarial calculations would dictate.

One can see two reasons why the universal program might fare better in the political arena. First, individuals might be confused, thinking that the program is simply a pension system in which retires receive benefits based solely on their individual tax payments. Second, a universal system creates a natural constituency of support among the elderly and those nearing retirement. Even those who over an entire lifetime may have contributed far more to the pension system than they receive as retires will benefit when old from the system's continuation. In summary, dedicated taxes may serve several purposes other than to act as user fees.

While the mechanisms associated with each purpose may be different, all involve altering the level of public spending relative to what would occur in the absence of tax dedication. We have seen one of these mechanisms, voter confusion, in the other examples discussed above.

All mechanisms relate to the political process, but not in the simple sense of determining policies by sorting out winners and losers. As with the other fiscal anomalies already discussed, dedicated tax funding has obvious social costs. There are also some potential benefits, at least to some groups in the population, but one can have little assurance that the overall practice provides a net benefit to society as a whole.

Conclusions

Richard Musgrave contributed much to our understanding of what constitutes good public finance practice, and therefore also what does not. In this paper, I have presented four examples of the practice of public finance that pose challenges for our theories. In each case, the practices exist even though there are potential alternatives that could make society better off without necessarily creating losers, at least among domestic residents. These fiscal anomalies suggest that our theories need to take seriously several factors that may receive too little attention at present.

First, the structure of a particular policy may affect its salience on the part of individuals. Perhaps individuals are less aware of the progressivity of a fiscal system when this progressivity is achieved in pieces rather than with one particular tax instrument. They may not recognize the taxes implicit in import quotas, particularly if those quotas are given away rather than auctioned off. And they may not understand that public pension systems also incorporate progressive redistribution.

Most research to date has focused on the salience of tax policies to individuals with respect to their own decisions, but their decisions as voters should also be affected and governments can be expected to take this into account.

Second, individuals may have notions of fairness regarding the regulation of socially harmful activities that conflict with the perspectives economists take. To economists, speeding and polluting are examples of activities where government intervention is needed to get prices right, to make sure that social costs are properly accounted for so that the socially appropriate amount of the activity occurs and is allocated efficiently across different individuals.

To other individuals, there may be no acceptable level of activities that cause social damage, and it is immoral to use a market mechanism to allocate these activities, even if the market mechanism simulates a tax policy that would not be viewed so negatively, and even if the mechanism makes everyone individually better off.

Third, people may be disposed to think about fairness in terms of individual policies, rather than considering the fiscal system as a whole. Thus, they may see it as fair to limit any one person's receipt of a particular tax benefit or agricultural support payment, even if such limits have no other justification. Citizens may insist that the value added tax be progressive, even though the VAT is not a good vehicle for achieving progressivity. And they may think that high-income speeders should be assessed higher fines, even if the income tax already achieves a desirable degree of redistribution. Why they are disposed to think this way, and the extent to which this is an ingrained predisposition, is not clear.

Fourth, taxpayers may take a more positive view of paying taxes if they have a sense of what the taxes pay for. This means that government programs may rely on dedicated taxes even when there is no natural linkage between the taxes and spending, and even though matching taxes to expenditures is otherwise generally undesirable when one is seeking an efficient public sector. Beyond the obvious observation that the practice of public finance would be easier (if less interesting) to explain if we were all economists, how should a public finance theorist respond to these conclusions?

Some of what we observe may indeed reflect the fact that we are not all economists and may not understand how economic policies work. Unless we undertake a major program of universal economics education, however, and perhaps even if we do so, our theory needs to adapt to this lack of understanding. What we observe also appears to reflect a different way of thinking about fairness and the benefits of public policy, a way of thinking that is not easily modelled or described in a logically consistent manner and may not be overcome by one lesson, or several lessons, in economics. Modelling such beliefs is a challenge, but a necessary one to confront if we are to develop public policies that are not only socially beneficial but are also perceived to be so. In short, we have much work to do.

11

RBI Guidelines on Credit Risk Management

Reserve Bank of India (RBI) has come out with draft guidelines on Credit Default Swap (CDS) per notification dated May 2007. The guidelines could not have come at a more opportune time, as several players are waiting eagerly to get appropriate instruments to manage credit risk in their portfolio.

The guidelines initially are addressed to commercial banks and primary dealers only and the scope is limited to usage of Credit Default Swap by the banks and primary dealers for sale and purchase of credit protection in respect of single resident reference entity. Down the line, it seems that insurance companies and mutual funds also would get to participate in the exciting field of credit derivatives.

For the uninitiated, credit derivatives are synthetic instruments for transfer of credit risk in a financial transaction or a portfolio consisting of financial assets. Most commonly used form of credit risk transfer that we in India are conversant with, is securitization. Securitization has focus on selling assets with credit risk. Banks can sell their loans directly or they can securitize. or pool together their assets with credit risk and sell parts of the pool to outside investors. Either way it reduces credit risk because the credit exposure is transferred to the new owner. Unfortunately, these methods are insufficient for managing the credit exposure of many financial institutions. Credit derivatives are financial contracts that provide insurance against credit-related losses. These contracts give investors, debt issuers, and banks new techniques for managing credit risk that complement the loan sales and asset securitization methods. A credit derivative is usually a bilaterally entered contract. The value of the contract is derived from the credit risk of the underlying like a bond, a bank loan, or some other credit instrument. The value of a credit derivative is linked to the change in credit quality of these instruments. Different variants of credit derivatives are Credit Default Swap, Total Return Swap, Credit Linked Notes, Collateralized Debt/Loan Obligations (CDO/CLO), both index tranched and bespoke, Credit Spread Options etc. CDOs on CDOs or CDO2 are new variants of credit derivatives.

Since most of these are well known to most of the discerning readers, we are dwelling on the draft guidelines of Reserve Bank of India and are submitting observations hereunder as to what according to us are required to be additionally addressed to make the world of credit derivatives in India more meaningful and in line with the expectation of the market:

At the very beginning we draw attention to a statement in the draft that declares that the document does not supersede any previous guidelines. While this is partially true, a clearer statement on why the draft guidelines of 2003 are not pursued to logical end could have put things in proper perspective.

It is not also understood as to why the scope is kept limited to Banks and PDs and that too in respect of single resident reference entity, leaving other financial institutions and retail assets outside the purview. At a time when infrastructure development through public private partnership is encouraged and deepening and widening of debt market is spoken about, the option is required to be extended to other financial institutions as well including but not limited to registered NBFCs and institutions dedicated to infrastructure financing in particular.

It is the experience of the undersigned that Public Sector Banks with overseas presence write protections freely in respect of Credit Linked Notes referencing to FCCBs issued by Indian corporates in the international market. It is not clear whether the Banks will continue to be permitted to write such protections in the international market but not in the domestic market.

We expected RBI to appreciate the problems of NBFCs more closely and to appreciate that not all NBFCs that are in the business of creation of physical assets in the country are doing so for narrow business gains. Some of them are in the business to address the gap in the physical infrastructure of the country that deters foreign investments to come in. Unfortunately they are in the finishing segment of the infrastructure vertical and are not yet officially recognized as infrastructure activities.

It is well known that the NBFCs, particularly Asset Finance Companies run huge asset liability mismatches in their books in the absence of alternative source of funding other than credit lines from Banks. In order to address this issue they normally enter in to bilateral deals for sale of assets or undertake vanilla securitization. Recent guidelines of RBI indirectly restricting flow of credit to NBFC ND SI have further put such NBFCs in a spot as assets they finance are funded at a much cheaper rate in the market than the rate at which they can raise resources from Banks.

In the absence of variety of players interested in loans proposed to be sold/securitized, the counter parties are almost always banks only. Availability of CDS to NBFCs would have afforded some alternatives (CDOs in particular) to them to go for tranched securitization and sell them to different players according to the risk appetite/comfort level. CDOs take a debt portfolio and partition the credit risk to suit different investors' demands. This is done by placing a basket of bonds into an SPV, and issuing a series of notes against the basket, which consecutively bears the losses on the portfolio. The arrival of the credit default swap has enabled product structurers to replicate cash CDO portfolios without actually using the underlying debt – the synthetic CDO.

From the point of view of regulatory oversight also RBI would rather like to encourage securitization/CDOs than continuing with popular bilateral deals where isolation of assets from the seller (true sale) and establishing bankruptcy remoteness of seller (putting the beneficial cash flow from the sold assets beyond the reach of the transferor, or any consolidated affiliate of the transferor, and their creditors either by a single transaction or a series of transactions taken as a whole even in the event of bankruptcy or receivership of the transferor or any consolidated affiliate), appear at times to be extremely di fficult and tend to vary from one legal expert to another. Besides, tranched securitization will attract many players in to the debt market thereby lending solidity to its process of maturity.

As far as the institutional mechanism to facilitate credit derivative transaction is concerned, RBI has stopped short of announcing the initiatives they are required to take. In order to make credit derivatives attractive, it is important that indices like the CDX and iTraxx indices are launched to serve as true benchmarks in credit trading. Constructed as baskets of a sample of single-name default swaps with standardized maturity dates and coupons, they instantly give the market the liquidity it needs. Understandably Indian market does not have adequate data to build such indices. However, our Rating Agencies are eminently competent to provide a solution for this going forward and a role for them should be defined in the guidelines.

RBI may also contemplate identification and approval of select legal firms to undertake legal due diligence and sign off on all contracts that represent transfer of credit risk whether through securitization/ loan sales route or through credit derivatives. At a time when Indian economy is getting integrated and transnational are evincing interests in the Indian market, such calibration of the institutional mechanism is felt to be essential prerequisite. In this context it may be stated that though the guidelines have referred to ISDA Master Agreement, contemporary literature suggests that the ISDA is not to be taken as an omnibus solution. According to Mr. Joris Vlug of Zanders & Partners, "In a more 'volatile' world it is sensible and strongly recommended to thoroughly negotiate ISDA schedules.

At least two main items in the schedule should receive special attention. One is the fact that the parties (especially corporates) tend to forget that a trigger for a termination event in an ISDA schedule automatically triggers other funding facilities through the cross default sections in those funding facilities. The second concern is the tendency of banks to propose a schedule, which is not realistic from the other party's point of view, either due to stringent covenants or unrealistic terms and conditions. Remember one important thing: an ISDA Agreement is a bilateral agreement, so you must negotiate thoroughly." Select legal firms may give necessary consultancy in this context and enable deals to go through without any doubt about their enforceability, particularly when the concept of 'restructuring', 'modified restructuring' and 'modified modified restructuring' as default events create some doubts/haziness.

Besides, taking a cue from SOX (Sarbanes Oxley) compliance requirements, RBI might as well obligate entities using credit derivatives to induct in their Audit Committees with at least one independent financial expert who is conversant with derivatives and derivative accounting. Such members along with others in the Audit Committee, may be requested to examine internal controls at a desired level of detail (e.g., about the structure of derivatives, the risks they hedge, the model used for their mark-to-market, their hedge effectiveness over time, the management and procedural controls between the front and back offices, and the conformance with trading policies and limits etc.). It is stated "treasurers who are infrequent users of derivatives may not have adequate systems, controls and processes in place.

They may also be unaware of the leverage implicit in the transactions, and could end up with transactions that have a huge negative impact on their financial statements. The identified expert in the Audit Committee should develop a statement that specifies what hedging techniques and instruments should be used to support strategy. This involves de tailed descriptions of the risk appetite, forecasted transactions, partial term hedges and other issues. Without it the risk policy is often left to the whims of treasury officials, who could pursue policies that are at odds with the board's wishes."

RBI has rightly prescribed that banks should address issues regarding conflicts of interest while structuring CDS. For that matter it is equally important for securitization and other credit derivatives too. Like in treasury operations, the concept of middle office is equally important in credit derivative transactions. In this context the prescription given by Mr. Joel Bessis in the following statement is worth recalling: " Even though banks have always followed well-known diversification principles, classical emphasis of credit analysis is at the transaction level. Portfolio analysis that has significant potential to improve risk return trade off calls for *separation of origination from portfolio management.*"

Lastly, given the fact that process automation in different banks and PDs are at different levels of maturity, giving across the board authority level to write protection might not be free from risks. The more comprehensive the process automation is the lesser is the degree of operational risk. Hence a benchmark requirement of process automation could have been made mandatory for writing derivative contracts.

While concluding, we draw attention to the recommendations of the Joint Forum of Basel Committee on Banking Supervision (BCBS) on the issue of Credit Risk Transfer (CRT) in October 2004. BCBS proposes that any CRT/player in CRT space should satisfy the following tests:

1. Whether the instruments/transactions accomplish a clean risk transfer,
2. The degree to which CRT market participants understand the risks involved, and

3. Whether CRT activities are leading to undue concentrations of credit risk inside or outside the regulated financial sector.

It has also been stated, "some transactions are not really intended to transfer a large portion of credit risk in the first place. For example, some structured transactions may only transfer the "catastrophic" risks associated with the most extreme set of portfolio outcomes; these risks may be more macroeconomic than credit events. It is therefore important that all participants have a good understanding of the relevant transactions and the circumstances in which they do and do not transfer credit risk."

Leverage

In finance, leverage is a general term for any technique to multiply gains and losses. Common ways to attain leverage are borrowing money, buying fixed assets and using derivatives. Important examples are:

- A public corporation may leverage its equity by borrowing money. The more it borrows, the less equity capital it needs, so any profits or losses are shared among a smaller base and are proportionately larger as a result.
- A business entity can leverage its revenue by buying fixed assets. This will increase the proportion of fixed, as opposed to variable, costs, meaning that a change in revenue will result in a larger change in operating income.
- Hedge funds often leverage their assets by using derivatives. A fund might get any gains or losses on $20 million worth of crude oil by posting $1 million of cash as margin.

Measuring Leverage

A good deal of confusion arises in discussions among people who use different definitions of leverage. The term is used differently in investments and corporate finance, and has multiple definitions in each field.

Investments

Accounting leverage is total assets divided by total assets minus total liabilities. Notional leverage is total notional amount of assets plus total notional amount of liabilities divided by equity. Economic leverage is volatility of equity divided by volatility of an unlevered investment in the same assets. To understand the differences, consider the following positions, all funded with $100 of cash equity.

- Buy \$100 of crude oil. Assets are \$100 (\$100 of oil), there are no liabilities. Accounting leverage is 1 to 1. Notional amount is \$100 (\$100 of oil), there are no liabilities and there is \$100 of equity. Notional leverage is 1 to 1. The volatility of the equity is equal to the volatility of oil, since oil is the only asset and you own the same amount as your equity, so economic leverage is 1 to 1.
- Borrow \$100 and buy \$200 of crude oil. Assets are \$200, liabilities are \$100 so accounting leverage is 2 to 1. Notional amount is \$200, equity is \$100 so notional leverage is 2 to 1. The volatility of the position is twice the volatility of an unlevered position in the same assets, so economic leverage is 2 to 1.
- Buy \$100 of crude oil, borrow \$100 worth of gasoline and sell the gasoline for \$100. You now have \$100 cash, \$100 of crude oil and owe \$100 worth of gasoline. Your assets are \$200, liabilities are \$100 so accounting leverage is 2 to 1. You have \$200 notional amount of assets plus \$100 notional amount of liabilities, with \$100 of equity, so your notional leverage is 3 to 1. The volatility of your position might be half the volatility of an unlevered investment in the same assets, since the price of oil and the price of gasoline are positively correlated, so your economic leverage might be 0.5 to 1.
- Buy \$100 of a 10-year fixed-rate treasury bond, and enter into a fixed-for-floating 10-year interest rate swap to convert the payments to floating rate. The derivative is off-balance sheet, so it is ignored for accounting leverage. Accounting leverage is therefore 1 to 1. The notional amount of the swap does count for notional leverage, so notional leverage is 2 to 1. The swap removes most of the economic risk of the treasury bond, so economic leverage is near zero.

Leverage and ROE

If we have to check real effect of leverage on ROE, we have to study financial leverage. Financial leverage refers to the use of debt to acquire additional assets. Financial leverage may decrease or increase return on equity in different conditions. Financial over-leveraging means incurring a huge debt by borrowing funds at a lower rate of interest and utilizing the excess funds in high risk investments in order to maximize returns.

Leverage and Risk

The most obvious risk of leverage is that it multiplies losses. A corporation that borrows too much money might face bankruptcy during a business downturn, while a less-levered corporation might survive. An investor who buys a stock on 50% margin will lose 40% of his money if the stock declines 20%.

There is an important implicit assumption in that account, however, which is that the underlying levered asset is the same as the unlevered one. If a company borrows money to modernize, or add to its product line, or expand internationally, the additional diversification might more than offset the additional risk from leverage. Or if an investor uses a fraction of his or her portfolio to margin stock index futures and puts the rest in a money market fund, he or she might have the same volatility and expected return as an investor in an unlevered equity index fund, with a limited downside. So while adding leverage to a given asset always adds risk, it is not the case that a levered company or investment is always riskier than an unlevered one. In fact, many highly-levered hedge funds have less return volatility than unlevered bond funds, and public utilities with lots of debt are usually less risky stocks than unlevered technology companies.

Popular Risks

There is a popular prejudice against leverage rooted in the observation that people who borrow a lot of money often end up badly. But the issue here is those people are not leveraging anything, they're borrowing money for consumption.

In finance, the general practice is to borrow money to buy an asset with a higher return than the interest on the debt. That at least might work out. People who consistently spend more than they make have a problem, but it's overspending (or underearning), not leverage. The same point is more controversial for governments.

People sometimes borrow money out of desperation rather than calculation. That also is not leverage. But it is true that leverage sometimes increases involuntarily. When Long-Term Capital Management collapsed with over 100 to 1 leverage, it wasn't that the principals tried to run the firm at 100 to 1 leverage, it was that as equity eroded and they were unable to liquidate positions, the leverage level was beyond their control. One hundred to one leverage was a symptom of their problems, not the cause (although, of course, part of the cause was the 27 to 1 leverage the firm was running before it got into trouble, and the 55 to 1 leverage it had been forced up to by mid-August 1998 before the real troubles started). But the point is the fact that collapsing entities often have a lot of leverage does not mean that leverage causes collapses.

Involuntary leverage is a risk. It means that as things get bad, leverage goes up, multiplying losses as things continue to go down. This can lead to rapid ruin, even if the underlying asset value decline is mild or temporary. The risk can be mitigated by negotiating the terms of leverage, and by leveraging only liquid assets.

Forced Position Reductions

A common misconception is that levered entities are forced to reduce positions as they lose money. This is only true if the entity is run at maximum leverage. For example, if a person has $100, borrows another $100 and buys $200 worth of oil, he has 2 to 1 accounting leverage. If the price of oil declines 25%, he has $50 of equity supporting $150 worth of oil, 3 to 1 accounting leverage. If 2 to 1 is the maximum his counterparties will allow him, he has to sell one-third of his position to pay his debt down to $50. Now if oil goes back up to the original price, he has only $83 of equity. He lost 17 percent of his equity, even though the p (say) $10 of cash margin to enter into $200 of long oil futures contracts. Now if the price of oil declines 25%, the investor has to put up an additional $50 of margin, but she still has $40 of unencumbered cash. She may or may not wish to reduce the position, but she is not forced to do so. The point is that it is using maximum leverage that can force position reductions, not simply using leverage. It often surprises people to learn that hedge funds running at 10 to 1 or higher notional leverage ratios hold 80 percent or 90 percent cash.

12

Risk Identification – Risk Factor and Kinds

Risk is all-pervasive. Wherever there is uncertainty, risk prevails. The concept of risk is omnipresent from the existence of mankind, but now it has become more relevant due to interdependence of economies throughout the globe. The recent financial crises in the developed economies not only affect domestic companies negatively, but are also capable of wiping of the entire net worth of companies. What appears to be safe for generations may not be safe now. The need of the hour is to look into these phenomena cautiously rather than suspiciously.

Risk management is the current favorite strategy, globally. It has helped global enterprises to face situations such as the Y2K problem or protecting against data loss in the aftermath of 9/11. It is impossible to predict all the incidents/events and their intensity in advance and to protect oneself against it. However, there is a well-laid procedure that can help predict possible threats and take remedial measures to reduce losses.

It is done in three stages.

Risk Identification: This is the first step towards mitigation/reduction of risk. The various sources of risk in today's market place are interest rate risk, market risk, inflation risk, business risk, financial risk, liquidity risk, technology risk, political risk, sovereign risk, counterparty risk etc. Any of these risks can affect business adversely. Good knowledge of these sources can help to take appropriate action at the right times. One must try to understand the possible impact of these risks on the business and prepare a course of action to mitigate the adverse affect. Now regulators of many countries are making it mandatory to have a risk management committee that will understand the risk implications of existing or new products and suggest the measures required to be taken.

Risk Measurement: This is the second stage. One can choose from various risk-measurement models according to compatibility and the complexity of requirement. There are various risk measurement models available for different types of risk, such as VAR (delta normal method, historical simulation method, and Monte Carlo simulation method), stress testing, cash flow at risk, Merton model, credit scoring models, credit risk portfolio models, and so on. The most commonly used among these is the VAR.

The basic objective of all the models is to learn about the maximum loss a company can suffer in worst-case scenarios. Scenario analysis, stress test and the Monte Carlo simulation method give enormous scope to management teams to use real time situations to get close-to-accurate results.

Risk Mitigation: Once an estimate of the risk is made, the next job is to mitigate that risk. This is crucial since it involves cost, effort, time, and resources.

There are a few risks that can not be mitigated like war, natural calamities, changes in economic policy, industrial recession etc.

However, many risks can be insured or protected. Portfolio diversification in negatively correlated areas is one way to mitigate the impact of market risk. There are various derivative instruments available to reduce credit/counterparty risk; but in the current financial crisis it is difficult to rely on them. The recommendations of Counterparty Risk Management Policy Group II report further strengthens the global financial system by identifying private sector initiatives that will reduce the risk of global financial shocks and limit losses.

Liquidity risk can be addressed by matching the maturities of asset and liabilities in an organization. Further, investing a portion of an organization's portfolio in highly liquid and sovereign bonds will support the organization in liquidity crises, besides earning regular returns.

Operational risk can be due to data loss, human failure, fraud and forgery etc. Operational risk can be avoided with proper precaution, comprehensive backup policy (including mirror image) at some remote area and foolproof management policy. To avoid frauds, policy makers put themselves in the shoes of person wants to commit fraud and make rules to plug the loopholes. One should always keep in mind that lack of proper checks and control may lead to financial disaster which could have been avoided in the cases like Barings Bank, Sumitomo, Daiwa Bank, and Allied Irish Bank.

Market risk refers to the risk to an institution resulting from movements in market prices, in particular, changes in interest rates, foreign exchange rates, and equity and commodity prices.

Credit Risk Philosophy

The credit risk philosophy is a statement of principles and objectives that outlines the institution's willingness to assume credit risk and will vary with the nature and complexity of its business, the extent of other risks assumed, its ability to absorb losses and the minimum expected return acceptable for a specific level of risk.

General Areas of Credit

The general areas of credit in which an institution is prepared to engage usually specify product lines, types of credit facilities, types of borrowers, or industries in which an institution may focus its marketing efforts or may establish constraints restricting an institution's activities.

Approval Authorities

Clearly defined and appropriate levels of authorities for credit approval, provisions or write-offs help ensure that credit decisions are prudent and acceptable, that the integrity and credibility of the credit process is protected by fair, consistent and objective credit decisions, and that the risk is acceptable given the expected return.

Approval limits may relate to size, security or other criteria, such as industry sector. Authorities may be absolute, incremental or a combination thereof and may also be individual, pooled, or shared within a committee.

The delegation of authority needs to be clearly documented, and must include as a minimum:

- the absolute and or incremental credit approval authority being delegated;
- the provision or write-off authority being delegated;
- the officers, positions or committees to whom authority is being delegated;
- the ability of recipients to further delegate risk approval and write-off authority; and

- the restrictions, if any, placed on the use of delegated risk-approval and write-off authorities.

The degree of delegation of authority will depend on a number of variables including:

- the institution's risk philosophy and credit culture;
- the quality of the credit portfolio;
- the degree of market responsiveness required;
- the types of risks being assessed; and
- the experience of lending officers.

Portfolio Concentration Limits

Concentration occurs when an institution's portfolio contains an excessive level of credits to :

- a single counterparty;
- a group of associated counterparties;
- an industry;
- one type of credit facility; or
- a class of security

Excessive concentration renders an institution vulnerable to adverse changes in the area in which the credit is concentrated, and to security impairment.

Sound and prudent portfolio management and control involve the minimization of concentration risk by developing and implementing policies and procedures to ensure the diversification of the credit portfolio. At a minimum, credit diversification policies must be:

- stated clearly;
- include goals for portfolio mix; and
- place exposure limits on single counterparties and groups of associated counterparties and related entities, key industries or economic sectors and new or existing products.

Determination of whether or not concentration exists is a matter of judgment. In circumstances where a member institution's credit portfolio is centred in one industry sector, diversification of credit risk may be achieved by the provision of credit to borrowing categories that respond differently to economic cycles, or across various product lines.

The principal criteria in determining single counterparties are:

- the capability of the borrower to satisfy its commitments without support from external sources; and

- the independence of the borrower from the obligations (financial or otherwise) of others.

Associated counterparties may be a group of persons related financially or by common ownership, management, research and development, marketing or any combination thereof. Identification of associated counterparties requires analysis of the impact of these factors on the financial dependency of the parties involved.

To ensure that an institution is not excessively exposed to a single or associated counterparty, credit limits need to be established within the context of the member's aggregate exposure to such counterparties, in terms of both the total credit extended and the total investment in security instruments issued by such counterparties.

Single counterparty and associated counterparty groupings need to be reviewed regularly to ensure that prior considerations have not changed to an extent that would warrant reclassification.

Credit Granting, Documentation and Collection Process

The most significant risk that an institution faces in the credit granting and collection process is default. Default occurs if a counterparty does not perform its obligations according to the terms of the credit agreement.

To minimize its exposure to loss through default, each institution must give proper consideration to, and conduct an assessment of, each credit (and the credit risks associated with each credit or type of credit) prior to the approval or the disbursement of funds, and ensure that credits are appropriately documented. These procedures to evaluate and document each credit proposal need to be accompanied by clearly defined procedures for collection and regular monitoring.

Evaluating Credit Proposals

Although some well constructed credits can deteriorate because of unforeseen circumstances, most credit problems stem from disregarding or inadequately assessing basic lending principles, including:

- the purpose of the credit and source of repayment;
- the character, integrity and reputation of the borrower to promptly and willingly repay debts or fulfil contractual obligations;
- the borrower's capacity to repay, based on historical financial trends and cash flow projections; and

- the adequacy of collateral.

For commercial credits, the borrower's business or management capability and the status of the borrower's industry and its position within that industry also need to be considered.

Major influences on the credit approval process are an institution's market share, growth or profitability. An overemphasis on any of these factors may expose member institutions to undue risks resulting from:

- a relaxation in credit quality standards, including the assumption of borrowers' risks, the excessive granting of subordinated credit, or the provision of credit with overgenerous terms, conditions or amounts; or
- an adjustment of target market criteria or entrance into untested markets or products.

To develop and maintain a sound credit portfolio, each institution must have a prudent and effective formal evaluation process that provides for an independent and objective assessment of credit proposals. In this context, where circumstances warrant, consideration should be given to the formation and use of specialist credit groups for significant product lines, types of credit facilities, and the sectors in which the institution is engaged.

A strong credit process independent of the marketing function is an effective means of ensuring that credit risks are appropriately analysed and reviewed, and are within the parameters of the institution's credit policies. The details of the analysis, however, will vary with the areas of credit the institution is engaging in. Commercial credits require extensive analysis; a retail portfolio may not require the same degree of assessment. In all cases, sufficient analysis must be made to properly assess the integrity of the borrower, the borrower's ability t repay, and, where applicable, the value of collateral pledged.

Credit Collection Process

All licensees need to have in place procedures governing the collection of principal, interest and fees to ensure that such payments are received on a timely basis, in accordance with the terms of repayment, and are appropriately recorded.

Although most credits are ultimately repaid in full, it is recognized that all institutions are exposed to risk of default and, therefore, some credit write-offs may be expected.

A reduction in credit quality needs to be recognized at an early stage when there are still a number of strategic options open to the institution in managing its default risk. These options include referral to an internal credit workout group, where values suggest the need for renegotiations of the terms of the credit, and reorganization or liquidation of the borrower in order to minimize potential loss to the institution. Renegotiations must not, however, be used to disguise serious weaknesses in a credit. Recovery efforts require a well-conceived strategy and timetable.

Credit Portfolio Monitoring and Control

Failure to establish adequate procedures to effectively monitor and control the credit function within established guidelines has resulted in credit problems for many institutions. Compromising credit policies and procedures has been another major cause of credit problems.

Accordingly, each institution needs to develop and implement comprehensive procedures and information systems to effectively monitor and control the characteristics and quality of its credit portfolio. These procedures need to define prudent criteria for identifying and reporting potential problem accounts to ensure that such accounts are identified for more frequent review, followed up with appropriate corrective action, classified as unsatisfactory where appropriate, and that provisions are made where necessary.

Categorization of the credit portfolio by credit characteristic, risk rating and regular review of individual and groups of credits within the portfolio, and independent internal credit inspections or audits are integral elements of effective and prudent portfolio monitoring and control.

Portfolio Characteristics

In order to track portfolio diversification characteristics, each institution needs to have in place a system to enable credits to be grouped by single and associated groups of counterparties, types of credit facilities, and industries.

Credit Rating System

Each institution needs to have a credit rating system that defines risk-rating criteria and rates credits according to those criteria.

Internal credit ratings provide an effective tool for monitoring the level and trends in the quality of individual credits and the credit portfolio by highlighting credits or segments of the portfolio that warrant special attention.

At a minimum, a rating system should permit credits to be classified as:

- satisfactory or acceptable risk;
- below standard risk (or substandard); and
- unsatisfactory risk or doubtful (for example, credits in which payments are contractually past due, credits in which partial or complete provisions for loss have been made, or credits not adequately supported by collateral, where appropriate).

Furthermore, each institution needs to develop and implement appropriate policies for classifying credits as non-accrual and conservative accounting policies for recognizing revenue related to such accounts. Usually, credits are classified non-accrual whenever there is serious doubt as to the ultimate collectibility of principal or interest, whenever, a provision for loss has been recorded against the account, or where interest owing remains uncollected 90 days following its contracted or scheduled date for payment.

Normally, revenue should not be recognized through the capitalization of interest in any manner, except where this was specifically agreed upon with the client and formed part of the original terms of the credit and the loan continues to be adequately collateralized or is otherwise in good standing. Usually, commercial credit needs to be rated individually. Retail portfolios, however, consisting of relatively smaller credits of a similar nature, may permit the adoption of procedures that rate all credits as satisfactory, unless there are indications to the contrary, with only unsatisfactory credits requiring individual attention.

Credit Review

Most outstanding credits and commitments to extend credit are contingent upon borrowers maintaining specific credit standards. Consequently, lending institutions need to regularly monitor the status of borrowers and re-evaluate individual credits and commitments, and their ratings, particularly credit to owners and directors. Reliance on unreviewed credits and optimistic economic forecasts can lead to a serious undetected deterioration of the credit portfolio. Accordingly, the credit risk management programme of each institution must include procedures governing the regular formal review and, where applicable, the re-rating of individual credits.

An effective internal credit review system couples independent review with regular analysis and re-rating of credits by account officers. Because of their frequent contact with borrowers, account officers are in a position to detect changes in a borrower's operations or financial condition. This permits these officers to identify potential problems before they may be discovered by independent credit reviewers. Accordingly, credit review systems must ensure that an account officer is monitoring credit quality and, where applicable, underlying security on an on-going basis.

The nature, complexity and degree of analysis and the quantity of credits re-evaluated under a credit review process will vary with the type and sophistication of credits in the portfolio. Each commercial credit should be reviewed at least annually; retail credits, however, may need less frequent individual review. Credits on the security of real estate may require more frequent review.

Common objectives of effective credit review systems include:

- ensuring that the institution is aware of borrowers current financial condition;
- ensuring that collateral security is adequate and enforceable relative to borrowers' current circumstances;
- ensuring that credits are in compliance with their covenants and margins;
- providing early identification and classification of potential problem credits; and
- providing current information regarding the quality of the loan portfolio.

Internal Credit Inspection/Audit

Internal credit inspections/audits verify the continuing adequacy and applicability of credit risk management policies and procedures, provide an independent assessment of the credit portfolios' existence, quality and value, the integrity of the credit process, and promotes detection of problems relating thereto. Assessments should, at a minimum, randomly test all aspects of credit risk management in order to determine that:

- credit activities are in compliance with the institution's credit and accounting policies and procedures, and with the laws and regulations to which these credit activities are subject;
- credits exist, are duly authorized, and are accurately recorded and appropriately valued on the books of the institution;

- credits are appropriately rated;
- credit files are complete;
- potential problem accounts are being identified on a timely basis and determine whether the institution's provision for credit losses is adequate; and
- credit risk management information reports are adequate and accurate.

Assessments of the credit risk management activities should be presented to the institution's Board of Directors on a timely basis for review.

Conflict of Interest and Confidentiality

Each institution needs to have in place procedures to prevent conflicts of interest and preserve confidentiality. Conflict of interest in the credit process occurs if persons use their connections or influence to obtain funds for themselves or their interests. Conflict of interest may lead to the extension of credit on an unsound basis – because individuals within the credit process may be subject to influence by such persons and, therefore, may not be in a position to evaluate and reject credit applications on the same basis as credit requests from other persons dealing with the institution at arm's length.

Releasing confidential information without a client's prior consent may adversely impact upon the reputation and stature of an institution and may bring the institution into disrepute.

Role of the Board of Directors

The Board of Directors of each institution is ultimately responsible for the integrity of the institution's credit risk management function. In discharging its responsibility, a Board of Directors usually charges management with developing credit policies for the Board's approval, and developing and implementing procedures to manage and control the structure and quality of the institution's credit portfolio, and the level of credit risk assumed, within these policies, and ensuring that such policies remain adequate, comprehensive and prudent.

A Board of Directors needs to have a means of ensuring compliance with the credit risk management program. A Board of Directors generally ensures compliance through periodic reporting by management and internal inspectors/auditors. The reports must provide sufficient information to satisfy the Board of Directors that the institution is complying with its credit risk management policies. At a minimum, a Board of Directors should:

- review and approve credit risk management policies recommend by the institution's management;
- review periodically, but at least once a year, the credit risk management programme;
- ensure the selection and appointment of qualified and competent management to administer the credit risk function;
- ensure that an internal inspection/audit function reviews the credit operations to assess whether or not the institution's policies and procedures are being adhered to, and whether the policies effectively contribute to the achievement of corporate objectives;
- review credits to, or guaranteed by, officers of the institution, including policies related thereto;
- review credits to directors or firms in which they are partners, directors or officers including policies related thereto;
- review credits to corporations controlled by the institution, or their officers or directors, including policies related thereto;
- ratify credits exceeding the level of authority delegated to management and be aware of credits that, while worthy of consideration, are not within the purview of existing credit policies of the institution;
- review significant credit exposures;
- review trends in portfolio quality and the adequacy of the institution's provision for credit losses; and
- outline the content and frequently of management reports to the board on credit risk management.

Role of Management

The management of each institution is responsible for implementing the institution's credit risk management policies and ensuring that procedures are put in place to manage and control credit risk and the quality of the credit portfolio in accordance with these policies.

Although specific credit risk management responsibilities will vary from one institution to another, management at each institution is responsible for:

- developing and recommending credit risk management policies for approval by the Board of Directors;
- implementing the credit risk management policies;

- ensuring that credit risk is managed and controlled within the credit risk management programme;
- ensuring the development and implementation of appropriate reporting systems with respect to the content, format and frequency of information concerning the credit portfolio and credit risk, to permit the effective analysis and the sound and prudent management and control of existing and potential credit risk exposure;
- monitoring and controlling the nature and composition of the institution's credit portfolio;
- monitoring the quality of the credit portfolio and ensuring that the portfolio is soundly and conservatively valued, uncollectible credits written off, and probable losses adequately provided for;
- ensuring that an internal inspection/audit function reviews and assesses the credit portfolio and credit risk management programme;
- developing lines of communication to ensure the timely dissemination of credit risk management policies and procedures and other credit risk management information to all individuals involved in the credit process; and
- reporting comprehensively on significant credit activities, the composition and quality of the credit portfolio, and the credit risk management program to the Board of Directors at least once a year.

Credit Risk Rating and Pricing

Credit risk is the primary financial risk in the banking system and exists in virtually all income-producing activities. How a bank selects and manages its credit risk is critically important to its performance over time; indeed, capital depletion through loan losses has been the proximate cause of most institution failures. Identifying and rating credit risk is the essential first step in managing it effectively.

Well-managed credit risk rating systems promote bank safety and soundness by facilitating informed decision making. Rating systems measure credit risk and differentiate individual credits and groups of credits by the risk they pose. This allows bank management and examiners to monitor changes and trends in risk levels. The process also allows bank management to manage risk to optimize returns. Credit risk ratings are also essential to other important functions, such as:

- Credit approval and underwriting C Risk ratings should be used to determine or influence who is authorized to approve a credit, how much credit will be extended or held, and the structure of the credit facility (collateral, repayment terms, guarantor, etc.).
- Loan pricingC Risk ratings should guide price setting. The price for taking credit risk must be sufficient to compensate for the risk to earnings and capital. Incorrect pricing can lead to risk/return imbalances, lost business, and adverse selection.1
- Relationship management and credit administration C A credit's risk rating should determine how the relationship is administered. Higher risk credits should be reviewed and analysed more frequently, and higher risk borrowers normally should be contacted more frequently. Problem and marginal relationships generally require intensive supervision by management and problem loan/workout specialists.
- Allowance for loan and lease losses (ALLL) and capital adequacy C Risk ratings of individual credits underpin the ALLL. Every credit's inherent loss should be factored into its assigned risk rating with an allowance provided either individually or on a pooled basis. The ALLL must be directly correlated with the level of risk indicated by risk ratings. Ratings are also useful in determining the appropriate amount of capital to absorb extraordinary, unexpected credit losses.
- Portfolio management information systems (MIS) and board reporting C Risk rating reports that aggregate and stratify risk and describe risk's trends within the portfolio are critical to credit risk management and strategic decision making.
- Traditional and advanced portfolio management C Risk ratings strongly influence banks' decisions to buy, sell, hold, and hedge credit facilities.

Expectations of Bank Credit Risk Rating Systems

No single credit risk rating system is ideal for every bank. The attributes described below should be present in all systems, but how banks combine those attributes to form a process will vary. The OCC expects the following of a national bank's risk rating system:

- The system should be integrated into the bank's overall portfolio risk management. It should form the foundation for credit risk measurement, monitoring, and reporting, and it should support management's and the board's decision making.
- The board of directors should approve the credit risk rating system and assign clear responsibility and accountability for the risk rating process. The board should receive sufficient information to oversee management's implementation of the process.
- All credit exposures should be rated. (Where individual credit risk ratings are not assigned, e.g., small-denomination performing loans, banks should assign the portfolio of such exposures a composite credit risk rating that adequately defines its risk, i.e., repayment capacity and loss potential.)
- The risk rating system should assign an adequate number of ratings. To ensure that risks among pass credits (i.e., those that are not adversely rated) are adequately differentiated, most rating systems require several pass grades.
- Risk ratings must be accurate and timely.
- The criteria for assigning each rating should be clear and precisely defined using objective (e.g., cash flow coverage, debt-to-worth, etc.) and subjective (e.g., the quality of management, willingness to repay, etc.) factors.
- Ratings should reflect the risks posed by both the borrower's expected performance and the transaction's structure. • The risk rating system should be dynamic — ratings should change when risk changes.
- The risk rating process should be independently validated (in addition to regulatory examinations).
- Banks should determine through back-testing whether the assumptions implicit in the rating definitions are valid _ that is, whether they accurately anticipate outcomes. If assumptions are not valid, rating definitions should be modified.
- The rating assigned to a credit should be well supported and documented in the credit file.

Developments in Bank Risk Rating Systems

Many banks are developing more robust internal risk rating processes in order to increase the precision and effectiveness of credit risk measurement and management. This trend will continue as banks implement advanced portfolio risk management practices and improve their processes for measuring and allocating economic capital to credit risk. Further, expanded risk rating system requirements are anticipated for banks that assign regulatory capital for credit risk in accordance with the Basel Committee on Bank Supervision's proposed internal-ratings-based approach to capital. More and more banks are:

- Expanding the number of ratings they use, particularly for pass credits;
- Using two rating systems, one for risk of default and the other for expected loss;
- Linking risk rating systems to measurable outcomes for default and loss probabilities; and
- Using credit rating models and other expert systems to assign ratings and support internal analysis.

Pass Risk Ratings

Probably the most significant change has been the increase in the number of rating categories (grades), especially in the pass category. Precise measurement of default and loss probability facilitates more accurate pricing, allows better ALLL and capital allocation, and enhances early warning and portfolio management. Today's credit risk management practices require better differentiation of risk within the pass category. It is difficult to manage risk prospectively without some stratification of the pass ratings. The number of pass ratings a bank will find useful depends on the complexity of the portfolio and the objectives of the risk rating system.

Less complex, community banks may find that a few pass ratings — for example, a rating for loans secured by liquid, readily marketable collateral; a "watch" category; and one or two other pass categories — are sufficient to differentiate the risk among their pass-rated credits. Larger, more complex institutions will generally require the use of several more pass grades to achieve their risk identification and portfolio management objectives.

Linking Internal and External (Public) Ratings

Public rating agencies provide independent credit ratings and analysis to keep the investment public informed about the credit condition of the obligors and instruments they rate. Banks' ability to purchase investment securities has long been tied to ratings supplied by "nationally recognized rating agencies"2 under 12 USC 24. For the past several years, more and more loans are receiving public ratings, and banks are increasingly using public ratings in their risk management systems.

Banks are starting to map their internal risk ratings to public ratings. They use public ratings to create credit models and to fill gaps in their own default and loss data. Banks also obtain public ratings for loans and pools of loans to add liquidity to the portfolio. Public agency ratings are recognized and accepted in the corporate debt markets because of the depth of their issuer and default databases and because such ratings have been tested and validated over time.

While public agency ratings, bank ratings, and regulator ratings tend to respond similarly to financial changes and economic events, agency ratings may not have the same sensitivity to change that the OCC expects of bank risk ratings.

Agency ratings can provide examiners one view of an obligor's credit risk; however, the examiner's risk rating must be based on his/her own analysis of the facts and circumstances affecting the credit's risk. Banks whose internal risk rating systems incorporate public agency ratings must ensure that their internal credit risk ratings change when risk changes, even if there has been no change in the public rating.

Automated Scoring Systems

While statistical models that estimate borrower risk have long been used in consumer lending and the capital markets, commercial credit risk models have only recently begun to gain acceptance. Increasing information about credit risk and rapid advances in computer technology have improved modelling techniques for both consumer and commercial credit. Because of these advancements, the internal risk rating processes at some large banks can and do rely considerably on credit models.

These banks use models to confirm internal ratings, assign finer ratings within broad categories, and supplement judgmentally assigned ratings. Most commercial credit scoring models attempt to estimate an obligor's probability of default and to assign a quantitative risk score based on those probabilities. Generally, they do not take into account a facility's structural elements, such as collateral, that can moderate the impact of a borrower's default.

Most credit scoring models are either statistical systems or expert systems:

1. A statistical system relies on quantitative factors that, according to the model vendor's research, are indicators of default. Examples of these models include Zeta®, KMV's Credit Monitor®, Moody's RiskCalc®, and Standard & Poor's CreditModel®.
2. An expert system attempts to duplicate a credit analyst's decision making. Examples include Moody's RiskScore® and FAMAS LA Encore® models. One of the biggest impediments to the development of commercial credit scoring models has been the lack of data. Until recently, most banks did not maintain the data on commercial loan portfolios needed to develop the statistical analysis for modelling. However, after the credit events of the late 1980s and early 1990s, banks began to develop these databases. Because defaults and losses have been rare in recent years, constructing the databases with the number of observations necessary (thousands in some cases) has been difficult. Furthermore, these models have not yet been tested through a full business cycle. Whether they will be accurate during a recession, when safety and soundness concerns are most acute, remains a question. Like other models, automated commercial credit scoring systems should be carefully evaluated and periodically validated. Until banks gain more experience with them under a range of market conditions, they should use such systems to supplement more traditional tools of credit risk management: credit analysis, risk selection at origination, and individual loan review. Additional information about models can be found in OCC Bulletin 2000-16, "Model Validation," dated May 30, 2000; the OCC's Risk Analysis Division (RAD) can also provide technical assistance.

Risk Rating Process Controls

A number of interdependent controls are required to ensure the proper functioning of a bank's risk rating process.

Board of Directors and Senior Management

The board and senior management must ensure that a suitable framework exists to identify, measure, monitor, and control credit risk. Board-approved policies and procedures should guide the risk rating process.

These policies and procedures should establish the responsibilities of various departments and personnel. The board and management also must instill a credit culture that demands timely recognition of risk and has little tolerance for rating inaccuracy. Unless the board and senior management meet these responsibilities, their ability to oversee the loan portfolio can be severely hampered.

Reviewing and Updating Credit Risk Ratings

The benefits of rating risk are more fully realized if ratings are dynamic. The loan officer (or whoever is primarily responsible for rating) should review and update risk ratings whenever relevant new information is received.

All credits should receive a formal review at least annually to ensure that risk ratings are accurate and up-to-date. Large credits, new credits, higher risk pass and problem credits, and complex credits should be reviewed more frequently. In order to gain efficiencies, smaller, performing credits may be excluded from periodic reviews and reviewed as exceptions. Such loans tend to pose less risk transaction by transaction.

Management Information Systems

MIS are an important control because they provide feedback about the risk rating system. In addition to static data, risk rating system MIS should generate, or enable the user to calculate, the following information:

- The volume of credits whose ratings changed more than one grade (i.e., "double downgrades");
- Seasoning of ratings (the length of time credits stay in one grade);
- The velocity of rating changes (how quickly are they changing);
- Default and loss history by rating category;
- The ratio of rating upgrades to rating downgrades; and
- Rating changes by line of business, loan officer, and location.

MIS reports should display information by both dollar volume and item count, because some reports can be skewed by changes in one large account.

Credit Review

An independent third party should verify loan ratings. For many banks these verifications are conducted by credit review personnel, but other divisions or outsourcing may be acceptable. These verifications help to ensure accuracy and consistency, and augment oversight of the entire credit risk management process. The verifications' formality and scope should correspond to the portfolio's complexity and inherent risk. The credit review function should be sufficiently staffed (both in numbers and in expertise) and appropriately empowered to independently validate and communicate the effectiveness of the risk rating system to the board and senior management. Smaller banks that do not have separate credit review departments can satisfy this requirement by using staff who are not directly involved with the approval or management of the rated credits to perform the review.

Internal Audit

Internal audit is another control point in the credit risk rating process. Typically, internal audit will test the integrity of risk rating data and review documentation. Additionally, they may test internal processes and controls for perfecting, valuing, and managing collateral; verify that other control functions, such as credit review, are operating as they should; and validate risk rating data inputs to the credit risk management information system.

Back-Testing

Systems that quantify risk ratings in terms of default probabilities or expected loss should be back-tested. Back-tests should show that the definitions' default probabilities and expected loss rates are largely confirmed by experience. Banks using credit models or other systems that use public rating agency default or transition information should demonstrate how their ratings are equivalent to agency ratings.

For those risk rating systems not explicitly tied to statistical probabilities, banks should be able to show that credits with more severe ratings exhibit higher defaults and losses. Although the default and loss levels are not explicitly defined in this type of rating system, the system should rank-order risk and should aggregate pools of similarly risky loans using an objective measurement of risk.

Examining the Risk Rating Process

Examiners evaluate a bank's internal risk rating process by considering whether:

- Individual risk ratings are accurate and timely.
- The overall system is effective relative to the risk profile and complexity of the bank's credit exposures.

To determine whether a bank's risk ratings are accurate, examiners will review a sample of loans and compare internal bank ratings with those assigned by OCC staff. Examiners should be most concerned when rating inaccuracies understate risk; however, any significant inaccuracy should be criticized because it will distort the picture of portfolio risk and diminish the effectiveness of interdependent portfolio management processes. Accurate risk ratings, in both the pass and problem categories, are critical to sound credit risk management, especially the determination of ALLL and capital adequacy.

When examiners discover significant risk rating inaccuracies (generally, greater than 5 percent of the number of credits reviewed, or 3 percent of the dollar amount), they must investigate to determine the root causes and decide whether to expand their loan review sample. Determining factors include:

- The nature and pattern of rating inaccuracies, for example, inaccuracies within pass categories, problem credits that are passed, missed ratings with a few large credits or several smaller credits, and inaccuracies in a specific portfolio or location;
- The severity of inaccuracy, i.e., how many grades away the rating is from what it should be;
- The adequacy of the ALLL and capital; and
- Whether inaccurate risk ratings distort overall portfolio risk and the bank's financial statements.

Examiners' analysis of risk rating accuracy and the bank's agreement or disagreement should be documented on an OCC line sheet and, if necessary, in a formal write-up for the Report of Examination.

Reviewing the ratings of individual credits discloses much about how well the overall process is functioning. In their review of the risk rating process, examiners should determine:

- Whether there is a sufficient number of ratings to distinguish between the various types of credit risk the bank assumes;
- The effectiveness of risk rating process controls;
- Whether line lenders, management, and key administrative and control staff understand and effectively use and support the risk rating process; and
- The effectiveness of the risk rating system as a part of the bank's overall credit risk management process.

Whether reviewing individual credit ratings or the risk rating process, examiners should be alert for impediments or disincentives that may prevent the system from functioning properly. Such situations may include:

- Compensation programs that fail to reinforce lenders' and management's responsibility to properly administer, analyse, and report the risk in their portfolios. Worse yet, compensation programs that encourage lenders and management to understate risk in order to boost risk-adjusted returns or to generate incremental business by lowering risk-based pricing.
- Relationship management structures that may encourage lenders and management to "hide" problems for fear of losing control over a customer relationship (e.g., having to transfer management responsibilities to a workout division or specialist).
- Inexperience, incompetence, or unfounded optimism among lenders and management. Some account officers and managers have lent money only when the economy is favorable and may not be adept at recognizing or handling problems. Others may be unduly optimistic and may overlook obvious signs of increased risk.

Whatever the cause, it can be relatively easy for loan officers and line managers to rate credits a step, or more, above what they deserve. When examiners encounter such practices, they must ensure that required corrective actions address the root cause of the problem.

Rating Credit Risk

Examiners rate credit risk and expect national banks to rate credit risk based on the borrower's *expected performance,* i.e., the likelihood that the borrower will be able to service its obligations in accordance with the terms. Payment performance is a future event; therefore, examiners' credit analyses will focus primarily on the borrower's ability to meet its future debt service obligations.

Generally, a borrower's expected performance is based on the borrower's financial strength as reflected by its historical and projected balance sheet and income statement proportions, its performance, and its future prospects in light of conditions that may occur during the term of the loan. Expected performance should be evaluated over the foreseeable future — not less than one year. While the borrower's history of meeting debt service requirements must always be incorporated into any credit analysis, risk ratings will be less useful if overly focused on past performance. Credit risk ratings are meant to measure risk rather than record history. An example follows:

> *A business borrower is in the third year of a seven-year amortizing term loan. The borrower has enjoyed good business conditions and financial health since the inception of the loan, has made payments as scheduled, and is current. However, the borrower's business prospects and financial capacity are weakening and are expected to continue to weaken in the upcoming year. As a result, the borrower's projected cash flow will be insufficient to cover the required debt service. In this simple example, the risk rating should be changed now when the borrower's risk of default increases rather than later when cash flow coverage becomes negative or when default occurs. When credits are classified because of the borrower's or credit structure's well-defined weaknesses, examiners normally will await correction of the weaknesses and a period of sustained performance under reasonable repayment terms before upgrading the credit rating. The mere existence of a plan for improvement, by itself, does not warrant an upgrade.*

For certain types of loans, however, examiners will base their risk ratings on a combination of the loans' current and historical performance. Such loans include retail credits and smaller (as a percentage of capital) commercial loans amortizing in accordance with reasonable repayment terms. These loans, which normally will not be reviewed individually, will be classified based on their performance status and the quality of the underwriting.

The primary consideration in examiners' credit risk assessment is the strength of the primary repayment source. The OCC defines primary repayment source as a sustainable source of cash. This cash, which must be under the borrower's control, must be reserved, explicitly or implicitly, to cover the debt obligation.

In assigning a rating, examiners assess the strength of the borrower's repayment capacity, in other words, the probability of default, where default is the failure to make a required payment in full and on time. As the primary repayment source weakens and default probability increases, collateral and other protective structural elements have a greater bearing on the rating.

The regulatory definition of substandard illustrates this progression. Examiners first assess the paying capacity of the borrower; then, they analyse the sound worth of any pledged collateral. Almost all credit transactions are expected to have secondary or even tertiary sources of repayment (collateral, guarantor support, third-party refinancing, etc.).

Despite the secondary support, the rating assessment, until default has occurred or is highly probable, is generally based on the expected strength of the primary repayment source.

In some instances, loans are so poorly structured that they require classification even though the likelihood of default is low. Examples are loans with deferred interest payments or no meaningful amortization.

Examiners will assign a rating to each credit that they review. The assigned rating applies to the amount that the bank is *legally committed to fund.* To determine this amount, an examiner may need to review the promissory note, loan agreement, or other such contract used to document the credit transaction. Ratings assigned to unfunded balances are designated "contingent."

Because the amount of credit risk is based on the borrower's expected performance over the foreseeable future, examiners will assess performance expectations over at least the upcoming 12 months. However, examiners will incorporate all relevant factors in a credit rating, regardless of timing conventions.

Assigning Regulatory Credit Classifications

The regulatory agencies use a common risk rating scale to identify problem credits. The regulatory definitions are used for all credit relationships — commercial, retail, and those that arise outside lending areas, such as from capital markets. The regulatory ratings special mention, substandard, doubtful, and loss identify different degrees of credit weakness. Credits that are not covered by these definitions are "pass" credits, for which no formal regulatory definition exists, i.e., regulatory ratings do not distinguish among pass credits.

Examiners are expected to assign ratings in accordance with the guidance in this booklet, regardless of the system the bank employs. Regulatory Definitions3 Special mention (SM) — "A special mention asset has potential weaknesses that deserve management's close attention. If left uncorrected, these potential weaknesses may result in deterioration of the repayment prospects for the asset or in the institution's credit position at some future date. Special mention assets are not adversely classified and do not expose an institution to sufficient risk to warrant adverse classification."

Special mention assets have potential weaknesses that may, if not checked or corrected, weaken the asset or inadequately protect the institution's position at some future date. These assets pose elevated risk, but their weakness does not yet justify a substandard classification. Borrowers may be experiencing adverse operating trends (declining revenues or margins) or an illproportioned balance sheet (e.g., increasing inventory without an increase in sales, high leverage, tight liquidity). Adverse economic or market conditions, such as interest rate increases or the entry of a new competitor, may also support a special mention rating.

Nonfinancial reasons for rating a credit exposure special mention include management problems, pending litigation, an ineffective loan agreement or other material structural weakness, and any other significant deviation from prudent lending practices.

The special mention rating is designed to identify a specific level of risk and concern about asset quality. Although an SM asset has a higher probability of default than a pass asset, its default is not imminent. Special mention is not a compromise between pass and substandard and should not be used to avoid exercising such judgment. Classified assets are exposures rated substandard, doubtful, or loss. Classified assets do not include pass and special mention exposures.

Substandard C "A substandard asset is inadequately protected by the current sound worth and paying capacity of the obligor or of the collateral pledged, if any. Assets so classified must have a well-defined weakness, or weaknesses, that jeopardize the liquidation of the debt. They are characterized by the distinct possibility that the bank will sustain some loss if the deficiencies are not corrected."

Substandard assets have a high probability of payment default, or they have other well-defined weaknesses. They require more intensive supervision by bank management. Substandard assets are generally characterized by current or expected unprofitable operations, inadequate debt service coverage, inadequate liquidity, or marginal capitalization. Repayment may depend on collateral or other credit risk mitigants.

For some substandard assets, the likelihood of full collection of interest and principal may be in doubt; such assets should be placed on nonaccrual. Although substandard assets in the aggregate will have a distinct potential for loss, an individual asset's loss potential does not have to be distinct for the asset to be rated substandard. Doubtful C "An asset classified doubtful has all the weaknesses inherent in one classified substandard with the added characteristic that the weaknesses make collection or liquidation in full, on the basis of currently existing facts, conditions, and values, highly questionable and improbable."

A doubtful asset has a high probability of total or substantial loss, but because of specific pending events that may strengthen the asset, its classification as loss is deferred. Doubtful borrowers are usually in default, lack adequate liquidity or capital, and lack the resources necessary to remain an operating entity. Pending events can include mergers, acquisitions, liquidations, capital injections, the perfection of liens on additional collateral, the valuation of collateral, and refinancing.

Generally, pending events should be resolved within a relatively short period and the ratings will be adjusted based on the new information. Because of high probability of loss, nonaccrual accounting treatment is required for doubtful assets. Loss C "Assets classified loss are considered uncollectible and of such little value that their continuance as bankable assets is not warranted. This classification does not mean that the asset has absolutely no recovery or salvage value, but rather that it is not practical or desirable to defer writing off this basically worthless asset even though partial recovery may be effected in the future."

With loss assets, the underlying borrowers are often in bankruptcy, have formally suspended debt repayments, or have otherwise ceased normal business operations. Once an asset is classified loss, there is little prospect of collecting either its principal or interest. When access to collateral, rather than the value of the collateral, is a problem, a less severe classification may be appropriate. However, banks should not maintain an asset on the balance sheet if realizing its value would require long-term litigation or other lengthy recovery efforts. Losses are to be recorded in the period an obligation becomes uncollectible.

Rating Specialized Credits

Some specialized types of lending have unique attributes that examiners must consider when assigning a risk rating.

- "Commercial Real Estate and Construction Lending," November 1995;
- "Leasing Finance," January 1998;
- "Agricultural Lending," December 1998; and
- "Accounts Receivable and Inventory Financing," March 2000.

Retail Credit. The same rating principles are used for retail and commercial loans, but the principles are applied differently for retail loans. Because retail credits are usually relatively small-balance, homogeneous exposures, the Federal Financial Institutions Council (FFIEC) agencies rate retail credits primarily on payment performance. Payment performance is a proxy for the strength of repayment capacity.

This approach promotes consistency and efficiency. Classification guidance for retail credit is detailed in the FFIEC's "Uniform Retail Credit Classification and Account Management Policy" (Uniform Policy) issued June 20, 2000. This policy statement establishes standards for classification of retail credit based on delinquency status, loan type, collateral protection, and other events influencing repayment, such as bankruptcy, death, and fraud.

Examiners should refer to the Uniform Policy for details. While the Uniform Policy should be followed in most circumstances, examiners always have the prerogative to rate a retail credit's risk more stringently, if appropriate, regardless of its payment status or collateral position. A harsher rating may be appropriate when underwriting standards or risk selection standards are compromised at loan inception, when the poor performance of a portfolio or individual transactions is masked by liberal cure programs (re-aging, extensions, deferrals, or renewals), or when a review of borrower repayment capacity justifies such a rating.

Foreign Assets. The evaluation of a bank's foreign assets must include a number of special considerations. Country risk factors, such as political, social, and macroeconomic conditions and events that are beyond the control of individual counterparties, can adversely affect otherwise good credit risks. For example, depreciation in a country's exchange rate increases the cost of servicing external debt and can increase the credit risk associated with even the strongest counterparties in a foreign country.

For countries in which the aggregate exposure of U.S. banks is considered significant, the Interagency Country Exposure Review Committee (ICERC) evaluates and assigns ratings for "transfer risk." The ICERC-assigned transfer risk ratings are applicable to most types of foreign assets held by an institution. The ICERC-assigned transfer risk ratings are:

- The only ratings applicable to sovereign exposures in a reviewed country and

- The least severe risk rating that can be applied to all other cross-border and cross-currency exposures of U.S. banks in an ICERC-reviewed country.

However, because transfer risk is only one component of country risk, examiners should not criticize banks whose internally assigned risk rating for a country is more severe than the ICERC-assigned transfer risk rating.

And because the ICERC does not evaluate the credit risk of individual private sector exposures in a country, examiners may assign such exposures credit risk ratings that are more severe than the country's ICERC-assigned transfer risk rating. For any given private sector exposure, the applicable rating is the more severe of either the ICERC-assigned transfer risk rating for the country or the examiner-assigned credit risk rating (including ratings assigned by the Shared National Credit Program).

The "Guide to the Interagency Country Exposure Review Committee Process," issued in November 1999, for additional information on the special considerations and rules that are applicable in banks with foreign exposures.

Loans Purchased at a Discount. When a bank purchases a loan at a discount, the loan's book value will be less than the contract amount. Such a loan should receive a thorough credit risk evaluation and be assigned a rating that reflects its default probability and loss potential. Before a pass rating is assigned to a discounted loan, the reduced book value must sufficiently offset any weakened repayment capacity, high leverage, strained liquidity, or structural weakness.

Investment Securities. Information about the classification of investment securities is contained in BC 127 (rev), "Uniform Agreement on the Classification of Assets and Appraisal of Securities Held by Banks," April 26, 1991 and FAS 115, "Accounting for Certain Investments in Debt and Equity Securities."

The Credit Risk Evaluation Process

The risk rating process starts with a thorough analysis of the borrower's ability to repay and the support provided by the structure and any credit risk mitigants. When analysing the risk in a credit exposure, examiners will consider:

- The borrower's current and expected financial condition, i.e., cash flow, liquidity, leverage, free assets;

- The borrower's ability to withstand adverse, or "stressed," conditions;
- The borrower's history of servicing debt, whether projected and historical repayment capacity are correlated, and the borrower's willingness to repay;
- Underwriting elements in the loan agreement, such as loan covenants, amortization, and reporting requirements;
- Collateral pledged (amount, quality, and liquidity), control over collateral, and other credit risk mitigants; and
- Qualitative factors such as the caliber of the borrower's management, the strength of its industry, and the condition of the economy.

Financial Statement Analysis

There is no substitute for rigorous analysis of a borrower's financial statements. The balance sheet, income statement, sources and uses of funds statement, and financial projections provide essential information about the borrower's initial and ongoing repayment capacity. Quantitative analysis of revenues, profit margins, income and cash flow, leverage, liquidity, and capitalization should be sufficiently detailed to identify trends and anomalies that may affect borrower performance.

The balance sheet deserves as much attention as the income statement. The balance sheet can provide an early warning of credit problems, for example, if assets degrade or the relative level of assets and liabilities changes.

Commercial borrowers generate their revenue, income, and liquidity from their assets, so examiners should analyse the composition of these accounts and how their proportions change. Capitalization and liquidity also warrant careful analysis because they imply a borrower's ability to withstand an economic slowdown or unplanned events.

Cash Flow

Business cash flow is the operating revenue derived from ordinary business activities less operating costs paid (not simply incurred), plus noncash expenses such as depreciation and amortization. Although the concept is simple, cash flow calculations are often complex. Many businesses calculate cash flow differently because of the nature of their operations and cash conversion cycle.

Changes in "working capital" accounts should be reviewed to understand the cash flow implications. Uses of cash flow should be scrutinized — debt repayment is not the only use of cash flow. Changes, actual or planned, in capital expenditures must be closely reviewed. A troubled borrower will often cut capital expenditures in order to generate cash for debt service. Although this may provide short-term relief, such reductions can imperil a business's future. Shortfalls in cash flow or debt service coverage are usually the most obvious indications of a problem credit.

Ratio Analysis and Benchmarks

Financial ratios provide vital information about balance sheet and income statement proportions (debt to equity, income to revenues, etc.). Comparing a borrower's financial ratios with prior periods and industry or peer group norms can identify potential weaknesses. Whenever a ratio deviates significantly from that of its peers, examiners should conduct further analysis to identify the root cause.

Analysis of Projections

While current and historical information is necessary to establish a borrower's condition and financial track record, projections estimate expected performance. Examiners should analyse how projections vary from historical performance and assess whether the borrower is likely to achieve them. Projections should be analysed under multiple scenarios — downside, breakeven, best case, most likely case — and stress-tested periodically. Borrowers that quickly or repeatedly fall short of their projections lack credibility. Examiners' conclusion that a borrower will not be able to perform at projected levels should be factored into the loan's risk rating.

Qualitative Considerations

Underwriting

Underwriting is the process by which banks structure a credit facility to minimize risks and generate optimal returns for the risks assumed. Sound underwriting provides protections such as coordinating repayment with cash flow, covenants, and collateral, thereby increasing the likelihood of collection. When competition or other pressures cause a bank to weaken its underwriting and structural protections, credit risk increases. Although structural weaknesses may not have an immediate effect on performance, they do affect the probability and severity of future problems.

At times, structural weaknesses can be so severe that the loan deserves an SM rating or classification. Examiners should not defer or forgo criticism of fundamental underwriting flaws because they have become the "competitive norm."

Management

The importance of a business borrower's management — competency and integrity— can not be overstated. The ability of the commercial entity's managers to guide it, exploit opportunities, develop and execute plans, and react to market changes is extremely important to its financial well being. The unexpected loss of one or two key employees can be detrimental to a company, particularly a small or mid-size firm. Even the most experienced management teams can be challenged by high growth, which is one of the most common reasons for business failure.

Industry

The purpose of industry analysis is to understand the conditions in which a business operates and the changes — cyclical, competitive, and technological— that it is likely to experience. Most industries exhibit some degree of cyclical volatility and some industries are exposed to seasonal variances, too. Such volatility affects the operating performance and financial condition of a company. Technological change and new competitors or substitute products can also affect performance.

Credit Risk Mitigation

Credit risk can be moderated by enhancing the loan structure. Parties to a loan can arrange for mitigants such as collateral, guarantees, letters of credit, credit derivatives, and insurance during or after the loan is underwritten. Although these mitigants have similar effects, there are important distinctions, including the amount of loss protection, that must be considered when assigning risk ratings. For example, a letter of credit may affect a loan's risk rating differently than a credit derivative.

Credit mitigants primarily affect loss when a loan defaults and, except for certain guarantees, generally do not lessen the risk of default. Therefore, their impact on a rating should be negligible until the loan is classified. Examiners should be alert for ratings that overstate how much of a loan's credit risk is mitigated. Account officers at times assign less severe ratings based on the existence of collateral or other mitigants rather than undertaking a realistic assessment of the value the bank can recover. The following discussion of the primary forms of mitigation provides guidance for determining an appropriate rating for a credit with a weak or potentially weak borrower and a credit mitigant. There are few hard and fast rules. Examiners should consider each credit facility separately, giving due consideration to every factor in the rating.

Collateral

Collateral, the most common form of credit risk mitigation, is any asset that is pledged, hypothecated, or assigned to the lender and that the lender has the right to take possession of if the borrower defaults. The lender's rights must be perfected through legal documents that provide a security interest, mortgage, deed of trust, or other form of lien against the asset. The process of perfecting the lender's interest varies by type of asset and by locality. Once the lender has taken possession of the collateral, loan losses can be reduced or eliminated through sale of the assets.

The level of loss protection is a function of the assets' value, liquidity, and marketability. Realistic collateral valuation is important at loan inception and throughout the loan's life, but it becomes increasingly important as the borrower's financial condition and performance deteriorate. Collateral valuations should include analysis of the value under duress — that is, what will the collateral be worth when it must be liquidated. The appropriate value may be a fair market, orderly liquidation, or forced liquidation valuation, depending on the borrower's circumstances. Rarely will a "going concern" valuation be appropriate when a loan becomes collateral-dependent. Proceeds from the sale will be diminished by costs related to repossession, holding, and selling the assets. Examiners should assess the validity of the bank's methods of valuing the collateral and determine whether the resulting values are reasonable.

When financial results show that the borrower is not able to repay the loan as structured, the loan should be considered collateral-dependent, classified, and reserved for in accordance with FAS 114, "Accounting by Creditors for Impairment of a Loan." Absent other credit risk mitigation, the portion of the loan covered by the proceeds from liquidating conservatively valued collateral normally should be classified substandard. Any remaining loan balance should be classified doubtful or loss depending on other factors.

Loan Guarantees

Loans may be guaranteed by related or unrelated businesses and individuals. Guarantor strength is often a major consideration when deciding whether to grant a loan, especially to start-up businesses. A guarantor's financial statement should be analysed to ensure that the guarantor can perform as required, if necessary, and that the statement acknowledges the guarantee. Because the by-laws of some corporations prohibit them from assuming contingent liabilities, examiners may need to determine whether a guarantee is properly authorized.

Guarantee agreements should be as precise as possible, stating the specific credit facilities being guaranteed, under what circumstances the guarantor will be expected to perform, and what benefit the guarantor received for providing the guarantee. Guarantees can be unconditional or conditional. An unconditional guarantee generally extends liability equal to that of the primary obligor; in other words, the guarantor assumes the full responsibilities of the borrower. A conditional guarantee requires the creditor to meet a condition before the guarantor becomes liable. Guarantees can also be limited to a specific transaction, in amount, to interest or principal, and in duration.

If a guarantee is to enhance a credit's risk rating, the guarantor must display the capacity and willingness to support the debt. A presumption of willingness is usually appropriate until financial support becomes necessary. At that point, willingness must be demonstrated. Once demonstrated, a strong guarantee can mitigate the risk of default or loss and justify a more favorable rating, despite an obligor's well-defined weaknesses. When adequate evidence of guarantor performance is lacking, the guarantee should not have a beneficial effect on the risk rating. Guarantors who attempt to invalidate their obligations through litigation or protracted renegotiations retard, rather than improve, a loan's collectibility.

Government guarantees are a special case. Credits with a U.S. government agency guarantee are usually accorded a pass rating. Most government guarantees are conditioned on bank management's performance (proper diligence and reporting), and mismanagement can void the guarantee and eliminate the rating enhancement. Although the incidence of mismanagement is very low, a rating enhancement may not be appropriate for banks with significant credit administration problems affecting the guaranteed credits. State or municipal guarantees usually have the same effect as U.S. government guarantees, although the bank must analyse and document the financial strength of these government entities. Guarantees from foreign governments require analysis of sovereign risk.

"Comfort letters," a common convention in international financing, are statements, usually from a domestic parent company, acknowledging a foreign subsidiary's debt. Many bankers maintain that comfort letters are guarantees, structured to avoid accounting conventions that require the parent to reflect guaranteed debt on its own financial statements. However, comfort letters are not legally binding, and in some instances they have not been honored. Therefore, they generally do not enhance a credit's rating. But when the parent has a demonstrated track record of honoring such commitments, or has a strong continuing interest in maintaining the financial condition of the borrowing entity, a comfort letter might enhance a risk rating. For example, if the borrower is the parent's sole supplier of an essential manufacturing component, risk is probably mitigated and the loan rating can be improved.

Letters of Credit

A letter of credit (L/C) is a form of guarantee issued by a financial institution. An L/C rarely protects against default risk, unless it specifically can be drawn on for loan payments. An L/C issuer is typically more creditworthy than a guarantor. When an L/C that protects against default is obtained from a high-quality institution, it may effectively prevent default and losses. The issuer's low credit risk substantially mitigates the borrower's higher credit risk. Before a loss scenario could develop, both the borrower and the L/C issuer would have to default.

The risk rating of a credit that is backed by an L/C issued by a high-quality institution generally should be rated no worse than substandard. However, examiners should evaluate the specific conditions that a borrower must meet before the L/C can be drawn on. When there is a distinct possibility that the borrower will fail to meet those conditions, the L/C should not have a beneficial effect on the rating. An L/C can be irrevocable, which means all parties must agree to its cancellation, or revocable, which means the L/C can be canceled or amended at the discretion of the issuer. Revocable letters do not mitigate credit risk.

A standby L/C pays only when the obligor fails to perform. Examiners should evaluate the protections provided by a standby L/C just as they do that of other L/Cs.

Credit Derivatives

Credit derivatives can be used to manage capital, manage loan portfolios, and mitigate risk in individual transactions. Only credit derivatives for individual transactions have a bearing on risk ratings. Most of these credit derivatives mitigate loss, but they do not materially mitigate default risk.

Credit derivatives for individual loan transactions are usually purchased after the loan has been underwritten. In a typical credit derivative transaction, the protection purchaser (the creditor bank), for a fee, transfers some or all of a loan's credit risk to the protection seller. Standard types of derivatives are credit default swaps, total return swaps, credit-linked notes, and credit spread options.

Credit derivatives have unique structural characteristics and complexities that can diminish or eliminate their ability to reduce credit risk. In determining how much a derivative enhances a credit's rating (if indeed it does so at all), examiners should determine whether the derivative's protection is compromised by any of the following circumstances:

- The events that trigger payment are tied to a reference asset that may have different terms and conditions than the loan held by the bank. The residual exposure in this transaction is known as basis risk.
- The bank has forward credit exposure because the derivative has a shorter maturity than the bank loan. A timing mismatch can also occur when the protection does not take effect until some future date.
- The derivative has a materiality clause that limits protection to amounts over a designated threshold. In other words, the bank retains the first loss position.
- The definition of default or any other credit event that triggers the seller's payment is less rigorous for the swap or the reference asset than for the bank's loan. This is known as contract basis risk.
- The protection seller is materially at risk of default. If this seller and the reference asset are correlated (that is, if they are subject to many of the same economic and market forces), the risk to the protection buyer increases.
- Language in credit derivatives' contracts is complex and can be subject to different interpretations.

Credit Insurance

Credit insurance, a recent innovation for commercial loans, is not yet used extensively. Examiners should look for coverage-limiting insurance underwriting specifications such as deductible amounts and exclusion of certain loss events. Additionally, the insurer's financial strength and default risk should be evaluated. If the underwriting is acceptable and the insurer is strong, insurance can enhance a credit's risk rating in much the way an L/C does.

Accounting Issues

Accounting issues are intertwined with credit risk ratings, particularly at the classified level where the credit risk rating often dictates the accounting treatment. A brief discussion of accounting issues follows.

Rebooking Charged-off Credit

In 1997, the instructions to the call report were brought into compliance with generally accepted accounting principles (GAAP) and the practice of rebooking charged-off loans was disallowed. Under GAAP, when a bank charges off a loan or lease in part or full, the bank establishes a new cost basis. Once the loan's cost basis has been decreased, it cannot be increased later.

Nonaccrual

A loan that is on nonaccrual or about to be placed on nonaccrual has severe problems such that the full collection of interest and principal is highly questionable. Nonaccrual loans will almost always be classified. A bank places a loan on nonaccrual according to criteria in the call report instructions. The general rule is that an asset should be placed on nonaccrual when principal or interest is 90 days or more past due, unless the asset is well-secured and in the process of collection. A "well-secured" asset is secured by a lien or pledge of collateral that has a realizable value sufficient to discharge the debt fully (including accrued interest), or it is secured by the guarantee of a financially responsible party.

An asset is "in the process of collection" if collection of the asset is proceeding in due course through legal action (including the enforcement of a judgment), or through efforts not involving legal action that are reasonably expected to result in the loan's repayment or in its restoration to a current status in the near future. A 30-day collection period has generally been applied to determining when a loan is "in the process of collection." Customarily, an asset can remain in that status more than 30 days only when it can be demonstrated that the timing and amount of repayment is reasonably certain.

There is no requirement that a loan must be delinquent for 90 days before it is placed on nonaccrual. Once reasonable doubt exists about a loan's collectibility, the loan should be placed on nonaccrual. When payment performance depends on the borrower drawing on lines of credit, the bank advancing additional loan funds, or the bank extending excessively lenient repayment terms, the loan should be considered for nonaccrual status.

Loans propped up in this way are often referred to as "performing – nonperforming" loans. A borrower's financial statement can be adequate evidence of a high probability of default and exposure to loss; when it is, the loan should be placed on nonaccrual. While an asset is in nonaccrual status, some or all of the cash interest payments received may be treated as interest income on a cash basis as long as the remaining book balance of the asset is deemed to be fully collectible.

Consumer loans and loans secured by one-to four-family residential properties are not required to be placed on nonaccrual when the loan becomes 90 days delinquent. Each bank should formulate its own policies on these assets to ensure that net income is not being materially overstated. Examiners should evaluate the bank's accrual policy for these loans. In doing so, they should consider the portfolio size, 90-day roll rate to loss, and whether the nonaccrual criteria apply.

The call report instructions govern the reversal of previously accrued but uncollected interest and the treatment of subsequent payments on nonaccrual assets. When a loan is placed on nonaccrual, all previously accrued but uncollected interest should be reversed, unless the loan is secured by a U.S. government guarantee.

For interest accrued in the current accounting period, the bank makes an adjusting entry directly against the interest income account. For prior accounting periods, the bank charges the ALLL if provisions for possible interest loss were made. If accrued interest provisions have not been made, the entire amount is charged against interest income. An asset may be restored to accrual status when all principal and interest is current and the bank expects full repayment of the remaining contractual principal and interest, or when the asset otherwise becomes well-secured and is in the process of collection. The following assets do not have to meet these requirements to be restored to accrual status:

- Formally restructured loans qualifying for accrual status.
- Assets acquired at a discount from an unaffiliated third party.

- Loans that remain past due, but for which the borrower has resumed full payment of interest and principal according to contractual specifications. Such loans qualify only if (1) all contractual amounts due can reasonably be expected to be repaid within a prudent period and (2) repayment has been in accordance with the contract for a sustained period (usually at least six months).

Formally Restructured Loans

Restructured debt should be identified by the bank's internal credit review system and closely monitored by management. When analysing a formally restructured loan, the examiner should focus on the borrower's ability to repay the credit in accordance with its modified terms.

The assignment of special mention status to a formally restructured credit would be appropriate if potential weaknesses remain after the restructuring. It would be appropriate to classify a formally restructured extension of credit adversely when well-defined weaknesses exist that jeopardize the orderly repayment of the credit under its modified terms. Restructured loans require a period of sustained performance, generally six months, under the restructured terms before being upgraded to a pass rating. For a further discussion of troubled debt restructuring, see the glossary section of the call report instructions.

Loans Purchased at Discount

A bank purchasing a credit at a discount from its face amount must book the loan at the purchase price. Ordinarily, the discount is recognized as an adjustment of yield over the remaining contractual life of the loan. However, if the loan is acquired at a discount because full payment is not expected, the discount should be accounted for in accordance with the guidance in AICPA Bulletin 6, "Amortization of Discounts on Certain Acquired Loans," August 1989.

13

Credit Risk: Concepts and Process of Risk Management

Credit risk is an investor's risk of loss arising from a borrower who does not make payments as promised. Such an event is called a default. Another term for credit risk is default risk.

Investor losses include lost principal and interest, decreased cash flow, and increased collection costs, which arise in a number of circumstances:

- A consumer does not make a payment due on a mortgage loan, credit card, line of credit, or other loan
- A business does not make a payment due on a mortgage, credit card, line of credit, or other loan
- A business or consumer does not pay a trade invoice when due
- A business does not pay an employee's earned wages when due
- A business or government bond issuer does not make a payment on a coupon or principal payment when due
- An insolvent insurance company does not pay a policy obligation
- An insolvent bank won't return funds to a depositor
- A government grants bankruptcy protection to an insolvent consumer or business.

Types of Credit Risk

- Default risk
- Credit spread risk
- Downgrade risk.

Mitigating Credit Risk

Lenders mitigate credit risk using several methods:

- Risk-based pricing: Lenders generally charge a higher interest rate to borrowers who are more likely to default, a practice called risk-based pricing. Lenders consider factors relating to the loan such as loan purpose, credit rating, and loan-to-value ratio and estimates the effect on yield (credit spread).
- Covenants: Lenders may write stipulations on the borrower, called covenants, into loan agreements:
    - o Periodically report its financial condition
    - o Refrain from paying dividends, repurchasing shares, borrowing further, or other specific, voluntary actions that negatively affect the company's financial position
    - o Repay the loan in full, at the lender's request, in certain events such as changes in the borrower's debt-to-equity ratio or interest coverage ratio.
- Credit insurance and credit derivatives: Lenders and bond holders may hedge their credit risk by purchasing credit insurance or credit derivatives. These contracts transfer the risk from the lender to the seller (insurer) in exchange for payment. The most common credit derivative is the credit default swap.
- Tightening: Lenders can reduce credit risk by reducing the amount of credit extended, either in total or to certain borrowers. For example, a distributor selling its products to a troubled retailer may attempt to lessen credit risk by reducing payment terms from *net 30* to *net 15.*
- Diversification: Lenders to a small number of borrowers (or kinds of borrower) face a high degree of unsystematic credit risk, called concentration risk. Lenders reduce this risk by diversifying the borrower pool.
- Deposit insurance: Many governments establish deposit insurance to guarantee bank deposits of insolvent banks. Such protection discourages consumers from withdrawing money when a bank is becoming insolvent, to avoid a bank run, and encourages consumers to holding their savings in the banking system instead of in cash.

Credit Risk Related Acronyms

ACPM Active credit portfolio management

EAD Exposure at default

EL Expected loss

ERM Enterprise risk management

LGD Loss given default

PD Probability of default

KMV quantitative credit analysis solution developed by credit rating agency Moody's.

Risk-return Spectrum

The risk-return spectrum is the relationship between the amount of return gained on an investment and the amount of risk undertaken in that investment. The more return sought, the more risk that must be undertaken.

The Progression

There are various classes of possible investments, each with their own positions on the overall risk-return spectrum. The general progression is: short-term debt; long-term debt; property; high-yield debt; equity. There is considerable overlap of the ranges for each investment class. All this can be visualised by plotting expected return on the vertical axis against risk (represented by standard deviation upon that expected return) on the horizontal axis. This line starts at the risk-free rate and rises as risk rises. The line will tend to be straight, and will be straight at equilibrium.

For any particular investment type, the line drawn from the risk-free rate on the vertical axis to the risk-return point for that investment has a slope called the Sharpe ratio.

Short-term Loans to Good Government Bodies

A lowest end is short-dated loans to government and government-guaranteed entities (usually semi-independent government departments). The lowest of all is the risk-free rate of return. The risk-free rate has zero risk (most modern major governments will inflate and monetise their debts rather than default upon them), but the return is positive because there is still both the time-preference and inflation premium components of minimum expected rates of return that must be met or exceeded if the funding is to be forthcoming from providers. The risk-free rate is commonly approximated by the return paid upon 30-day or their equivalent, but in reality that rate has more to do with the monetary policy of that country's central bank than the market supply conditions for credit.

Mid- and Long-term Loans to Good Government Bodies

The next types of investment is longer-term loans to government, such as 3-year bonds. The range width is larger, and follows the influence of increasing risk premium required as the maturity of that debt grows longer. Nevertheless, because it is debt of good government the highest end of the range is still comparatively low compared to the ranges of other investment types discussed below. Also, if the government in question is not at the highest jurisdiction (i.e., is a state or municipal government), or the smaller that government is, the more along the risk-return spectrum that government's securities will be.

Mid- and Long-term Loans to Blue-chip Corporations

Overlapping the range for short-term debt is the longer term debt from those same well-rated corporations. These are higher up the range because the maturity has increased. The overlap occurs of the mid-term debt of the best rated corporations with the short-term debt of the nearly-but-not perfectly-rated corporations.

In this arena, the debts are called investment grade by the rating agencies. The lower the credit rating, the higher the yield and thus the expected return.

High-yield Debt

After the returns upon all classes of investment-grade debt come the returns on speculative grade high-yield debt (also known derisively as junk bonds). These may come from mid and low rated corporations, and less politically stable governments.

Equity

Equity returns are the profits earned by businesses after interest and tax. Even the equity returns on the highest rated corporations are notably risky. Small-cap stocks are generally riskier than large-cap; companies that primarily service governments, or provide basic consumer goods such as food or utilities, tend to be less volatile than those in other industries. Note that since stocks tend to rise when corporate bonds fall and vice-versa, a portfolio containing a small percentage of stocks can be less risky than one containing only debts.

Options and Futures

Option and futures contracts often provide leverage on underlying stocks, bonds or commodities; this increases the returns but also the risks. Note that in some cases, derivatives can be used to hedge, decreasing the overall risk of the portfolio due to negative correlation with other investments.

Why the Progression?

The existence of risk causes the need to incur a number of expenses. For example, the more risky the investment the more time and effort is usually required to obtain information about it and monitor its progress. For another, the importance of a loss of X amount of value is greater than the importance of a gain of X amount of value, so a riskier investment will attract a higher risk premium even if the forecast return is the same as upon a less risky investment. Risk is therefore something that must be compensated for, and the more risk the more compensation required.

If an investment had a high return with low risk, eventually everyone would want to invest there. That action would drive down the actual rate of return achieved, until it reached the rate of return the market deems commensurate with the level of risk. Similarly, if an investment had a low return with high risk, all the present investors would want to leave that investment, which would then increase the actual return until again it reached the rate of return the market deems commensurate with the level of risk. That part of total returns which sets this appropriate level is called the risk premium.

Default (finance)

In finance, default occurs when a debtor has not met his or her legal obligations according to the debt contract, e.g. has not made a scheduled payment, or has violated a loan covenant (condition) of the debt contract. A default is the failure to pay back a loan. Default may occur if the debtor is either unwilling or unable to pay their debt. This can occur with all debt obligations including bonds, mortgages, loans, and promissory notes.

Distinction from Insolvency and Bankruptcy

The term default should be distinguished from the terms insolvency and bankruptcy.

- "Default" essentially means a debtor has not paid a debt which he or she is required to have paid.

- "Insolvency" is a legal term meaning that a debtor is unable to pay his or her debts.
- "Bankruptcy" is a legal finding that imposes court supervision over the financial affairs of those who are insolvent or in default.

Sovereign Defaults

A sovereign default is a failure by the government of a sovereign state to pay back its debt in full.

If potential lenders or bond purchasers begin to suspect that a government may fail to pay back its debt, they may demand a high interest rate in compensation for the risk of default. A dramatic rise in the interest rate faced by a government due to fear that it will fail to honor its debt is sometimes called a sovereign debt crisis. Governments may be especially vulnerable to a sovereign debt crisis when they rely on financing through short-term bonds, since this creates a situation of maturity mismatch between their short-term bond financing and the long-term asset value of their tax base. They may also be vulnerable to a sovereign debt crisis due to currency mismatch if they are unable to issue bonds in their own currency, as a decrease in the value of their own currency may then make it prohibitively expensive to pay back their foreign-denominated bonds

Since a sovereign government, by definition, controls its own affairs, it cannot be obliged to pay back its debt. Nonetheless, a government which defaults may be excluded from further credit; some of its overseas assets may be seized; and it may face political pressure from its own domestic bondholders to pay back its debt. Therefore governments rarely default on the entire value of their debt. Instead, they often enter into negotiations with their bondholders to agree on a delay or partial reduction of their debt payments, which is often called a debt restructuring or 'haircut'.

Some economists have argued that, in the case of acute insolvency crises, it can be advisable for regulators and multilateral lenders to preemptively engineer the orderly restructuring of a nation's public debt-also called "orderly default" or "controlled default". In the case of Greece, these experts generally believe that a delay in organising an orderly default would wind up hurting the rest of Europe even more.

The International Monetary Fund often assists in sovereign debt restructurings. To ensure that funds will be available to pay the remaining part of the sovereign debt, it often makes its loans conditional on austerity measures within the country, such as tax increases or reductions in public sector jobs and services. A recent example is the Greek bailout agreement of May 2010.

Sovereign borrowers such as nation-states generally are not subject to bankruptcy courts in their own jurisdiction, and thus may be able to default without legal consequences. One example is with North Korea, which in 1987 defaulted on some of its loans. In such cases, the defaulting country and the creditor are more likely to renegotiate the interest rate, length of the loan, or the principal payments. In the 1998 Russian financial crisis, Russia defaulted on its internal debt (GKOs), but did not default on its external Eurobonds. As part of the Argentine economic crisis in 2002, Argentina defaulted on $1 billion of debt owed to the World Bank.

List of Sovereign Debt Crises

The following list includes episodes in which risk premia on sovereign bonds have risen sharply, as well as a partial list of actual sovereign defaults and debt restructuring.

- Latin American debt crisis (1980s)
- 1994 economic crisis in Mexico
- 1998 Russian financial crisis
- Argentine debt restructuring (2002)
- 2010 European sovereign debt crisis.

Orderly Defaults

In times of acute insolvency crises, it can be advisable for regulators and lenders to preemptively engineer the methodic restructuring of a nation's public debt-also called "orderly default" or "controlled default". Experts who favour this approach to solve a national debt crisis typically argue that a delay in organising an orderly default would wind up hurting lenders and neighboring countries even more.

Strategic Default

A strategic default is the decision by a borrower to stop making payments (i.e., to default) on a debt despite having the financial ability to make the payments.

This is particularly associated with residential and commercial mortgages, in which case it usually occurs after a substantial drop in the house's price such that the debt owed is (considerably) greater than the value of the property — the property has negative equity or is "underwater" — and is expected to remain so for the foreseeable future, such as following the bursting of a real estate bubble. Such borrowers are called "walkaways."

Prevalence Post-housing Bubble

Distinguished economists Paul Krugman and Hal Varian have acknowledged that strategic default will be an inevitable result of the collapse of the finance and property bubble of the era following 2006. They also note that this is one of the few ways of freeing people from the burden of mortgage debt. Once free of the mortgage debtors are free to use their income for other expenditures. A study in September 2009 from the credit reporting agency Experian and consulting outfit Oliver Wyman estimated that close to a fifth of troubled mortgages in the U.S. involved borrowers who were strategically defaulting.

Sovereign Strategic Default

As with Strategic default when a debtor *chooses* to default on a loan sovereign borrowers such as nation-states also can choose to default on a loan. Ecuador's president Rafael Correa in 2008 had given the order not to approve a debt interest payment.

Consumer Default

Consumer default frequently concern arrears in rent or mortgage payments, consumer credit, or utility payments. A European Union wide analysis identified certain risk groups, such as single households, being unemployed – even after correcting for the (significant) impact of having a low income-, being young (especially being younger than around 50 years old, with somewhat different results for the New Member States, where the elderly more often at risk as well), being unable to rely on social networks, etc. Even internet illiteracy has been associated with increased default, potentially caused by these households being less likely to find their way to the social benefits they are often entitled to. While effective non-legal debt counseling is usually the preferred-more economic and less disruptive-option, consumer default can end-up in legal debt settlement or consumer bankruptcy procedures, the last ranging from 1-year procedures in the UK to 6-year procedures in Germany.

Settlement (Finance)

Settlement of securities is a business process whereby securities or interests in securities are delivered, usually against (in simultaneous exchange for) payment of money, to fulfil contractual obligations, such as those arising under securities trades.

In the U.S., the settlement date for marketable stocks is usually 3 (three) business days after the trade is executed, and for listed options and government securities it is usually 1 (one) day after the execution.

As part of performance on the delivery obligations entailed by the trade, settlement involves the delivery of securities and the corresponding payment.

A number of risks arise for the parties during the settlement interval, which are managed by the process of clearing, which follows trading and precedes settlement. Clearing involves modifying those contractual obligations so as to facilitate settlement, often by netting and novation.

Nature of Settlement

Settlement involves the delivery of securities from one party to another. Delivery usually takes place against payment, but some deliveries are made without a corresponding payment (sometimes referred to as a *free delivery*). Examples of a delivery without payment are the delivery of securities collateral against a loan of securities, and a delivery made pursuant to a margin call.

Traditional (Physical) Settlement

Prior to modern financial market technologies and methods such as depositories and securities held in electronic form, securities settlement had involved the physical movement of paper instruments, or certificates and transfer forms. Payment was usually made by paper check upon receipt by the registrar or transfer agent of properly negotiated certificates and other requisite documents.

Physical settlement securities still exist in modern markets today mostly for private (restricted or unregistered) securities as opposed to those of publicly (exchange) traded securities, however payment of money today is typically made via electronic funds transfer (in the U.S., a bank wire transfer made through the Federal Reserve's Fedwire system). Physical/paper settlement involves higher risks, inasmuch as paper instruments, certificates, and transfer forms are subject to risks electronic media are not more or less such as loss, theft, counterfeit, and forgery.

The U.S. securities markets experienced what became known as "the paper crunch," as settlement delays threatened to disrupt the operations of the securities markets which led to the formation of electronic settlement via a Central Securities Depository, specifically the Depository Trust Company (DTC), and ultimately its parent, the Depository Trust & Clearing Corporation. In the United Kingdom, the weakness of paper-based settlement was exposed by a programme of privatisation of nationalised industries in the 1980s, and the Big Bang of 1986 led to an explosion in the volume of trades, and settlement delays became significant. In the market crash of 1987, many investors sought to limit their losses by selling their securities, but found that the failure of timely settlement left them exposed.

Electronic Settlement

The electronic settlement system came about largely as a result of *Clearance and Settlement Systems in the World's Securities Markets*, a major report in 1989 by the Washington-based think tank, the Group of Thirty. This report made nine recommendations with a view to achieving more efficient settlement. This was followed up in 2003 with a report, Clearing and Settlement: A Plan of Action, with 20 recommendations. In an electronic settlement system, electronic settlement takes place between participants. If a non-participant wishes to settle its interests, it must do so through a participant acting as a custodian. The interests of participants are recorded by credit entries in securities accounts maintained in their names by the operator of the system. It permits both quick and efficient settlement by removing the need for paperwork, and the simultaneous delivery of securities with the payment of a corresponding cash sum (called delivery versus payment, or DVP) in the agreed upon currency.

Legal Significance

After the trade and before settlement, the rights of the purchaser are contractual and therefore personal. Because they are merely personal, their rights are at risk in the event of the insolvency of the vendor. After settlement, the purchaser owns securities and their rights are proprietary. Settlement is the delivery of securities to complete trades. It involves upgrading personal rights into property rights and thus protects market participants from the risk of the default of their counterparties.

Immobilisation and Dematerialisation

Immobilisation and dematerialisation are the two broad goals of electronic settlement. Both were identified by the influential report by the Group of Thirty in 1989.

Immobilisation

Immobilisation entails the use of securities in paper form and the use of a Central Securities Depository or more than one, which is/are electronically linked to a settlement system. Securities (either constituted by paper instruments or represented by paper certificates) are immobilised in the sense that they are held by the depository at all times. In the historic transition from paper-based to electronic practice, immoblisation often serves as a transitional phase prior to dematerialisation. The Depository Trust Company in New York is the largest immobilizer of securities in the world. Euroclear and Clearstream Banking, Luxembourg are two important examples of international immobilisation systems. Both originally settled eurobonds, but now a wide range of international securities are settled through them including many types of sovereign debt and equity securities.

Dematerialisation

Dematerialisation involves dispensing of paper instruments and certificates altogether. Dematerialised securities exist only in the form of electronic records. The legal impact of dematerialisation differs in relation to bearer and registered securities respectively.

Direct and Indirect Holding Systems

In a direct holding system, participants hold the underlying securities directly. The settlement system does not stand in the chain of ownership, but merely serves as a conduit for communications of participants to issuers.

Security (Finance)

A security is generally a fungible, negotiable financial instrument representing financial value. Securities are broadly categorized into:

- debt securities (such as banknotes, bonds and debentures),
- equity securities, e.g., common stocks; and,
- derivative contracts, such as forwards, futures, options and swaps.

The company or other entity issuing the security is called the issuer. A country's regulatory structure determines what qualifies as a security. For example, private investment pools may have some features of securities, but they may not be registered or regulated as such if they meet various restrictions.

Securities may be represented by a certificate or, more typically, "non-certificated", that is in electronic or "book entry" only form. Certificates may be *bearer*, meaning they entitle the holder to rights under the security merely by holding the security, or *registered*, meaning they entitle the holder to rights only if he or she appears on a security register maintained by the issuer or an intermediary.

They include shares of corporate stock or mutual funds, bonds issued by corporations or governmental agencies, stock options or other options, limited partnership units, and various other formal investment instruments that are negotiable and fungible.

Debt and Equity

Securities are traditionally divided into debt securities and equities.

Debt

Debt securities may be called debentures, bonds, deposits, notes or commercial paper depending on their maturity and certain other characteristics. The holder of a debt security is typically entitled to the payment of principal and interest, together with other contractual rights under the terms of the issue, such as the right to receive certain information. Debt securities are generally issued for a fixed term and redeemable by the issuer at the end of that term. Debt securities may be protected by collateral or may be unsecured, and, if they are unsecured, may be contractually "senior" to other unsecured debt meaning their holders would have a priority in a bankruptcy of the issuer. Debt that is not senior is "subordinated".

Corporate bonds represent the debt of commercial or industrial entities. Debentures have a long maturity, typically at least ten years, whereas notes have a shorter maturity. Commercial paper is a simple form of debt security that essentially represents a post-dated check with a maturity of not more than 270 days.

Money market instruments are short term debt instruments that may have characteristics of deposit accounts, such as certificates of deposit, and certain bills of exchange. They are highly liquid and are sometimes referred to as "near cash". Commercial paper is also often highly liquid. Euro debt securities are securities issued internationally outside their domestic market in a denomination different from that of the issuer's domicile. They include eurobonds and euronotes. Eurobonds are characteristically underwritten, and not secured, and interest is paid gross. A euronote may take the form of euro-commercial paper (ECP) or euro-certificates of deposit.

Government bonds are medium or long term debt securities issued by sovereign governments or their agencies. Typically they carry a lower rate of interest than corporate bonds, and serve as a source of finance for governments. U.S. federal government bonds are called *treasuries*. Because of their liquidity and perceived low risk, treasuries are used to manage the money supply in the open market operations of non-US central banks.

Sub-sovereign government bonds, known in the U.S. as municipal bonds, represent the debt of state, provincial, territorial, municipal or other governmental units other than sovereign governments.

Supranational bonds represent the debt of international organizations such as the World Bank, the International Monetary Fund, regional multilateral development banks and others.

Derivatives

A derivative is a financial instrument whose value depends on underlying variables. The most common derivatives are futures, options, and swaps but may also include other tradeable assets such as a stock or commodity or non-tradeable items such as the temperature (in the case of weather derivatives), the unemployment rate, or any kind of (economic) index. A derivative is essentially a contract whose payoff depends on the behaviour of a benchmark.

One of the oldest derivatives is rice futures, which have been traded on the Dojima Rice Exchange since the eighteenth century.

Derivatives are broadly categorized by the relationship between the underlying asset and the derivative (e.g., forward, option, swap); the type of underlying asset (e.g., equity derivatives, foreign exchange derivatives, interest rate derivatives, commodity derivatives or credit derivatives); the market in which they trade (e.g., exchange-traded or over-the-counter); and their pay-off profile. Derivatives can be used for speculating purposes ("bets") or to hedge ("insurance"). For example, a speculator may sell deep in-the-money naked calls on a stock, expecting the stock price to plummet, but exposing himself to potentially unlimited losses. Very commonly, companies buy currency forwards in order to limit losses due to fluctuations in the exchange rate of two currencies.

Hedging

Derivatives allow risk related to the price of the underlying asset to be transferred from one party to another. For example, a wheat farmer and a miller could sign a futures contract to exchange a specified amount of cash for a specified amount of wheat in the future. Both parties have reduced a future risk: for the wheat farmer, the uncertainty of the price, and for the miller, the availability of wheat. However, there is still the risk that no wheat will be available because of events unspecified by the contract, such as the weather, or that one party will renege on the contract. Although a third party, called a clearing house, insures a futures contract, not all derivatives are insured against counter-party risk.

From another perspective, the farmer and the miller both reduce a risk and acquire a risk when they sign the futures contract: the farmer reduces the risk that the price of wheat will fall below the price specified in the contract and acquires the risk that the price of wheat will rise above the price specified in the contract (thereby losing additional income that he could have earned). The miller, on the other hand, acquires the risk that the price of wheat will fall below the price specified in the contract (thereby paying more in the future than he otherwise would have) and reduces the risk that the price of wheat will rise above the price specified in the contract. In this sense, one party is the insurer (risk taker) for one type of risk, and the counter-party is the insurer (risk taker) for another type of risk.

Hedging also occurs when an individual or institution buys an asset (such as a commodity, a bond that has coupon payments, a stock that pays dividends, and so on) and sells it using a futures contract. The individual or institution has access to the asset for a specified amount of time, and can then sell it in the future at a specified price according to the futures contract. Of course, this allows the individual or institution the benefit of holding the asset, while reducing the risk that the future selling price will deviate unexpectedly from the market's current assessment of the future value of the asset.

Derivatives can serve legitimate business purposes. For example, a corporation borrows a large sum of money at a specific interest rate. The rate of interest on the loan resets every six months. The corporation is concerned that the rate of interest may be much higher in six months. The corporation could buy a forward rate agreement (FRA), which is a contract to pay a fixed rate of interest six months after purchases on a notional amount of money. If the interest rate after six months is above the contract rate, the seller will pay the difference to the corporation, or FRA buyer. If the rate is lower, the corporation will pay the difference to the seller. The purchase of the FRA serves to reduce the uncertainty concerning the rate increase and stabilize earnings.

Speculation and Arbitrage

Derivatives can be used to acquire risk, rather than to insure or hedge against risk. Thus, some individuals and institutions will enter into a derivative contract to speculate on the value of the underlying asset, betting that the party seeking insurance will be wrong about the future value of the underlying asset. Speculators look to buy an asset in the future at a low price according to a derivative contract when the future market price is high, or to sell an asset in the future at a high price according to a derivative contract when the future market price is low. Individuals and institutions may also look for arbitrage opportunities, as when the current buying price of an asset falls below the price specified in a futures contract to sell the asset.

Speculative trading in derivatives gained a great deal of notoriety in 1995 when Nick Leeson, a trader at Barings Bank, made poor and unauthorized investments in futures contracts. Through a combination of poor judgment, lack of oversight by the bank's management and regulators, and unfortunate events like the Kobe earthquake, Leeson incurred a US$1.3 billion loss that bankrupted the centuries-old institution.

Types—OTC and Exchange-traded

In broad terms, there are two groups of derivative contracts, which are distinguished by the way they are traded in the market:

- Over-the-counter (OTC) derivatives are contracts that are traded (and privately negotiated) directly between two parties, without going through an exchange or other intermediary. Products such as swaps, forward rate agreements, and exotic options are almost always traded in this way. The OTC derivative market is the largest market for derivatives, and is largely unregulated with respect to disclosure of information between the parties, since the OTC market is made up of banks and other highly sophisticated parties, such as hedge funds. Reporting of OTC amounts are difficult because trades can occur in private, without activity being visible on any exchange. According to the Bank for International Settlements, the total outstanding notional amount is US$684 trillion (as of June 2008). Of this total notional amount, 67% are interest rate contracts, 8% are credit default swaps (CDS), 9% are foreign exchange contracts, 2% are commodity contracts, 1% are equity contracts, and 12% are other. Because OTC derivatives are not traded on an exchange, there is no central counter-party. Therefore, they are subject to counter-party risk, like an ordinary contract, since each counter-party relies on the other to perform.

- Exchange-traded derivative contracts (ETD) are those derivatives instruments that are traded via specialized derivatives exchanges or other exchanges. A derivatives exchange is a market where individuals trade standardized contracts that have been defined by the exchange. A derivatives exchange acts as an intermediary to all related transactions, and takes Initial margin from both sides of the trade to act as a guarantee. The world's largest derivatives exchanges (by number of transactions) are the Korea Exchange (which lists KOSPI Index Futures & Options), Eurex (which lists a wide range of European products such as interest rate & index products), and CME Group (made up of the 2007 merger of the Chicago Mercantile Exchange and the Chicago Board of Trade and the 2008 acquisition of the New York Mercantile Exchange). According to BIS, the combined turnover in the world's derivatives exchanges totaled USD 344 trillion during Q4 2005. Some types of derivative instruments also may trade on traditional exchanges. For instance, hybrid instruments such as convertible bonds and/or convertible preferred may be listed on stock or bond exchanges. Also, warrants (or "rights") may be listed on equity exchanges. Performance Rights, Cash xPRTs and various other instruments that essentially consist of a complex set of options bundled into a simple package are routinely listed on equity exchanges. Like other derivatives, these publicly traded derivatives provide investors access to risk/reward and volatility characteristics that, while related to an underlying commodity, nonetheless are distinctive.

Common Derivative Contract Types

There are three major classes of derivatives:

1. Futures/Forwards are contracts to buy or sell an asset on or before a future date at a price specified today. A futures contract differs from a forward contract in that the futures contract is a standardized contract written by a clearing house that operates an exchange where the contract can be bought

and sold, whereas a forward contract is a non-standardized contract written by the parties themselves.

2. Options are contracts that give the owner the right, but not the obligation, to buy (in the case of a call option) or sell (in the case of a put option) an asset. The price at which the sale takes place is known as the strike price, and is specified at the time the parties enter into the option. The option contract also specifies a maturity date. In the case of a European option, the owner has the right to require the sale to take place on (but not before) the maturity date; in the case of an American option, the owner can require the sale to take place at any time up to the maturity date. If the owner of the contract exercises this right, the counter-party has the obligation to carry out the transaction.
3. Swaps are contracts to exchange cash (flows) on or before a specified future date based on the underlying value of currencies/exchange rates, bonds/interest rates, commodities, stocks or other assets.

More complex derivatives can be created by combining the elements of these basic types. For example, the holder of a swaption has the right, but not the obligation, to enter into a swap on or before a specified future date.

Stock

The capital stock (or just stock) of a business entity represents the original capital paid into or invested in the business by its founders. It serves as a security for the creditors of a business since it cannot be withdrawn to the detriment of the creditors. Stock is distinct from the property and the assets of a business which may fluctuate in quantity and value.

Shares

The stock of a business is divided into multiple shares, the total of which must be stated at the time of business formation. Given the total amount of money invested in the business, a share has a certain declared face value, commonly known as the par value of a share. The par value is the *de minimis* (minimum) amount of money that a business may issue and sell shares for in many jurisdictions and it is the value represented as capital in the accounting of the business. In other jurisdictions, however, shares may not have an associated par value at all. Such stock is often called non-par stock. Shares represent a fraction of ownership in a business. A business may declare different types (*classes*) of shares, each having distinctive ownership rules, privileges, or share values.

Ownership of shares is documented by issuance of a stock certificate. A stock certificate is a legal document that specifies the amount of shares owned by the shareholder, and other specifics of the shares, such as the par value, if any, or the class of the shares.

Types of Stock

Stock typically takes the form of shares of either common stock or preferred stock. As a unit of ownership, common stock typically carries voting rights that can be exercised in corporate decisions. Preferred stock differs from common stock in that it typically does not carry voting rights but is legally entitled to receive a certain level of dividend payments before any dividends can be issued to other shareholders. Convertible preferred stock is preferred stock that includes an option for the holder to convert the preferred shares into a fixed number of common shares, usually anytime after a predetermined date. Shares of such stock are called "convertible preferred shares" (or "convertible preference shares" in the UK)

New equity issues may have specific legal clauses attached that differentiate them from previous issues of the issuer. Some shares of common stock may be issued without the typical voting rights, for instance, or some shares may have special rights unique to them and issued only to certain parties. Often, new issues that have not been registered with a securities governing body may be restricted from resale for certain periods of time.

Preferred stock may be hybrid by having the qualities of bonds of fixed returns and common stock voting rights. They also have preference in the payment of dividends over common stock and also have been given preference at the time of liquidation over common stock. They have other features of accumulation in dividend.

Stock Derivatives

A stock derivative is any financial instrument which has a value that is dependent on the price of the underlying stock. Futures and options are the main types of derivatives on stocks. The underlying security may be a stock index or an individual firm's stock, e.g. single-stock futures.

Stock futures are contracts where the buyer is long, i.e., takes on the obligation to buy on the contract maturity date, and the seller is short, i.e., takes on the obligation to sell. Stock index futures are generally not delivered in the usual manner, but by cash settlement.

A stock option is a class of option. Specifically, a call option is the right (*not* obligation) to buy stock in the future at a fixed price and a put option is the right (*not* obligation) to sell stock in the future at a fixed price. Thus, the value of a stock option changes in reaction to the underlying stock of which it is a derivative. The most popular method of valuing stock options is the Black Scholes model. Apart from call options granted to employees, most stock options are transferable.

Equity Derivative

In finance, an equity derivative is a class of derivatives whose value is at least partly *derived* from one or more underlying equity securities. Options and futures are by far the most common equity derivatives, however there are many other types of equity derivatives that are actively traded.

Option Valuation

The theoretical value of an option is evaluated according to any of several mathematical models. These models, which are developed by quantitative analysts, attempt to predict how the value of an option changes in response to changing conditions. For example how the price changes with respect to changes in time to expiration or how an increase in volatility would have an impact on the value.

Hence, the risks associated with granting, owning, or trading options may be quantified and managed with a greater degree of precision, perhaps, than with some other investments. Exchange-traded options form an important class of options which have standardized contract features and trade on public exchanges, facilitating trading among independent parties. Over-the-counter options are traded between private parties, often well-capitalized institutions that have negotiated separate trading and clearing arrangements with each other.

Other Option Types

Another important class of options, particularly in the U.S., are employee stock options, which are awarded by a company to their employees as a form of incentive compensation. Other types of options exist in many financial contracts, for example real estate options are often used to assemble large parcels of land, and prepayment options are usually included in mortgage loans. However, many of the valuation and risk management principles apply across all financial options.

Option Styles

Naming conventions are used to help identify properties common to many different types of options. These include:

- European option – an option that may only be exercised on expiration.
- American option – an option that may be exercised on any trading day on or before expiry.
- Bermudan option – an option that may be exercised only on specified dates on or before expiration.
- Barrier option – any option with the general characteristic that the underlying security's price must pass a certain level or "barrier" before it can be exercised.
- Exotic option – any of a broad category of options that may include complex financial structures.
- Vanilla option – any option that is not exotic.

Valuation Models

The value of an option can be estimated using a variety of quantitative techniques based on the concept of risk neutral pricing and using stochastic calculus. The most basic model is the Black-Scholes model. More sophisticated models are used to model the volatility smile. These models are implemented using a variety of numerical techniques. In general, standard option valuation models depend on the following factors:

- The current market price of the underlying security,
- the strike price of the option, particularly in relation to the current market price of the underlying (in the money vs. out of the money),
- the cost of holding a position in the underlying security, including interest and dividends,
- the time to expiration together with any restrictions on when exercise may occur, and
- an estimate of the future volatility of the underlying security's price over the life of the option.

More advanced models can require additional factors, such as an estimate of how volatility changes over time and for various underlying price levels, or the dynamics of stochastic interest rates. The following are some of the principal valuation techniques used in practice to evaluate option contracts.

Black-Scholes

Following early work by Louis Bachelier and later work by Edward O. Thorp, Fischer Black and Myron Scholes made a major breakthrough by deriving a differential equation that must be satisfied by the price of any derivative dependent on a non-dividend-paying stock. By employing the technique of constructing a risk neutral portfolio that replicates the returns of holding an option, Black and Scholes produced a closed-form solution for a European option's theoretical price. At the same time, the model generates hedge parameters necessary for effective risk management of option holdings.

While the ideas behind the Black-Scholes model were ground-breaking and eventually led to Scholes and Merton receiving the Swedish Central Bank's associated Prize for Achievement in Economics (a.k.a., the Nobel Prize in Economics), the application of the model in actual options trading is clumsy because of the assumptions of continuous (or no) dividend payment, constant volatility, and a constant interest rate. Nevertheless, the Black-Scholes model is still one of the most important methods and foundations for the existing financial market in which the result is within the reasonable range.

Stochastic Volatility Models

Since the market crash of 1987, it has been observed that market implied volatility for options of lower strike prices are typically higher than for higher strike prices, suggesting that volatility is stochastic, varying both for time and for the price level of the underlying security. Stochastic volatility models have been developed including one developed by S.L. Heston. One principal advantage of the Heston model is that it can be solved in closed-form, while other stochastic volatility models require complex numerical methods.

Model Implementation

Once a valuation model has been chosen, there are a number of different techniques used to take the mathematical models to implement the models.

Trading

The most common way to trade options is via standardized options contracts that are listed by various futures and options exchanges.

Listings and prices are tracked and can be looked up by ticker symbol. By publishing continuous, live markets for option prices, an exchange enables independent parties to engage in price discovery and execute transactions. As an intermediary to both sides of the transaction, the benefits the exchange provides to the transaction include:

- fulfilment of the contract is backed by the credit of the exchange, which typically has the highest rating (AAA),
- counterparties remain anonymous,
- enforcement of market regulation to ensure fairness and transparency, and
- maintenance of orderly markets, especially during fast trading conditions.

Over-the-counter options contracts are not traded on exchanges, but instead between two independent parties. Ordinarily, at least one of the counterparties is a well-capitalized institution. By avoiding an exchange, users of OTC options can narrowly tailor the terms of the option contract to suit individual business requirements. In addition, OTC option transactions generally do not need to be advertised to the market and face little or no regulatory requirements. However, OTC counterparties must establish credit lines with each other, and conform to each others clearing and settlement procedures.

With few exceptions, there are no secondary markets for employee stock options. These must either be exercised by the original grantee or allowed to expire worthless.

The Basic Trades of Traded Stock Options (American Style)

These trades are described from the point of view of a speculator. If they are combined with other positions, they can also be used in hedging. An option contract in US markets usually represents 100 shares of the underlying security.

Long Call

A trader who believes that a stock's price will increase might buy the right to purchase the stock (a call option) rather than just purchase the stock itself. He would have no obligation to buy the stock, only the right to do so until the expiration date. If the stock price at expiration is above the exercise price by more than the premium (price) paid, he will profit.

If the stock price at expiration is lower than the exercise price, he will let the call contract expire worthless, and only lose the amount of the premium. A trader might buy the option instead of shares, because for the same amount of money, he can control (leverage) a much larger number of shares.

Long Put

A trader who believes that a stock's price will decrease can buy the right to sell the stock at a fixed price (a put option). He will be under no obligation to sell the stock, but has the right to do so until the expiration date. If the stock price at expiration is below the exercise price by more than the premium paid, he will profit. If the stock price at expiration is above the exercise price, he will let the put contract expire worthless and only lose the premium paid.

Short Call

A trader who believes that a stock price will decrease, can sell the stock short or instead sell, or "write," a call. The trader selling a call has an obligation to sell the stock to the call buyer at the buyer's option. If the stock price decreases, the short call position will make a profit in the amount of the premium. If the stock price increases over the exercise price by more than the amount of the premium, the short will lose money, with the potential loss unlimited.

Short Put

A trader who believes that a stock price will increase can buy the stock or instead sell, or "write", a put. The trader selling a put has an obligation to buy the stock from the put buyer at the put buyer's option. If the stock price at expiration is above the exercise price, the short put position will make a profit in the amount of the premium. If the stock price at expiration is below the exercise price by more than the amount of the premium, the trader will lose money, with the potential loss being up to the full value of the stock. A benchmark index for the performance of a cash-secured short put option position is the CBOE S&P 500 PutWrite Index (ticker PUT).

Option Strategies

Combining any of the four basic kinds of option trades (possibly with different exercise prices and maturities) and the two basic kinds of stock trades (long and short) allows a variety of options strategies. Simple strategies usually combine only a few trades, while more complicated strategies can combine several.

Strategies are often used to engineer a particular risk profile to movements in the underlying security. For example, buying a butterfly spread (long one X1 call, short two X2 calls, and long one X3 call) allows a trader to profit if the stock price on the expiration date is near the middle exercise price, X2, and does not expose the trader to a large loss.

An Iron condor is a strategy that is similar to a butterfly spread, but with different strikes for the short options – offering a larger likelihood of profit but with a lower net credit compared to the butterfly spread. Selling a straddle (selling both a put and a call at the same exercise price) would give a trader a greater profit than a butterfly if the final stock price is near the exercise price, but might result in a large loss. Similar to the straddle is the strangle which is also constructed by a call and a put, but whose strikes are different, reducing the net debit of the trade, but also reducing the risk of loss in the trade.

One well-known strategy is the covered call, in which a trader buys a stock (or holds a previously-purchased long stock position), and sells a call. If the stock price rises above the exercise price, the call will be exercised and the trader will get a fixed profit. If the stock price falls, the call will not be exercised, and any loss incurred to the trader will be partially offset by the premium received from selling the call. Overall, the payoffs match the payoffs from selling a put. This relationship is known as put-call parity and offers insights for financial theory. A benchmark index for the performance of a buy-write strategy is the CBOE S&P 500 BuyWrite Index (ticker symbol BXM).

Structure and Features

Warrants have similar characteristics to that of other equity derivatives, such as options, for instance:

- Exercising: A warrant is exercised when the holder informs the issuer their intention to purchase the shares underlying the warrant.

The warrant parameters, such as exercise price, are fixed shortly after the issue of the bond. With warrants, it is important to consider the following main characteristics:

- Premium: A warrant's "premium" represents how much extra you have to pay for your shares when buying them through the warrant as compared to buying them in the regular way.
- Gearing (leverage): A warrant's "gearing" is the way to ascertain how much more exposure you have to the underlying shares using the warrant as compared to the exposure you would have if you buy shares through the market.

- Expiration Date: This is the date the warrant expires. If you plan on exercising the warrant you must do so before the expiration date. The more time remaining until expiry, the more time for the underlying security to appreciate, which, in turn, will increase the price of the warrant (unless it depreciates). Therefore, the expiry date is the date on which the right to exercise no longer exists.
- Restrictions on exercise: Like options, there are different exercise types associated with warrants such as American style (holder can exercise anytime before expiration) or European style (holder can only exercise on expiration date).

Warrants are longer-dated options and are generally traded over-the-counter.

Secondary Market

Sometimes the issuer will try to establish a market for the warrant and to register it with a listed exchange. In this case, the price can be obtained from a broker. But often, warrants are privately held or not registered, which makes their prices less obvious.

Warrants can be easily tracked by adding a "w" after the company's ticker symbol to check the warrant's price. Unregistered warrant transactions can still be facilitated between accredited parties, and in fact several secondary markets have been formed to provide liquidity for these investments.

Comparison with Call Options

Warrants are very similar to call options. For instance, many warrants confer the same rights as equity options, and warrants often can be traded in secondary markets like options.

However, there also are several key differences between warrants and equity options:

- Warrants are issued by private parties, typically the corporation on which a warrant is based, rather than a public options exchange.
- Warrants issued by the company itself are dilutive. When the warrant issued by the company is exercised, the company issues new shares of stock, so the number of outstanding shares increases. When a call option is exercised, the owner of the call option receives an existing share from an assigned call writer (except in the case of employee stock options, where

new shares are created and issued by the company upon exercise). Unlike common stock shares outstanding, warrants do not have voting rights.

- Warrants are considered over the counter instruments, and thus are usually only traded by financial institutions with the capacity to settle and clear these types of transactions.
- A warrant's lifetime is measured in years (as long as 15 years), while options are typically measured in months. Even LEAPS (long-term equity anticipation securities), the longest stock options available, tend to expire in two or three years. Upon expiration, the warrants are worthless unless the price of the common stock is greater than the exercise price.
- Warrants are not standardized like exchange-listed options. While investors can write stock options on the ASX (or CBOE), they are not permitted to do so with ASX-listed warrants, since only companies can issue warrants, and while each option contract is over 1000 underlying ordinary shares (100 on CBOE), the number of warrants that must be exercised by the holder to buy the underlying asset depends on the conversion ratio set out in the offer documentation for the warrant issue.

Types of Warrants

A wide range of warrants and warrant types are available. The reasons you might invest in one type of warrant may be different from the reasons you might invest in another type of warrant.

- Equity warrants: Equity warrants can be call and put warrants.
    - o Callable warrants: Callable warrants give the Company the right to force the warrant holder to exercise the warrants into their predetermined number of shares at a predetermined price (or using a predetermined price formula) after certain contractual conditions are met
    - o Putable warrants: Putable warrants give the warrant holder the right to force the Company to issue the underlying securities at a predetermined price after certain contractual conditions are met.
- Covered warrants: A covered warrants is a warrant that has some underlying backing, for example the issuer will purchase the stock beforehand or will use other instruments to cover the option.

- Basket warrants: As with a regular equity index, warrants can be classified at, for example, an industry level. Thus, it mirrors the performance of the industry.
- Index warrants: Index warrants use an index as the underlying asset. Your risk is dispersed—using index call and index put warrants—just like with regular equity indexes. It should be noted that they are priced using index points. That is, you deal with cash, not directly with shares.
- Wedding warrants: are attached to the host debentures and can be exercised only if the host debentures are surrendered
- Detachable warrants: the warrant portion of the security can be detached from the debenture and traded separately.
- Naked warrants: are issued without an accompanying bond, and like traditional warrants, are traded on the stock exchange.

Traditional

Traditional warrants are issued in conjunction with a Bond (known as a warrant-linked bond), and represent the right to acquire shares in the entity issuing the bond. In other words, the writer of a traditional warrant is also the issuer of the underlying instrument. Warrants are issued in this way as a "sweetener" to make the bond issue more attractive, and to reduce the interest rate that must be offered in order to sell the bond issue.

Example

- Price paid for bond with warrants P_0
- Coupon payments C
- Maturity T
- Required rate of return r
- Face value of bond F

$$\text{Value of warrants} = P_0 - \left(\sum_{t=1}^{T} \frac{C}{(1+r)^t}\right) - \frac{F}{(1+r)^T}.$$

Third-party Warrants

Third-party warrant is a derivative issued by the holders of the underlying instrument. Suppose a company issues warrants which give the holder the right to convert each warrant into one share at $500. This warrant is company-issued. Suppose, a mutual fund that holds shares of the company sells warrants against those shares, also exercisable at $500 per share. These are called third-party warrants. The primary advantage is that the instrument helps in the price discovery process. In the above case, the mutual fund selling a one-year warrant exercisable at $500 sends a signal to other investors that the stock may trade at $500-levels in one year. If volumes in such warrants are high, the price discovery process will be that much better; for it would mean that many investors believe that the stock will trade at that level in one year. Third-party warrants are essentially long-term call options. The seller of the warrants does a covered call-write. That is, the seller will hold the stock and sell warrants against them. If the stock does not cross $500, the buyer will not exercise the warrant. The seller will, therefore, keep the warrant premium.

Uses of the Term Warrant other than as an Option on Equities

Warrant as a Check or IOU Issued by a Government Agency

The term warrant is sometimes used in the US to mean a warrant of payment which is a check or an IOU issued by a governmental agency. California differentiates between regular warrants, which can be exchanged immediately for cash and registered warrants which are IOUs.

In the late 1990s, when the State of California had a budget crisis due to a disagreement between the governor and the legislature, the state treasurer was forced to issue warrants paying 18% interest in lieu of being able to pay the state's bills with real money. The state had not issued warrants since before the Depression of the 1930s. Many institutions accepted them at face value because of the interest provision. Interestingly, the comptroller of Los Angeles County was buying the warrants because the county had surplus funds to take advantage of the higher interest rates on the warrants.

In some states, a warrant is a demand draft drawn on a government's treasury to pay its bills. Checks or electronic payments have replaced these warrants, but in Arkansas, some counties and school districts uses warrants for non-electronic payments

In finance, a warrant is a security that entitles the holder to buy stock of the company that issued it at a specified price, which is much lower than the stock price at time of issue. Warrants are frequently attached to bonds or preferred stock as a sweetener, allowing the issuer to pay lower interest rates or dividends. They can be used to enhance the yield of the bond, and make them more attractive to potential buyers.

Convertible Bonds

In finance, a convertible note (or, if it has a maturity of greater than 10 years, a convertible debenture) is a type of bond that the holder can convert into shares of common stock in the issuing company or cash of equal value, at an agreed-upon price. It is a hybrid security with debt-and equity-like features. Although it typically has a low coupon rate, the instrument carries additional value through the option to convert the bond to stock, and thereby participate in further growth in the company's equity value. The investor receives the potential upside of conversion into equity while protecting downside with cash flow from the coupon payments.

From the issuer's perspective, the key benefit of raising money by selling convertible bonds is a reduced cash interest payment. The advantage for companies of issuing convertible bonds is that, if the bonds are converted to stocks, companies' debt vanishes. However, in exchange for the benefit of reduced interest payments, the value of shareholder's equity is reduced due to the stock dilution expected when bondholders convert their bonds into new shares.

The convertible bond markets in the United States and Japan are of primary global importance. These two domestic markets are the largest in terms of market capitalisation. Other domestic convertible bond markets are often illiquid, and pricing is frequently non-standardised.

- USA: It is a highly liquid market compared to other domestic markets. Domestic investors have tended to be most active within US convertibles
- Japan: In Japan, the convertible bond market is more regulated than other markets. It consists of a large number of small issuers.
- Europe: Convertible bonds have become an increasingly important source of finance for firms in Europe. Compared to other global markets, European convertible bonds tend to be of high credit quality.
- Asia (ex Japan): The Asia region provides a wide range of choice for an investor. The maturity of Asian convertible bond markets vary widely.
- Canada: Canadian convertible bonds are exchange traded. Most of the Canadian convertible bond market consists of unsecured sub-investment grade bonds with high yields that are reflective of the issuer's risk of default.

- Domestics versus Euroconvertible bonds A further important classification is between the domestic and euroconvertibles markets. Euroconvertibles pay their interest gross and are free of transfer duty when bought, and are delivered into Euroclear or Clearstream for 7 day settlement. Domestics may have different settlement dates, they may pay their interest net of tax and be subject to transaction taxes. European euroconvertibles are generally highly liquid and have a pan-European investor base, dominated by hedge funds and proprietary desks. European domestic convertibles (such as in the UK and Italy) are dominated more by local investment institutions. Since the early nineteen-eighties, foreigners have been able to receive interest on U.S. domestic convertible bonds gross, and this has broadened the global investor base to embrace global hedge funds and other global investors. Likewise, foreigners have been able to receive interest gross on French convertibles (obligations convertibles or OCs), further blurring the differentiation between the domestic and euro CB markets. The pan-European CB market has substantially replaced the various domestic CB markets, and the driver behind this has been the ability of cross-border investors to receive interest payments gross.

Structure and Features

Like any typical bond, convertible bonds have an issue size, issue date, maturity date, maturity value, face value and coupon. They also have the following additional features:

- Conversion price: The nominal price per share at which conversion takes place.
- Conversion ratio: The number of shares each convertible bond converts into. It may be expressed per bond or on a per centum (per 100) basis.
- Parity (Conversion) value: Equity price × Conversion ratio.
- Conversion premium: Represent the divergence of the market value of the CB compared to that of the parity value.
- Call features: The ability of the issuer (on some bonds) to call a bond early for redemption, sometimes subject to certain share price performance. The intention is to encourage investors to convert early into equity (which has now become worth more than the bond's face value), by threatening repayment in cash for what is now a lower amount.

Uses for Issuers

- Lower fixed-rate borrowing costs. Convertible bonds allow issuers to issue debt at a lower cost. Typically, a convertible bond at issue yields 1% to 3% less than straight bonds.
- Locking into low fixed–rate long-term borrowing. For a finance director watching the trend in interest rates, there is an attraction in trying to catch the lowest point in the cycle to fund with fixed rate debt, or swap variable rate bank borrowings for fixed rate convertible borrowing. Even if the fixed market turns, it may still be possible for a company to borrow via a convertible carrying a lower coupon than ever would have been possible with straight debt funding.
- Higher conversion price than a rights issue strike price. Similarly, the conversion price a company fixes on a convertible can be higher than the level that the share price ever reached recently. Compare the equity dilution on a convertible issued on, say, a 20 or 30pct premium to the higher equity dilution on a rights issue, when the new shares are offered on, say, a 15 to 20pct discount to the prevailing share price.
- Voting dilution deferred. With a convertible bond, dilution of the voting rights of existing shareholders only happens on eventual conversion of the bond. However convertible preference shares typically carry voting rights when preference dividends are in arrears. Of course, the bigger voting impact occurs if the issuer decides to issue an exchangeable rather than a convertible.
- Increasing the total level of debt gearing. Convertibles can be used to increase the total amount of debt a company has in issue. The market tends to expect that a company will not increase straight debt beyond certain limits, without it negatively impacting upon the credit rating and the cost of debt. Convertibles can provide additional funding when the straight debt "window" may not be open. Subordination of convertible debt is often regarded as an acceptable risk by investors if the conversion rights are attractive by way of compensation.
- Maximising funding permitted under pre-emption rules. For countries, such as the UK, where companies are subject to limits on the number of shares that can be offered to non-shareholders non-pre-emptively, convertibles can raise more

money than via equity issues. Under the UK's 1989 Guidelines issued by the Investor Protection Committees (IPCs) of the Association of British Insurers (ABI) and the National Association of Pension Fund Managers (NAPF), the IPCs will advise their members not to object to non pre-emptive issues which add no more than 5pct to historic non-diluted balance sheet equity in the period from AGM to AGM, and no more than 7.5pct in total over a period of 3 financial years. The pre-emption limits are calculated on the assumption of 100pct probability of conversion, using the figure of undiluted historic balance sheet share capital (where there is assumed a 0pct probability of conversion). There is no attempt to assign probabilities of conversion in both circumstances, which would result in bigger convertible issues being permitted. The reason for his inconsistency may lie in the fact that the Pre Emption Guidelines were drawn up in 1989, and binomial evaluations were not commonplace amongst professional investors until 1991-92.

- Premium redemption convertibles such as the majority of French convertibles and zero-coupon Liquid Yield Option Notes (LYONs). provide a fixed interest return at issue which is significantly (or completely) accounted for by the appreciation to the redemption price. If, however, the bonds are converted by investors before the maturity date, the issuer will have benefited by having issued the bonds on a low or even zero-coupon. The higher the premium redemption price, (1) the more the shares have to travel for conversion to take place before the maturity date, and (2) the lower the conversion premium has to be at issue to ensure that the conversion rights are credible.
- Takeover paper. Convertibles have a place as the currency used in takeovers. The bidder can offer a higher income on a convertible than the dividend yield on a bid victim's shares, without having to raise the dividend yield on all the bidder's shares. This eases the process for a bidder with low-yield shares acquiring a company with higher-yielding shares. Perversely, the lower the yield on the bidder's shares, the easier it is for the bidder to create a higher conversion premium on the convertible, with consequent benefits for the mathematics of the takeover. In the 1980s, UK domestic convertibles accounted for about 80pct of the European convertibles market,

and over 80pct of these were issued either as takeover currency or as funding for takeovers. They had several cosmetic attractions.

The pro-forma fully-diluted earnings per share shows none of the extra cost of servicing the convertible up to the conversion day irrespective of whether the coupon was 10pct or 15pct. The fully diluted earnings per share is also calculated on a smaller number of shares than if equity was used as the takeover currency.

In some countries (such as Finland) convertibles of various structures may be treated as equity by the local accounting profession. In such circumstances, the accounting treatment may result in less pro-forma debt than if straight debt was used as takeover currency or to fund an acquisition. The perception was that gearing was less with a convertible than if straight debt was used instead. In the UK the predecessor to the International Accounting Standards Board (IASB) put a stop to treating convertible preference shares as equity. Instead it has to be classified both as (1) preference capital and as (2) convertible as well.

Nevertheless, none of the (possibly substantial) preference dividend cost incurred when servicing a convertible preference share is visible in the pro-forma consolidated pretax profits statement.

2010 U.S. Equity-Linked Underwriting League Table

Rank	*Underwriter*	*Market Share (%)*	*Amount ($m)*
1	J.P. Morgan	21.0	$7,359.72
2	Bank of America Merrill Lynch	15.3	$5,369.23
3	Goldman Sachs & Co	12.5	$4,370.56
4	Morgan Stanley	8.8	$3,077.95
5	Deutsche Bank AG	7.8	$2,748.52
6	Citi	7.5	$2,614.43
7	Credit Suisse	6.9	$2,405.97
8	Barclays Capital	5.6	$1,969.22
9	UBS	4.5	$1,589.20
10	Jefferies Group Inc	4.3	$1,522.50

The cosmetic benefits in (1) reported pro-forma diluted earnings per share, (2) debt gearing (for a while) and (3) pro-forma consolidated pre-tax profits (for convertible preference shares) led to UK convertible preference shares being the largest European class of convertibles in the early 1980s, until the tighter terms achievable on Euroconvertible bonds resulted in Euroconvertible new issues eclipsing domestic convertibles (including convertible preference shares) from the mid 1980s.

- Tax advantages. The market for convertibles is primarily pitched towards the non taxpaying investor. The price will substantially reflect (1) the value of the underlying shares, (2) the discounted gross income advantage of the convertible over the underlying shares, plus (3) some figure for the embedded optionality of the bond. The tax advantage is greatest with mandatory convertibles. Effectively a high tax-paying shareholder can benefit from the company securitising gross future income on the convertible, income which it can offset against taxable profits.

Convertible bonds are bonds that can be converted into shares of stock in the issuing company, usually at some pre-announced ratio. It is a hybrid security with debt-and equity-like features. It can be used by investors to obtain the upside of equity-like returns while protecting the downside with regular bond-like coupons.

Equity Futures, Options and Swaps

Investors can gain exposure to the equity markets using futures, options and swaps. These can be done on single stocks, a customized basket of stocks or on an index of stocks. These equity derivatives derive their value from the price of the underlying stock or stocks.

Stock Market Index Futures

Stock market index futures are futures contracts used to replicate the performance of an underlying stock market index. They can be used for hedging against an existing equity position, or speculating on future movements of the index. Indices for futures include well-established indices such as S&P, FTSE, DAX, CAC40 and other G12 country indices. Indices for OTC products are broadly similar, but offer more flexibility.

Equity Basket Derivatives

Equity basket derivatives are futures, options or swaps where the underlying is a non-index basket of shares. They have similar characteristics to equity index derivatives, but are always traded OTC (over the counter, i.e. between established institutional investors), as the basket definition is not standardized in the way that an equity index is. These are used normally for correlation trading.

Single-stock Futures

Single-stock futures are exchange-traded futures contracts based on an individual underlying security rather than a stock index. Their performance is similar to that of the underlying equity itself, although as futures contracts they are usually traded with greater leverage. Another difference is that holders of long positions in single stock futures typically do not receive dividends and holders of short positions do not pay dividends. Single-stock futures may be cash-settled or physically settled by the transfer of the underlying stocks at expiration, although in the United States only physical settlement is used to avoid speculation in the market....

Equity Index Swaps

An equity index swap is an agreement between two parties to swap two sets of cash flows on predetermined dates for an agreed number of years. The cash flows will be an equity index value swapped, for instance, with LIBOR. Swaps can be considered as being a relatively straightforward way of gaining exposure to an asset class you require. They can also be relatively cost efficient.

Equity Swap

An equity swap, like an equity index swap, is an agreement between two parties to swap two sets of cash flows. In this case the cash flows will be the price of an underlying stock value swapped, for instance, with LIBOR. A typical example of this type of derivative is the Contract for difference (CFD) where one party gains exposure to a share price without buying or selling the underlying share making it relatively cost efficient as well as making it relatively easy to transact.

Exchange-traded Derivatives

Other examples of equity derivative securities include exchange-traded funds and Intellidexes.

History

During Roman times, the empire contracted out many of its services to private groups called publicani. Shares in publicani were called "socii" (for large cooperatives) and "particulae" which were analogous to today's Over-The-Counter shares of small companies. Though the records available for this time are incomplete, Edward Chancellor states in his book *Devil Take the Hindmost* that there is some evidence that a speculation in these shares became increasingly widespread and that perhaps the first ever speculative bubble in "stocks" occurred.

The first company to issue shares of stock after the Middle Ages was the Dutch East India Company in 1606. The innovation of joint ownership made a great deal of Europe's economic growth possible following the Middle Ages. The technique of pooling capital to finance the building of ships, for example, made the Netherlands a maritime superpower. Before adoption of the joint-stock corporation, an expensive venture such as the building of a merchant ship could be undertaken only by governments or by very wealthy individuals or families.

Economic historians find the Dutch stock market of the 17th century particularly interesting: there is clear documentation of the use of stock futures, stock options, short selling, the use of credit to purchase shares, a speculative bubble that crashed in 1695, and a change in fashion that unfolded and reverted in time with the market (in this case it was headdresses instead of hemlines). Dr. Edward Stringham also noted that the uses of practices such as short selling continued to occur during this time despite the government passing laws against it.

This is unusual because it shows individual parties fulfilling contracts that were not legally enforceable and where the parties involved could incur a loss. Stringham argues that this shows that contracts can be created and enforced without state sanction or, in this case, in spite of laws to the contrary.

Shareholder

A shareholder (or *stockholder*) is an individual or company (including a corporation) that legally owns one or more shares of stock in a joint stock company. Both private and public traded companies have shareholders. Companies listed at the stock market are expected to strive to enhance shareholder value.

Shareholders are granted special privileges depending on the class of stock, including the right to vote on matters such as elections to the board of directors, the right to share in distributions of the company's income, the right to purchase new shares issued by the company, and the right to a company's assets during a liquidation of the company. However, shareholder's rights to a company's assets are subordinate to the rights of the company's creditors.

Shareholders are considered by some to be a partial subset of stakeholders, which may include anyone who has a direct or indirect equity interest in the business entity or someone with even a non-pecuniary interest in a non-profit organization. Thus it might be common to call volunteer contributors to an association stakeholders, even though they are not shareholders.

Although directors and officers of a company are bound by fiduciary duties to act in the best interest of the shareholders, the shareholders themselves normally do not have such duties towards each other.

However, in a few unusual cases, some courts have been willing to imply such a duty between shareholders. For example, in California, USA, majority shareholders of closely held corporations have a duty to not destroy the value of the shares held by minority shareholders.

The largest shareholders (in terms of percentages of companies owned) are often mutual funds, and, especially, passively managed exchange-traded funds.

Application

The owners of a company may want additional capital to invest in new projects within the company. They may also simply wish to reduce their holding, freeing up capital for their own private use.

By selling shares they can sell part or all of the company to many part-owners. The purchase of one share entitles the owner of that share to literally share in the ownership of the company, a fraction of the decision-making power, and potentially a fraction of the profits, which the company may issue as dividends.

In the common case of a publicly traded corporation, where there may be thousands of shareholders, it is impractical to have all of them making the daily decisions required to run a company. Thus, the shareholders will use their shares as votes in the election of members of the board of directors of the company.

In a typical case, each share constitutes one vote. Corporations may, however, issue different classes of shares, which may have different voting rights. Owning the majority of the shares allows other shareholders to be out-voted – effective control rests with the majority shareholder (or shareholders acting in concert). In this way the original owners of the company often still have control of the company.

Shareholder Rights

Although ownership of 50% of shares does result in 50% ownership of a company, it does not give the shareholder the right to use a company's building, equipment, materials, or other property. This is because the company is considered a legal person, thus it owns all its assets itself. This is important in areas such as insurance, which must be in the name of the company and not the main shareholder.

In most countries, boards of directors and company managers have a fiduciary responsibility to run the company in the interests of its stockholders. Nonetheless, as Martin Whitman writes:

> *...it can safely be stated that there does not exist any publicly traded company where management works exclusively in the best interests of OPMI [Outside Passive Minority Investor] stockholders. Instead, there are both "communities of interest" and "conflicts of interest" between stockholders (principal) and management (agent). This conflict is referred to as the principal/ agent problem. It would be naive to think that any management would forgo management compensation, and management entrenchment, just because some of these management privileges might be perceived as giving rise to a conflict of interest with OPMIs.*

Even though the board of directors runs the company, the shareholder has some impact on the company's policy, as the shareholders elect the board of directors. Each shareholder typically has a percentage of votes equal to the percentage of shares he or she owns. So as long as the shareholders agree that the management (agent) are performing poorly they can elect a new board of directors which can then hire a new management team. In practice, however, genuinely contested board elections are rare. Board candidates are usually nominated by insiders or by the board of the directors themselves, and a considerable amount of stock is held or voted by insiders. Owning shares does not mean responsibility for liabilities. If a company goes broke and has to default on loans, the shareholders are not liable in any way. However, all money obtained by converting assets into cash will be used to repay loans and other debts first, so that shareholders cannot receive any money unless and until creditors have been paid (often the shareholders end up with nothing).

Means of Financing

Financing a company through the sale of stock in a company is known as equity financing. Alternatively, debt financing (for example issuing bonds) can be done to avoid giving up shares of ownership of the company. Unofficial financing known as trade financing usually provides the major part of a company's working capital (day-to-day operational needs).

Trading

The shares of a company may in general be transferred from shareholders to other parties by sale or other mechanisms, unless prohibited. Most jurisdictions have established laws and regulations governing such transfers, particularly if the issuer is a publicly-traded entity.

The desire of stockholders to trade their shares has led to the establishment of stock exchanges. A stock exchange is an organization that provides a marketplace for trading shares and other derivatives and financial products. Today, investors are usually represented by a stock broker who buys and sells shares of a wide range of companies on the exchanges. A company may list its shares on an exchange by meeting and maintaining the listing requirements of a particular stock exchange. In the United States, through the inter-market quotation system, stocks listed on one exchange can also be traded on other participating exchanges, including the Electronic Communication Networks (ECNs), such as Archipelago or Instinet.

Many large non-U.S companies choose to list on a U.S. exchange as well as an exchange in their home country in order to broaden their investor base. These companies must maintain a block of shares at a bank in the US, typically a certain percentage of their capital. On this basis, the holding bank establishes American Depositary Shares and issues an American Depository Receipt (ADR) for each share a trader acquires. Likewise, many large U.S. companies list their shares at foreign exchanges to raise capital abroad.

Small companies that do not qualify and cannot meet the listing requirements of the major exchanges may be traded *over the counter* (OTC) by an off-exchange mechanism in which trading occurs directly between parties. The major OTC markets in the United States are the electronic quotation systems OTC Bulletin Board (OTCBB) and the Pink OTC Markets (*Pink Sheets*) where individual retail investors are also represented by a brokerage firm and the quotation service's requirements for a company to be listed are minimal. Shares of companies in bankruptcy proceeding are usually listed by these quotation services after the stock is delisted from an exchange.

Buying

There are various methods of buying and financing stocks. The most common means is through a stock broker. Whether they are a full service or discount broker, they arrange the transfer of stock from a seller to a buyer. Most trades are actually done through brokers listed with a stock exchange. There are many different stock brokers from which to choose, such as full service brokers or discount brokers. The full service brokers usually charge more per trade, but give investment advice or more personal service; the discount brokers offer little or no investment advice but charge less for trades. Another type of broker would be a bank or credit union that may have a deal set up with either a full service or discount broker.

There are other ways of buying stock besides through a broker. One way is directly from the company itself. If at least one share is owned, most companies will allow the purchase of shares directly from the company through their investor relations departments.

However, the initial share of stock in the company will have to be obtained through a regular stock broker. Another way to buy stock in companies is through Direct Public Offerings which are usually sold by the company itself. A direct public offering is an initial public offering in which the stock is purchased directly from the company, usually without the aid of brokers.

When it comes to financing a purchase of stocks there are two ways: purchasing stock with money that is currently in the buyer's ownership, or by buying stock on margin. Buying stock on margin means buying stock with money borrowed against the stocks in the same account. These stocks, or collateral, guarantee that the buyer can repay the loan; otherwise, the stockbroker has the right to sell the stock (collateral) to repay the borrowed money. He can sell if the share price drops below the margin requirement, at least 50% of the value of the stocks in the account. Buying on margin works the same way as borrowing money to buy a car or a house, using a car or house as collateral. Moreover, borrowing is not free; the broker usually charges 8–10% interest.

Stock Price Fluctuations

The price of a stock fluctuates fundamentally due to the theory of supply and demand. Like all commodities in the market, the price of a stock is sensitive to demand. However, there are many factors that influence the demand for a particular stock. The field of fundamental analysis and technical analysis attempt to understand market conditions that lead to price changes, or even predict future price levels.

A recent study shows that customer satisfaction, as measured by the American Customer Satisfaction Index (ACSI), is significantly correlated to the market value of a stock. Stock price may be influenced by analyst's business forecast for the company and outlooks for the company's general market segment.

Share Price Determination

At any given moment, an equity's price is strictly a result of supply and demand. The supply, commonly referred to as the *float*, is the number of shares offered for sale at any one moment. The demand is the number of shares investors wish to buy at exactly that same time. The price of the stock moves in order to achieve and maintain equilibrium. The product of this instantaneous price and the float at any one time is the market capitalization of the entity offering the equity at that point in time.

When prospective buyers outnumber sellers, the price rises. Eventually, sellers attracted to the high selling price enter the market and/or buyers leave, achieving equilibrium between buyers and sellers. When sellers outnumber buyers, the price falls. Eventually buyers enter and/or sellers leave, again achieving equilibrium.

Thus, the value of a share of a company at any given moment is determined by all investors voting with their money. If more investors want a stock and are willing to pay more, the price will go up. If more investors are selling a stock and there aren't enough buyers, the price will go down.

Of course, that does not explain how people decide the maximum price at which they are willing to buy or the minimum at which they are willing to sell.

In professional investment circles the efficient market hypothesis (EMH) continues to be popular, although this theory is widely discredited in academic and professional circles. Briefly, EMH says that investing is overall (weighted by a Stdev) rational; that the price of a stock at any given moment represents a rational evaluation of the known information that might bear on the future value of the company; and that share prices of equities are priced *efficiently*, which is to say that they represent accurately the expected value of the stock, as best it can be known at a given moment. In other words, prices are the result of discounting expected future cash flows.

The EMH model, if true, has at least two interesting consequences. First, because financial risk is presumed to require at least a small premium on expected value, the return on equity can be expected to be slightly greater than that available from non-equity investments:

if not, the same rational calculations would lead equity investors to shift to these safer non-equity investments that could be expected to give the same or better return at lower risk.

Second, because the price of a share at every given moment is an "efficient" reflection of expected value, then—relative to the curve of expected return—prices will tend to follow a random walk, determined by the emergence of information (randomly) over time. Professional equity investors therefore immerse themselves in the flow of fundamental information, seeking to gain an advantage over their competitors (mainly other professional investors) by more intelligently interpreting the emerging flow of information (news). The EMH model does not seem to give a complete description of the process of equity price determination.

For example, stock markets are more volatile than EMH would imply. In recent years it has come to be accepted that the share markets are not perfectly efficient, perhaps especially in emerging markets or other markets that are not dominated by well-informed professional investors.

Another theory of share price determination comes from the field of Behavioural Finance. According to Behavioural Finance, humans often make irrational decisions—particularly, related to the buying and selling of securities—based upon fears and misperceptions of outcomes. The irrational trading of securities can often create securities prices which vary from rational, fundamental price valuations. For instance, during the technology bubble of the late 1990s (which was followed by the dot-com bust of 2000–2002), technology companies were often bid beyond any rational fundamental value because of what is commonly known as the "greater fool theory".

The "greater fool theory" holds that, because the predominant method of realizing returns in equity is from the sale to another investor, one should select securities that they believe that someone else will value at a higher level at some point in the future, without regard to the basis for that other party's willingness to pay a higher price. Thus, even a rational investor may bank on others' irrationality.

Hybrid

Hybrid securities combine some of the characteristics of both debt and equity securities.

Preference shares form an intermediate class of security between equities and debt. If the issuer is liquidated, they carry the right to receive interest and/or a return of capital in priority to ordinary shareholders. However, from a legal perspective, they are capital stock and therefore may entitle holders to some degree of control depending on whether they contain voting rights.

Convertibles are bonds or preferred stock that can be converted, at the election of the holder of the convertibles, into the common stock of the issuing company. The convertibility, however, may be forced if the convertible is a callable bond, and the issuer calls the bond. The bondholder has about 1 month to convert it, or the company will call the bond by giving the holder the call price, which may be less than the value of the converted stock. This is referred to as a forced conversion.

Equity warrants are options issued by the company that allow the holder of the warrant to purchase a specific number of shares at a specified price within a specified time. They are often issued together with bonds or existing equities, and are, sometimes, detachable from them and separately tradable.

When the holder of the warrant exercises it, he pays the money directly to the company, and the company issues new shares to the holder. Warrants, like other convertible securities, increases the number of shares outstanding, and are always accounted for in financial reports as fully diluted earnings per share, which assumes that all warrants and convertibles will be exercised.

The Securities Markets

Primary and Secondary Market

In the U.S., the public securities markets can be divided into primary and secondary markets. The distinguishing difference between the two markets is that in the primary market, the money for the securities is received by the issuer of those securities from investors, typically in an initial public offering transaction, whereas in the secondary market, the securities are simply assets held by one investor selling them to another investor (money goes from one investor to the other).

An initial public offering is when a company issues public stock newly to investors, called an "IPO" for short. A company can later issue more new shares, or issue shares that have been previously registered in a shelf registration.

These later new issues are also sold in the primary market, but they are not considered to be an IPO but are often called a "secondary offering". Issuers usually retain investment banks to assist them in administering the IPO, obtaining SEC (or other regulatory body) approval of the offering filing, and selling the new issue. When the investment bank buys the entire new issue from the issuer at a discount to resell it at a markup, it is called a firm commitment underwriting. However, if the investment bank considers the risk too great for an underwriting, it may only assent to a best effort agreement, where the investment bank will simply do its best to sell the new issue.

For the primary market to thrive, there must be a secondary market, or aftermarket that provides liquidity for the investment security—where holders of securities can sell them to other investors for cash.

Otherwise, few people would purchase primary issues, and, thus, companies and governments would be restricted in raising equity capital (money) for their operations. Organized exchanges constitute the main secondary markets. Many smaller issues and most debt securities trade in the decentralized, dealer-based over-the-counter markets.

In Europe, the principal trade organization for securities dealers is the International Capital Market Association. In the U.S., the principal trade organization for securities dealers is the Securities Industry and Financial Markets Association, which is the result of the merger of the Securities Industry Association and the Bond Market Association.

The Financial Information Services Division of the Software and Information Industry Association (FISD/SIIA) represents a round-table of market data industry firms, referring to them as Consumers, Exchanges, and Vendors.

Listing and OTC Dealing

Securities are often listed in a stock exchange, an organized and officially recognized market on which securities can be bought and sold. Issuers may seek listings for their securities to attract investors, by ensuring there is a liquid and regulated market that investors can buy and sell securities in.

Growth in informal electronic trading systems has challenged the traditional business of stock exchanges. Large volumes of securities are also bought and sold "over the counter" (OTC). OTC dealing involves buyers and sellers dealing with each other by telephone or electronically on the basis of prices that are displayed electronically, usually by commercial information vendors such as Reuters and Bloomberg.

There are also eurosecurities, which are securities that are issued outside their domestic market into more than one jurisdiction. They are generally listed on the Luxembourg Stock Exchange or admitted to listing in London. The reasons for listing eurobonds include regulatory and tax considerations, as well as the investment restrictions.

Market

London is the centre of the eurosecurities markets. There was a huge rise in the eurosecurities market in London in the early 1980s. Settlement of trades in eurosecurities is currently effected through two European computerized clearing/depositories called Euroclear (in Belgium) and Clearstream (formerly Cedelbank) in Luxembourg. The main market for Eurobonds is the EuroMTS, owned by Borsa Italiana and Euronext. There are ramp up market in Emergent countries, but it is growing slowly.

Physical Nature of Securities

Certificated Securities

Securities that are represented in paper (physical) form are called certificated securities. They may be *bearer* or *registered.*

Bearer Securities

Bearer securities are completely negotiable and entitle the holder to the rights under the security (e.g. to payment if it is a debt security, and voting if it is an equity security). They are transferred by delivering the instrument from person to person. In some cases, transfer is by endorsement, or signing the back of the instrument, and delivery. Regulatory and fiscal authorities sometimes regard bearer securities negatively, as they may be used to facilitate the evasion of regulatory restrictions and tax. In the United Kingdom, for example, the issue of bearer securities was heavily restricted firstly by the *Exchange Control Act* 1947 until 1953. Bearer securities are very rare in the United States because of the negative tax implications they may have to the issuer and holder.

Registered Securities

In the case of registered securities, certificates bearing the name of the holder are issued, but these merely represent the securities.

A person does not automatically acquire legal ownership by having possession of the certificate. Instead, the issuer (or its appointed agent) maintains a register in which details of the holder of the securities are entered and updated as appropriate. A transfer of registered securities is effected by amending the register.

Non-certificated Securities and Global Certificates

Modern practice has developed to eliminate both the need for certificates and maintenance of a complete security register by the issuer. There are two general ways this has been accomplished.

Non-certificated Securities

In some jurisdictions, such as France, it is possible for issuers of that jurisdiction to maintain a legal record of their securities electronically. In the United States, the current "official" version of Article 8 of the Uniform Commercial Code permits non-certificated securities.

However, the "official" UCC is a mere draft that must be enacted individually by each of the U.S. states. Though all 50 states (as well as the District of Columbia and the U.S. Virgin Islands) have enacted some form of Article 8, many of them still appear to use older versions of Article 8, including some that did not permit non-certificated securities.

In the U.S. today, most mutual funds issue only non-certificated shares to shareholders, though some may issue certificates only upon request and may charge a fee. Shareholders typically don't need certificates except for perhaps pledging such shares as collateral for a loan.

Divided and Undivided Security

The terms "divided" and "undivided" relate to the proprietary nature of a security. Each divided security constitutes a separate asset, which is legally distinct from each other security in the same issue. Pre-electronic bearer securities were divided. Each instrument constitutes the separate covenant of the issuer and is a separate debt.

With undivided securities, the entire issue makes up one single asset, with each of the securities being a fractional part of this undivided whole. Shares in the secondary markets are always undivided. The issuer owes only one set of obligations to shareholders under its memorandum, articles of association and company law. A share represents an undivided fractional part of the issuing company. Registered debt securities also have this undivided nature.

Fungible and Non-fungible Security

The terms "fungible" and "non-fungible" are a feature of assets.

If an asset is fungible, this means that if such an asset is lent, or placed with a custodian, it is customary for the borrower or custodian to be obliged at the end of the loan or custody arrangement to return assets equivalent to the original asset, rather than the specific identical asset. In other words, the redelivery of fungibles is equivalent and not *in specie.*

In other words, if an owner of 100 shares of IBM transfers custody of those shares to another party to hold for a purpose, at the end of the arrangement, the holder need simply provide the owner with 100 shares of IBM identical to those received. Cash is also an example of a fungible asset. The exact currency notes received need not be segregated and returned to the owner. Undivided securities are always fungible by logical necessity. Divided securities may or may not be fungible, depending on market practice. The clear trend is towards fungible arrangements.

Regulation

In the United States, the public offer and sale of securities must be either registered pursuant to a registration statement that is filed with the U.S. Securities and Exchange Commission (SEC) or are offered and sold pursuant to an exemption therefrom. Dealing in securities is regulated by both federal authorities (SEC) and state securities departments. In addition, the brokerage industry is supposedly self policed by Self Regulatory Organizations (SROs), such as the Financial Industry Regulatory Authority (FINRA), formerly the National Association of Securities Dealers (or NASD) or the MSRB.

With respect to investment schemes that do not fall within the traditional puki ayam categories of securities listed in the definition of a security (Sec. 2(a)(1) of the 33 act and Sec. 3(a)(10) of the 34 act) the US Courts have developed a broad definition for securities that must then be registered with the SEC. When determining if there a is an "investment contract" that must be registered the courts look for an investment of money, a common enterprise and expectation of profits to come primarily from the efforts of others.

Bibliography

Aswathappa, K. : *Essential of Business Environment*, New Delhi, Himalaya Publishing House, 2001.

Basu, Kaushik. *Analytical Development Economics, The Less Developed Economy Revisited,* Cambridge, Mass.: MIT Press, 1997.

Beesley, Michael : *Corporate Social Responsibility: A Reassessment,* London, Crrom Helm, 1978.

Besley, T.: *How do Merket Failures Justify Interventions in Rural Credit Markets?,* Washington, D. C., World Bank, 1994

Carroll, A. : *Business and Society: Managing Corporate Social Performance,* Boston: Little, Brown & Company, 1981.

Cheruniam, F. : *Global Economy and Business Environment,* New Delhi, Himalaya Publishing House, 2001.

Dalrymple A : *Observations on the Copper Coinage wanted in Circars,* London, 1794.

Dixon, Robert L., and Harold E. Arnett: *The McGraw-Hill 36-Hour Accounting Course,* N.Y.: McGraw-Hill, 1993.

Dunfee, T. : *That Bind: A Social Contracts Approach to Business Ethics,* Boston, HBS HBS Harvard Business School, 1999.

Fetter F. A. : *The Gold Reserve: Its Function and its Maintenance,* Political Science Quarterly, 1896.

Gowdy, J., *Coevolution Economics: The Economy, Society and the Environment,* Kluwer, Boston, 1994.

Guarti, Luigi, *The Valuation of Finance*, Blackwell Publishing, 1994.

Guhan, S.: *The World Bank's Lending in South Asia*, Washington, Brookings Institution, 1995.

Harrigan, K. R.: *Strategies for Declining Businesses.* Lexington, MA: Heath, 1980

Hayek, F. A. *Individualism and Economic Order*, The University of Chicago Press, Chicago, 1948.

Jack Kemp: *A Monetary Agenda for the World Economy,* Boston, Quantum, 1984.

Larry J.: *Business Valuations, Advanced Topics,* Westport, CT, Quorum Books, 1997.

Le Prestre, Philippe: *The World Bank and the Environmental Challenge,* London, Associated University Presses, 1989.

Magliveras, Konstantinos D.: *Banks, Fraud and Crime,* Lloyd's of London Press, London, 2000.

Mayer, Martin: *The Bankers: The Next Generation.* N.Y.: Truman Talley Books/Dutton, 1997.

Neil H. : *Corporate Power and Social Responsibility: A Blueprint for the Future,* New York, Macmillan, 1973.

Peet, Richard, Born, Beate: *Unholy Trinity: The IMF, World Bank, and WTO,* New York, Zed Books, 2003.

Post , J.E. : *Business and Society,* New York, McGrawhill, 1988.

Probyn, Mr. : *Indian Coinage and Currency,* Effingham Wilson, London, 1897.

Reddy, Sumati : *Corporate Social Responsibility: The Environmental Aspects,* Hyderabad, ICFAI, 2004.

Ross, D.: *Economic Theory and Cognitive Science,* Cambridge, Mass., MIT Press, 2006.

Salancik, G. R.: *The External Control of Organizations, A Resource Dependence Perspective,* New York, 1978.

Sims, Ronald R. : *Ethics and Corporate Social Responsibility: Why Giants Fall,* New York, Praeger Publishers, 2003.

Smith, V. L.: *Papers in Experimental Economics,* Cambridge, Cambridge University Press, 1991.

Summner, Prof. : -4 *History of American Currency,* New York, 1874.

Tavakoli, Janet M.: *Credit Derivatives: A Guide to Instruments and Applications.* N.Y.: John Wiley & Sons, 1998.

Vogal, David : *Corporations and their Critics: Issues and Answers to the Problems of Corporate Social Responsibility,* New York, McGraw Hill, 1981.

Warwick, D. P.: *A Theory of Public Bureaucracy,* Cambridge, MA: Harvard University Press, 1975.

Wolfe, J.N.: *Value, Capital and Growth,* Chicago, Edinburgh University Press. 1968.

Wood, A.: *The Corporate Economy,* London: Macmillan, 1971.

Index

❑❑❑